Virtue in the Cave

Virtue in the Cave

Moral Inquiry in Plato's Meno

ROSLYN WEISS

UNIVERSITY PRESS

2001

OXFORD
UNIVERSITY PRESS

Oxford   New York

Athens   Auckland   Bangkok   Bogotá   Buenos Aires   Calcutta
Cape Town   Chennai   Dar es Salaam   Delhi   Florence   Hong Kong   Istanbul
Karachi   Kuala Lumpur   Madrid   Melbourne   Mexico City   Mumbai   Nairobi
Paris   São Paulo   Shanghai   Singapore   Taipei   Tokyo   Toronto   Warsaw

and associated companies in
Berlin   Ibadan

Published by Oxford University Press, Inc.
198 Madison Avenue, New York, New York 10016

Oxford is a registered trademark of Oxford University Press, Inc.

Library of Congress Cataloging-in-Publication Data
Weiss, Roslyn.
Virtue in the cave : moral inquiry in Plato's Meno / Roslyn Weiss.
p.   cm.
Includes bibliographical references and index.
ISBN 0-19-514076-1
1. Plato. Meno.   2. Vitue.   I. Title.
B377.W45   2001
170—dc21   00-061155

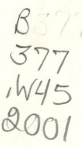
1 3 5 7 9 8 6 4 2
Printed in the United States of America
on acid-free paper

For Malcolm Brown

. . . when I was looking for a single virtue,
I found a swarm of virtues in your possession. — Plato, *Meno*

Acknowledgments

This book was made possible by a number of institutions, foundations, and people. It began in 1990 as a book on Socrates and the teachability of virtue. I acknowledge, with gratitude, the foundation and institutions that supported the project in that form: the National Endowment for the Humanities, the University of Delaware, and the Center for Hellenic Studies in Washington, D.C., where I spent the academic year 1990–1991 as a junior fellow.

The project was revived again several years later, in 1998—this time, as an interpretation of Plato's *Meno*. I am most grateful to the Earhart Foundation for its generous support and to Lehigh University for granting me a semester's leave. I wish to express my appreciation as well for the ongoing support provided by the Clara H. Stewardson Chair.

I wrote the major part of the book during my leave from Lehigh in the spring of 1999. When I returned to Lehigh in the fall, I led my colleagues, participants in the Lehigh Philosophy Faculty Seminar, through the manuscript—week by week, chapter by chapter. The spirited exchanges we had greatly improved the quality of the work. The seminar participants were Robert Barnes, Mark Bickhard, Robin Dillon, Barbara Frankel, Steven Goldman, Alexander Levine, Ralph Lindgren, Michael Mendelson, and Joan Straumanis.

I had the privilege of presenting papers on various aspects of the book while it was in preparation. I wish to thank the following institutions for affording me the opportunity to speak: Tel Aviv University, Ben Gurion University of the Negev, the University of Arizona, and St. Francis College. Fortune smiled on me when Ivor Ludlam was present at the talk I gave at Tel Aviv University. I have been blessed to be the beneficiary of Ivor's generous friendship, his expertise in Greek, his wit, and his love for and erudition in Plato and the classics generally. Three anonymous readers for Oxford University Press, whose identities I do not know, offered long, thoughtful, and thorough critiques of the manuscript; I took their criticisms and suggestions very seriously in preparing the final draft of this book.

My husband, Sam, provided technical assistance, from start to finish. I thank my husband, along with our beloved children, Miriam and Dena, for their unflagging support. I am grateful, as always, to my parents, Eleanor and Abraham Kestenbaum, for nature and nurture.

Malcolm Brown, to whom I dedicate this book, opened my eyes to the wonders of Plato. There is no greater gift.

Contents

Virtue in the Cave

Introduction

In the Cave

For even if one should happen to say the
whole truth, nevertheless, he himself does not
know; but belief is fashioned over all things.

Xenophanes, DK 21B34,
trans. McKirahan (1994)

Is the *Meno* just another in a series of "Socratic" excursions into the
barren land of moral definition? Or does it, perhaps, mark the first
"Platonic" foray into the more fertile fields of metaphysics and epistemology? Is the target of its inquiry the nature of virtue, or is the
target of its inquiry inquiry itself?[1]

This book takes and defends the position that the *Meno* is a self-
conscious analysis and assessment of the worth, on the one hand,
and of the limitations, on the other, not of inquiry simpliciter but
of, specifically, moral inquiry, indeed dramatizing, even constituting
in itself, Socrates' "fight in word and deed" (*M.* 86c2–3)[2] for the
value of open-ended and never-ending investigation into things
moral.[3] On this view, the *Meno* is an apology for the Socratic enterprise, justifying it, however, not, as one might think, on such "Platonic" grounds as immortality of the soul and recollection theory,
but on its own terms: moral inquiry is vindicated in the *Meno* by its

---

1. According to Bedu-Addo (1984), 14, for example, "the *Meno* is primarily an
enquiry into the nature of knowledge and the manner whereby it may be acquired,
and . . . the nature of virtue and how we may acquire it are discussed only for the sake
of example." Cf. Thompson (1901), 63, for whom the *Meno*'s main purpose is "not
metaphysical but ethical."

2. All references to Stephanus pagination of the *Meno* are keyed to the Sharples
edition (1985). All translations are my own unless otherwise noted.

3. Would Socrates need to fight in word and deed for mathematical inquiry or
for inquiry of other kinds when their worth is vindicated by their results?

progress toward true opinion.[4] The *Meno* postpones moral *knowledge* to the indefinite future, to someday, to the time when there might appear among us the equivalent of Teiresias among the dead (*M.* 100a4). In the *Meno*, moral knowledge is not ours now, nor will it soon be ours; nor, indeed, are we but questions away from having it.[5] For in the *Meno*, moral knowledge is not human knowledge; it is, as Socrates says of it in the *Apology* (20e1), wisdom greater than human. From the *Meno*'s perspective, then, until such time as human beings attain wisdom greater than human, moral matters will remain matters of opinion.[6]

What ought human beings to do in their moral Cave,[7] where they do not, and cannot, know what they need to know most of all, namely, how they ought best to live? Socrates' answer, in the *Meno* as in the *Apology*, is that people ought to engage in lifelong moral inquiry, that they ought to live the only life worthy of their humanity: a life of critical reflection. In the *Meno*, Socrates takes up his god-given task to help others live the examined life.

In carrying out his task, the method Socrates employs is elenchus, a method that can examine and "refute" opinions but that has no hope of transcending opinion and yielding knowledge.[8] Through

4. The *Meno*, then, is self-conscious in a way that other elenctic dialogues are not: it discloses what they simply assume. Whereas Socratic elenchus proceeds on the assumption that there is great value in being rid of false opinions and replacing them with true ones, the *Meno* makes explicit that true opinion is a worthy substitute for knowledge as a practical guide to the conduct of human affairs. See Irwin (1977), 133–34: "Normally Socrates practises his method without reflection," but the *Meno* contains "examination and defence of the method itself."

5. Although it is thought that *M.* 85c9–d1 implies that true opinions become knowledge when he who possesses those opinions is asked "these same things many times and in many ways," I will argue in Chapter 3 that that possibility is actually excluded and that, as it turns out, questioning cannot convert true opinions into knowledge; it can only arouse opinions.

6. To say that moral matters are matters of opinion is not to say that all opinions are equally valid; after all, there are false opinions and true ones. It is to say, however, that moral disagreements are not susceptible to definitive resolution.

7. The reference is to the Cave of Plato's famed Allegory of the Cave in Book 7 of the *Republic*. That the character Socrates has some notion of the Cave even before he envisions a nonmaterial realm of pure intelligibles, of Forms, is evident from his pained awareness of the chasm that divides human wisdom, wisdom that is worth "little or nothing" (*Ap.* 23a7), from wisdom greater than human. By recognizing the deficiency of human wisdom when compared with wisdom greater than human, Socrates consigns ordinary human beings to the moral Cave, that is, to the realm of moral *opinion*.

8. Elenchus is the method by which Socrates tests the beliefs held by his interlocutors, beliefs that he suspects are, generally, false. Elenchus does not, however, provide a direct means for discovering truth. Socrates' own moral views do not seem to arise

elenchus—that is, through subjecting opinions to the test of reason—Socrates aims at reducing moral error. In the court of reason, he trusts, false opinions will fall by dint of their absurdity, that is, of their failure to cohere with those truths most deeply embedded in the human soul. True opinions, by contrast, will stand: because they resonate in perfect harmony with those deepest human truths, they will banish the contrary false beliefs that bring discord to the soul.[9] The doors to the court of reason, however, must forever remain open; for, in principle, any belief, even one that has been examined many times, might meet an argument that proves its undoing. Elenchus, then, never rests; its truths are never fully secure—not even when bound "by arguments of iron and adamant" (*Gorg.* 509a1–2).

out of elenchus; the proof of their truth resides, if anywhere, in the failure of his opponents' views to survive the elenchus or in the invariably ridiculous showing made by them in elenctic exchanges with him (*Gorg.* 509a). See Kahn (1992), 246–48. Socrates and his interlocutors are hardly equal partners in the elenctic exchange; it is doubtful, therefore, that Socrates stands to learn anything (rather than just gain confirmation for what he already believes) from his conversations with them. Indeed, as it is not unusual for an interlocutor's ridiculousness to manifest itself as soon as he states his morally dubious view, Socrates' view is frequently vindicated, as far as he is concerned, even before the elenchus begins; in such cases, the elenchus can benefit only the interlocutor who is shown the untenability of his view. Strictly speaking, no opinion is refuted absolutely by way of elenchus. What happens in elenctic exchange is that the interlocutor's asserted view generates a contradiction when either it itself or propositions it logically entails are taken in conjunction with other propositions to which Socrates secures the interlocutor's assent. It is only when the propositions to which the interlocutor agrees and which pose a threat to his original view turn out to be, as a matter of fact, true that the interlocutor's view will have been proved to be, as a matter of fact, false. Although elenchus does not refute the interlocutor's view except in this provisional way, that is, contingent upon the truth of the propositions to which he consents, nevertheless there is a sense in which the interlocutor is himself always refuted in elenchus: insofar as he is shown to be unable to sustain his view without contradiction, he forfeits his warrant to hold it.

9. Although, as we shall see, elenchus proceeds on the assumption that all human beings harbor within themselves true beliefs that it can help bring to light, not every elenchus actually deals in these truths. In conducting his *elenchoi*, Socrates relies on whatever propositions he can gain his interlocutor's assent to. Only sometimes are these the beliefs that Socrates supposes all human beings share deep down (beliefs such as that what is of value is to live well truly rather than merely to seem—whether to oneself or to others—to be living well; that the soul is more important than the body; that wisdom is superior to folly; that harmony is preferable to discord). At other times, Socrates proposes propositions that are simply too plausible, reasonable, or innocuous to be denied (see Kraut [1983], 63–64). At still other times, Socrates urges on his interlocutor propositions that he himself does not endorse or about whose soundness he is himself in doubt in order either to shake the interlocutor's misguided confidence in inadequate or morally repugnant views or to advance his own point of view.

Although the *Meno* acknowledges fully the limitations of elenchus, it recognizes at the same time that it is precisely these limitations that intensify the urgency of its practice: with moral knowledge beyond reach, where else but to elenchus can one turn for moral truth? Since the best human life, according to Socrates, is the life whose central concern is virtue, and since, in the Cave, knowledge of virtue is inaccessible, the best human life will be the life spent in the *search* for moral truth.[10]

The best human life, thus conceived, will hold no appeal for the wicked, the stupid, the intellectually lazy, or the arrogant. The wicked actually savor their odious ideas; the stupid are unable to test their opinions; the intellectually lazy prefer to be guided by the authority of others; the arrogant are too certain of their wisdom to question it. Socrates' divine mission is to convert those susceptible of conversion to a life of moral inquiry, to turn away from their evil or complacent ways those who are capable of being turned away. Despite Socrates' dutiful efforts undertaken at the god's command, however, the interlocutors he encounters in Plato's elenctic dialogues prove to be intransigent: if they come to the exchange wicked, stupid, lazy, or arrogant, so they leave it. Socrates' great problem in the *Meno* is that his interlocutor is Meno. The *Meno* is the fictitious record of Socrates' attempts at Meno's improvement. The present book is a reconstruction of Socrates' efforts on Meno's behalf.

Meno is an interlocutor hobbled in his pursuit of a good life by several deficiencies in his character. He is both slow to learn (how many times must Socrates remind Meno that justice, temperance, and piety are vital components of any adequate account of virtue? [see *M.* 73a7–9, d7–8, 78d3–4]) and unwilling to exert the requisite effort; he is eager above all for power and wealth; and he holds a rather inflated opinion of himself. Socrates no doubt wants to leave Meno in a better state than that in which he found him. But how will Socrates convince Meno or, for that matter, other ambitious and impatient young men who crave fairly instant "success" that the way to make their lives worth living is to spend them engaged in a practice whose conclusions are never certain and whose completion is never near? How can Socrates possibly win the battle for the worth of murky moral inquiry when he competes with others who not only

---

10. See Andic (1971), 264: "It is not putting the case too strongly . . . to say that virtue, for Socrates, is the inquiry into what virtue is."

lure the young with the promise of power and wealth but also dazzle them by answering "fearlessly and magnificently" all questions posed by anyone (*M.* 70b6–7)?[11]

In truth, Socrates can hope to persuade Meno of the importance of moral inquiry only if he masks its inconclusiveness. To this end he perpetrates, as he must, a mild deception: he invents a myth of recollection. No sooner does he espouse the sham doctrine that all learning is recollection, however, than he is compelled to compound this bit of dissimulation with another, that is, with a purported "demonstration" of how recollection works. Socrates' strategy in both the recollection myth and in the ensuing demonstration with Meno's slave-boy is to obscure the unique character of virtue. In the recollection myth he speaks simply of "virtue and other things," suggesting thereby that, as in other things, so in virtue, there can be a final answer. In the slave-boy-demonstration, he fosters the illusion that virtue is like other things by dressing up instruction in geometry as elenchus. But geometry is not learned by elenchus; surely, neither Meno nor Socrates learned it that way. Geometry is a *mathēma*, a teachable and learnable subject whose propositions are susceptible of conclusive proof. Of what value, then, is elenchus for teaching geometry? Elenchus is not, after all, a method for teaching; elenchus takes the place of teaching when teaching is an impossibility, that is, in the matter of virtue. Since the propositions of virtue do not, within the confines of the Cave, admit of certain proof, elenchus steps in to pursue, not knowledge, but the more modest true opinion.

The *Meno*, let us note, is the only Platonic dialogue that celebrates the practical worth of true opinion, equating its practical effectiveness with that of knowledge.[12] Although the dialogue recognizes the superiority of knowledge to true opinion in respect of stability, nevertheless, on the assumption that human beings are not going to

---

11. See Teloh (1986), 138: "For what should Socrates do to educate an interlocutor who is defective in one or more of the personality characteristics required for a serious dialectical discussion? . . . Socrates tries different educational techniques . . . when he finds people . . . unwilling and perhaps unable, due to prior bad education, to participate in dialogue."

12. One is hard-pressed to find kind words for true opinion (when contrasted with knowledge) in the Platonic corpus outside the *Meno.* The *Symposium* (202a) designates it as neither good nor bad: it is not quite knowledge if it is held without a reason but neither is it ignorance insofar as it is true. The *Republic* (6.506c-d) is harsher: those with true opinion divorced from knowledge are said to resemble blind men who go the right way; moreover, blindness is associated in this passage with what is ugly. For further discussion, see Chapter 4, n. 50.

attain knowledge of virtue, it recommends, in place of the ideal guidance that knowledge would provide, the comparably good guidance that true opinion provides.[13]

This book proceeds on assumptions that are best exposed at the outset. I shall, therefore, consider the most controversial of these now, however briefly and dogmatically. (Some of these matters are taken up at greater length—and with supporting argument—later on.) I shall present the book's assumptions as answers to the following questions:

1. Does Socrates believe moral knowledge to be impossible, or does he just think it difficult to come by?
2. Why is moral knowledge impossible?
3. What is the point of searching for moral knowledge if its attainment is impossible?
4. Does Socrates willfully deceive Meno in argument? Is he not, then, a sophist?
5. How does one tell when Socrates is being sincere and when he is being ironic or is dissembling?
6. Why does Socrates work so hard in the *Meno* to introduce and promote doctrines that he does not endorse?
7. If Socrates deliberately misleads, what makes what Socrates does philosophy?

Let me address each of these questions in turn.

1. Does Socrates believe moral knowledge to be impossible, or does he just think it difficult to come by? Socrates comes to accept that moral knowledge (though not, by any means, all knowledge) is not possible for ordinary human beings. The kind of wisdom that ordinary human beings possess is, at best, human wisdom; but moral wisdom is wisdom greater than human. Moral wisdom is something the gods—if there are gods—would have, as might godlike men (those who are the equivalent of "Teiresias among the dead"). The lesson Socrates learns from the oracle is that the wisest of human

---

13. At the end of the *Gorgias,* Socrates makes the same recommendation when he proposes that he and Callicles use as their "guide" *hēgemoni* (*Gorg.* 527e2; cf. *M.* 98b7, e12, 99a1–2, a4, b3), the *logos* that has now been disclosed to them, namely, that the best way of life is to practice justice and the rest of virtue. (Callicles' competing *logos* has turned out to be worthless [*Gorg.* 527e1–7].) It is clear that Socrates and Callicles have not achieved knowledge. That is why their guide is to be the *logos* that, alone among so many others, "survives refutation and remains steady" (*Gorg.* 527b2–4, trans. Zeyl [1987]). What else can this *logos* be but a true opinion?

beings is one who knows that he lacks wisdom with respect to "the most important things," *ta megista*, that is, regarding virtue (*Ap.* 22d–e).[14] If the height of human wisdom is the recognition of one's moral ignorance, then there is no human wisdom that is moral expertise. For someone to achieve moral expertise, he would have to ascend out of the Cave, out of the realm of opinion, and become, in some sense, divine. How might one do that? Socrates' method, the elenchus, proceeds on the assumption that no one can. It is a method that tests opinions—against other opinions. It shows some opinions to be better and others worse, some sets of beliefs to be more coherent and others less so. Yet the elenchus provides no tether strong enough to secure moral beliefs permanently. Indeed, one can never be certain that tomorrow will not bring a new and powerful argument that will cast doubt on an opinion held today. That is why, for Socrates, the best a human being can do, in death as in life, is to keep challenging and testing his own views in light of those of others (see *Ap.* 40e–41c).

2. Why is moral knowledge impossible? Moral knowledge is impossible, most obviously, because there simply is no decisive, objective test in ethics. Everyone has a different opinion, and even if some opinions are true and others false, there is no *final* way to settle the matter. There are no acknowledged moral experts. There are no widely recognized teachers. As Socrates points out in the *Euthyphro* (7b–c), if the gods dispute about number, weight, or measure, they will not dispute for long. If they do dispute for long, their dispute will be about moral matters: right and wrong, good and bad, noble and base. There is in ethics no counting, no scale, no yardstick. There is, to be sure, thinking and reason, but in moral matters, the premises upon which reason operates are just people's opinions. Progress is not ruled out; but certainty—knowledge—is.

Also, there is no suprahuman vantage point from which a human being can judge what is best for human beings. No human being stands to us as we stand, say, to the foals and calves whose good we seek to secure (see *Ap.* 20a–b), and no one can determine, in a comparable way, what our "good" is. The doctor treats our bodies, but he does not treat us. What is needed for moral knowledge

14. Cf. *Gorg.* 527e1–3, where the expression "the most important matters," *tōn megistōn*, refers to the question of which way of life is the best one, *ho tropos aristos tou biou*.

is some way of penetrating into the depths of human nature to discern human good. No ordinary mortal is so positioned as to be able to do that.

3. What is the point of searching for moral knowledge if its attainment is impossible? Knowledge is the goal of inquiry. And this is so regardless of whether knowledge is or is not a possible outcome of the inquiry. Thus, when people explore urgent moral questions, as when they explore urgent theological ones, their inquiry is spurred by their pressing need to *know*—even as they are aware in advance that they will never know. Xenophanes, for example, quoted at the beginning of this Introduction, delved deeply into the question of the divine nature—despite his full and explicit recognition that neither he nor any other human being could ever achieve knowledge concerning the gods.

Socrates wants desperately to know about moral matters; there is, for him, no more important human concern than how one ought to live. He encourages his associates to appreciate as he does how vital it is to have such knowledge and how shameful it therefore is not to have it (*Gorg.* 472c–d, 505e). Nevertheless, he does not think it possible for him, or others, to know. Like Xenophanes with respect to the gods, Socrates believes, with respect to virtue, that true opinion is the most that can be achieved by ordinary men. In the practical sense, then, Socrates' goal may be said to be true opinion. His ideal goal, however, unattainable as it may be, is knowledge.

4. Does Socrates willfully deceive Meno in argument? Is he not, then, a sophist? Socrates deals with each interlocutor as befits the interlocutor. The interlocutor's beliefs and character determine, to a very great extent, both Socrates' demeanor toward him and the kinds of argument he fashions to address him. In all Socrates' dealings, however, even those in which he baits, teases, befuddles, manipulates, or shames his interlocutor, Socrates has the interlocutor's best interests at heart. Socrates is a gadfly—and gadflies bite. Indeed, in some of his attempts to improve his interlocutors Socrates seems to employ a particularly unsavory tactic often associated with sophists: he uses deliberately fallacious arguments to trip up his opponents and to triumph over them. Is Socrates not, then, a sophist?[15]

Socrates in the *Apology* distinguishes himself from the sophists by emphasizing that he is not paid for his services as professional soph-

---

15. For fuller discussion see Weiss (2000).

ists are (*Ap.* 19d8–20a2; see also 33a–b). He thus refutes the charge, at least on his interpretation of it, that he "teaches others these same things," namely, how to make the weaker argument the stronger (*Ap.* 19c1). He also flatly rejects (*Ap.* 19c2–d7) the allegation that he "investigates the things under the earth and the heavenly things" (*Ap.* 19b4–5). The one thing that he does not deny is that he "makes the weaker argument the stronger" (*Ap.* 19b5–c1). Indeed, how could he? Does he not twist people's words? Does he not extract agreement from them without their having any understanding of how or why they have agreed? Does he not pursue the merely verbal advantage?

He does. Nevertheless, Socrates' assertion that he is not paid for his services says a lot about how he differs from sophists: he is a man who takes no money and hence a man who cannot be bought; insofar as he is not out to make money, he is free to converse with anyone—whether rich or poor; moreover, having to please no one, he can devote himself to the promotion of the genuine good of others—whether they like it or not. Socrates' end is thus pure, noble. Not so, however, his means. The crucial difference between him and the sophists lies in the motive behind their tactics—not in their tactics. Since Socrates, like the sophists, will do whatever he must in order to prevail, what sets him apart from them is that he will do so, of course, not for the sake of achieving fame and amassing fortune, but for the sake of improving the souls of those who have gone or might go astray.[16] Indeed, he, even more than sophists, cannot afford to lose. Socrates is a zealot. Philosophy is his religion, his divine mission. Like the man who so abhors violence that he will even fight to stop it if necessary,[17] so will Socrates prevaricate for the sake of truth, deceive for the sake of justice[18]—if necessary.[19]

16. For the sake of the soul's improvement, Socrates will permit most anything. See *Euthyd.* 285a6–b7, where Socrates says to Ctesippus, concerning the clownish sophists Euthydemus and Dionysodorus: "If they really know how to destroy men so as to make good and sensible people out of bad and stupid ones . . . then let us . . . permit them to destroy the boy for us and make him wise." To which Ctesippus replies: "I, too, Socrates, am ready to hand myself over to the visitors; and I give them permission to skin me even more thoroughly than they are doing now so long as my hide will in the end become . . . a piece of virtue" (*Euthyd.* 285c7–d1, trans. Sprague [1965]).

17. See Narveson (1965).

18. Socrates' willingness to use ignoble means for the sake of noble ends is consistent with the *Republic*'s round endorsement of the "noble lie" (*Rep.* 3.414b).

19. As we shall see, Socrates deceives only once he has exhausted all more direct

5. How does one tell when Socrates is being sincere and when he is being ironic or is dissembling? There are no hard and fast rules for detecting a Socratic ploy and, alas, no substitute for a keen eye, a finely tuned ear, and an openness to the dynamic of a dramatic exchange. Nevertheless, Plato will, not infrequently, aid the reader by dropping hints. In the *Meno*, for example, as we shall see, Plato indicates in a variety of ways that Socrates' response to "Meno's paradox" is less than forthright: myth replaces argument; conclusions reached are non sequiturs; there are disclaimers, sudden reversals, inaccurate reports of what has preceded, and a "demonstration" that is farcical on its face. Other dialogues similarly flag instances of Socratic dissimulation.

6. Why does Socrates work so hard in the *Meno* to introduce and promote doctrines that he does not endorse? The advancement of the thesis that all learning is recollection, by way of both myth and "demonstration," works on two levels. On one level, the thesis is intended to induce Meno to proceed with the inquiry. This end is no insignificant one for Socrates. Since, as he sees it, the unexamined life is not worth living for a man, it is of critical importance that he convince Meno, by whatever means, to continue to inquire.

On a second level, however, the recollection thesis has something to say to the reader. As I shall argue, what Socrates promotes, beneath the surface, is the value of true opinion as a substitute for knowledge—in the special case in which knowledge cannot be attained: virtue. Recollection, then, is not, in the final analysis, what Socrates pretends for Meno's sake that it is, namely, a process by which all forms of knowledge are learned. It is, instead, the process by which a questioner helps his interlocutor recover, not knowledge, but truth, and not all truth, but only moral truth, from out of the depths of his soul. What Socrates provides in the *Meno*, then, is nothing short of a defense of his life's work, the work of elenctic moral inquiry.

7. If Socrates deliberately misleads, what makes what Socrates does philosophy? Socratic philosophy, as Plato portrays it in the Platonic dialogues that have come to be known as "Socratic,"[20] is shock-

means of getting through to his interlocutor and has become convinced that nothing short of deception will work.

20. Plato's dialogues do, I think, fall into distinct groups, both stylistically and substantively. I mark off as "Socratic" those that neither contain any mention of what has come to be known as Platonic "Forms" nor would have any inkling of what such

ingly unprofessional. It takes place in the agora, not in the study. It is not written down. It is not systematic. It is frequently ad hominem. What, then, makes it philosophy? That it cares about wisdom, truth, and the best state of the soul. That it is indifferent to money, power, and fame. That it demands that one abide by one's principles even at the cost of one's life. That it requires of its practitioners a devotion to others that supersedes self-interest and even familial concern. That its loyalty is not to family and friends but to truth and justice. It is a mistake to think that all Socrates wants, qua philosopher, is to get people to think. No; he wants no less to get them to think rightly. He demands of people that they reorder their priorities, hold justice and temperance in esteem, and transcend conventional conceptions of success. He is a champion of right-thinking and right-doing. Not for him the cool, disengaged, disinterested speculation that has come to be called philosophy. For Socrates, arguments are not merely philosophy's tools; they are its weapons.

Virtue in the Cave proceeds, then, on the seven assumptions adumbrated above: (1) that Socrates, in the *Meno*, believes moral knowledge to be impossible for human beings to attain; (2) that moral knowledge is impossible to attain because there are, in morality, no conclusive tests; (3) that all inquiry is for the sake of knowledge, whether or not the inquirer believes knowledge to be a possible result; (4) that Socrates willfully deceives but is, nevertheless, no sophist; (5) that the dramatic action of the dialogues, as well as, frequently, Plato's strategically placed hints, help the reader discern when Socrates is not in earnest; (6) that Socrates introduces doctrines he does not endorse because, on the one hand, he hopes thereby to improve his interlocutor and because, on the other hand, they contain, beneath the surface, an important message for the reader; and (7) that what Socrates practices is indeed philosophy—if in a sense remote to us today.

The following is a brief synopsis of *Virtue in the Cave,* which follows closely the order of the text of the *Meno*:

"Forms" are, since it is these dialogues that bring to life the "Socrates" portrayed in the *Apology.* I resist the term "early," however, for there are, in my judgment, insufficient grounds for drawing conclusions about the relative chronology of the dialogues—except in those cases in which one dialogue seems clearly to refer back to another. I see no reason to suppose that Plato, a master imitator of the styles of others, could not imitate his own, writing at any time of his life a dialogue "Socratic" in style and content.

Chapter 1 (*M.* 70a–79e) replays Socrates' struggle to divest Meno of his fascination with power and money and to encourage him to place value instead on justice, temperance, and piety.

Chapter 2 (*M.* 79e–81e) tracks the mounting tensions between Socrates and Meno, tensions that lead to an impasse in their joint search for the nature of virtue, an impasse that culminates, finally, in "Meno's paradox." This chapter argues that the myth of recollection with which Socrates responds to the paradox does not represent Socrates' own beliefs but is, in the main, a ploy designed to keep Meno from abandoning the inquiry.

Chapter 3 (*M.* 81e–86c) resists the widespread tendency to suppress the frankly farcical nature of the slave-boy-demonstration[21] and permits it to be seen, instead, for what it really is: a lesson in geometry, complete with teacher, student, and new material taught. This chapter also discloses the deeper message of "recollection": since moral true opinions are always in the soul, they can be released and recovered through the Socratic method of elenctic questioning; geometry, however, and other kinds of knowledge are simply taught.

Chapter 4 (*M.* 86c–100c) portrays Socrates' reluctant relinquishment of the search for what virtue is, the inquiry for which he so doggedly fought in the belief that in it alone lies Meno's salvation. Taking its place is a consideration of Meno's preferred question of how virtue is acquired. Chapter 4 shows how Socrates seeks to benefit Meno even within the investigation's newly narrowed confines by persuading him that virtue comes to men neither by nature nor by teaching nor spontaneously. This chapter shows, too, how Socrates makes the case, sotto voce, for true opinion as the source of virtue.

The Conclusion explores the relationship between Plato's portrayal of Socrates in the *Meno* and his portrayal of Socrates in the Socratic dialogues generally and, especially, in the *Apology*. This chapter shows that the Socratic ideals and commitments featured in the *Meno*, namely, Socrates' high regard for true opinion and his determination to fight in word and deed for the worth of moral inquiry, are fully consonant with those in evidence in the *Apology* and in other Socratic dialogues. This chapter explains, too, how it is that even though the examined life fails to achieve moral knowledge, it is, nevertheless, for Socrates, a happy one, and the man who

---

21. See Rorty (1987), 323–24: "If *Socrates* intended to have a serious conversation with Meno's slave, *Plato* presents that conversation as a farce" (emphasis in original).

leads it, a good man. It contends that whereas for Socrates knowledge is certainly a sufficient condition for virtue, it is, as the *Meno* and the *Apology* both show, not a necessary one.[22]

Appendix I considers the relationship between the *Phaedo*'s and the *Meno*'s versions of the recollection thesis. In doing so, Appendix I addresses what is surely the most serious and most formidable objection to the interpretation advanced in this book of the *Meno*'s recollection thesis: how can the *Meno* be, as is argued here, mainly a strategic ploy on Socrates' part to keep Meno from abandoning the inquiry into the nature of virtue when recollection is integral to Plato's conception of learning in the *Phaedo* as well?[23] In response to this objection, Appendix I shows that the *Phaedo*'s discussion of recollection is no mere refinement or development of the *Meno*'s but represents, on the contrary, a radical departure from it. Thus, far from supporting the *Meno*'s version of recollection, the *Phaedo* provides good reason for abandoning it.

Appendix II explores the change in the status of moral inquiry brought about by the introduction in the *Republic* of the Theory of Forms. This appendix shows how and why, with the emergence in the *Republic* of philosophers defined not by their sheer love of wisdom but by their actual attainment of it, moral inquiry is abandoned: for the philosopher-kings, moral inquiry is replaced by the vision of the Forms; for the citizens they govern, it is replaced by the rulers' exercise of persuasion or, when necessary, of compulsion. Whereas the practice of elenchus is critical for men's moral improvement in the Cave, its inability to transcend opinion renders it obsolete once some human beings attain wisdom greater than human.

22. I will argue in the Conclusion that when Socrates contends in the elenctic dialogues that virtue is knowledge, what he contends is that knowledge is sufficient for virtue.

23. Appendix I shows that of all the other places in the Platonic corpus in which recollection purportedly appears, there is, in fact, only one dialogue (besides the *Meno* and *Phaedo*) in which it is actually found: the *Phaedrus*. Yet because of the heavily mythic presentation of recollection in the *Phaedrus*, the *Phaedrus*'s account, it is argued, cannot be taken at face value as providing confirmation of recollection as a serious Platonic theory of learning.

1

The Struggle over Definition

[Young people] are great-souled; there is
great souledness in thinking oneself worthy
of great things, a feeling that belongs to one
who is full of good hope. They would always
rather do noble deeds than useful ones.

Aristotle, *Rhetoric* 2.12.1389a

i. Meno

The action of the *Meno* is driven by the character Meno, by his passions, his personal traits, his associations, his ambitions. Meno is Socrates' project, the current object of Socrates' ongoing efforts to re-
form anyone he meets—young or old, foreigner or citizen—who
regards "the things worth the most [prudence, truth, and how one's
soul will be the best possible (*Ap.* 29e1–2)] as the least important,
and the paltrier things [having as much money as possible, reputation, and honor (*Ap.* 29d9–e1)] as most important" (*Ap.* 30a1–2,
trans. West and West [1984]).

Who is the character Meno? Meno is a young man, around twenty
years old,[1] from Thessaly, a place that, at least according to the *Crito*
(53d), is known for corruption. In the *Meno*, Thessaly is said to be

---

1. Morrison (1942) and Ryle (1976) contend that Meno must have been somewhat older. As Morrison puts it, 157–58: "It is difficult to believe that a youth of 20
would have been in charge of a company of mercenaries: and Xenophon, whose aim
was to denigrate Meno's morals, has a motive for exaggerating his youth." According
to Ryle, 3: "Meno is already a mature man with a household of his own, including
slaves; he is of high military rank; he has been acquainted for a long time with Aristippus and Gorgias . . . he is *'still'* handsome enough to have lovers, 76B" (emphasis
in original). Stokes (1963), 294, makes a similar argument. See Bluck (1961a), 123,
however, who argues that Meno must indeed be about twenty years old. It seems to
me that Meno is at the tail end of his youth: that is why he is young enough still to
have lovers.

known for horsemanship and wealth and, of late—that is, in the aftermath of Gorgias's visit—for wisdom as well (*M.* 70a5–b6).[2] Meno is of aristocratic birth, a man of means, and quite handsome.[3] The *Meno* notes his association with Aristippus, whom the dialogue identifies as his lover (*M.* 70b);[4] with Gorgias,[5] whose views he is depicted as adopting seemingly uncritically; and with Anytus, notorious for his participation—along with Meletus and Lycon—in prosecuting Socrates and seeking his execution.

The *Meno* opens, abruptly, with Meno's question concerning how a person comes to possess virtue. The question is for him a pressing one, not of theoretical but of immediate practical interest.[6] Indeed, Meno shows no inclination to investigate with Socrates the question that *is* theoretical, Socrates' question, What is virtue? It is clear that Meno has never before stopped to consider what human excellence really is, what will make his life a truly worthwhile one, where success genuinely lies. Like young Hippocrates in the *Protagoras*, who, in his eagerness to enter the ranks of the successful, awakens Socrates in the middle of the night to wangle from him an introduction to Protagoras, so Meno impatiently seeks to be assured either that he has already come by virtue—whether naturally or by having apprenticed

2. There is palpable irony in this Socratic observation: Gorgias has taught the Thessalians to answer any question, just as he does, "fearlessly and magnificently"— as is appropriate for those who have knowledge (*M.* 7b6–c3). Yet no one, of course— neither Gorgias nor, a fortiori, the Thessalians—could possibly know everything! Interestingly, what Gorgias prides himself on in the *Gorgias* is precisely the ability to speak well about things with respect to which he has no knowledge (see *Gorg.* 458e–459c).

3. Nehamas (1987), 283–84, contends that *kalos* at *M.* 71b6 means, not "good-looking," but rather "noble," arguing that whereas knowledge of who Meno is would need to precede knowledge of Meno's "essential" qualities (those that, for the Greeks, define a person: his geographical, familial, and social origins), such knowledge need not precede knowledge of every other (accidental) quality a person or thing may have. Yet, as Meno's good looks are prominently featured later on in the dialogue (at *M.* 76b4–5 and 80c3–5), it seems likely that here, too, it is Meno's good looks and not his nobility that Socrates intends by *kalos*. Moreover, *kalos* appears alongside *gennaios* (*M.* 71b7), so if we take *kalos* to mean "noble," what does it add to *gennaios*, "of noble birth"?

4. According to Xenophon, it was owing to Meno's relationship with Aristippus that Meno was given command of the mercenaries whom Cyrus had loaned to Aristippus and who took part, with Meno, in the Anabasis, the unsuccessful attempt on the Persian throne in 401 B.C.

5. Socrates counts Meno's lover, Aristippus, among the Thessalian lovers of Gorgias's wisdom, implying thereby that Gorgias's wisdom was seductive but, like Meno, lacked real substance.

6. Contra Ryle (1976), 3.

himself appropriately to Gorgias—or that there is some other way that he might still attain it. Moreover, just as Socrates must keep Hippocrates' enthusiasm at bay long enough to consider with him the nature of the "product" he intends to purchase from Protagoras, so must he frustrate Meno's determination to have his question quickly answered: he insists that before they discuss Meno's question of how virtue is attained, they attend to the logically antecedent question of what virtue is.

Meno does not find Socrates' question particularly difficult (*M.* 71e1).[7] He knows the answer; he has heard it from Gorgias. Furthermore, he expects Socrates to know it, too, as Socrates has also met Gorgias. It is clear from the start that Meno will not say what he thinks—he apparently does not do much independent thinking— but will say what he has memorized of the teachings of Gorgias (or, when necessary, of someone else). Meno's very name is, in fact, a pun on memory and memorization.[8] It is because Meno does not

---

7. Meno does not seem to distinguish, as Gorgias does (see n. 2), between speaking well about something and having knowledge of it. What Meno says in response to Socrates' request for a definition of virtue is that it is not difficult "to say," *eipein* (*M.* 71e1); he does not realize that his finding it easy to speak about virtue does not entail that he knows anything about it. Indeed, Meno has clearly never given the matter any thought. Later on in the dialogue, Meno notes with admiration that Gorgias never undertook to teach virtue and ridiculed those who did; what Gorgias sought to do, Meno says, was only to teach others to be clever at speaking (*M.* 95c). Nevertheless, when he himself repeats the clever things Gorgias has to say about virtue, Meno thinks he has learned from Gorgias what virtue is. For discussion of yet another consequence of Meno's failure to distinguish between speaking well about something and having knowledge of it, see Chapter 2, n. 3.

8. Klein (1965), 44. The pun on Meno's name is most pronounced in the passage in which Socrates says of himself that he is a poor rememberer: *Ou panu eimi mnēmōn, ō Menōn* (*M.* 71c8). Is it possible that Socrates, by claiming to be bad at remembering, implies that he, in contrast to Meno, *thinks?* See also MacDonough (1978), 174, who notes another pun associated with Meno's name: *menō* (see *M.* 97e4, e8, 98a2, a8), "to abide" or "to remain steadfast." Steadfastness, MacDonough rightly recognizes, is not a quality that Meno possesses: after his third failure to produce an adequate definition, he no longer wishes to continue the discussion. This root also appears at *M.* 77a1–2, where Socrates wants Meno to stay and Meno says he would stay (*perimenoim'*) if Socrates would give him more answers like the one in which he defined color in terms of effluences. *Menein*, I might add, is a constant theme in the *Crito* as well, playing on the connection between, on the one hand, Socrates' decision to remain in prison and, on the other, the abidingness of the moral principles upon which he draws in reaching that decision. Punning on names is not uncommon in Plato. Meletus, Socrates' accuser, is the man who presumably (but not really) cares about the young; *meletē* is the Greek word for "care" (see *Ap.* 24c8; *Euthyph.* 2d2, d4, 3a3; and West and West [1984], 73, who take note of this pun). The name Crito suggests the

do much thinking, because he is not truly reflective, that he is, as Thompson (1901), xx, says, "a bad *pupil*" (emphasis in original).

The Meno of our dialogue craves power and money. As he seeks to define virtue, his definition initially embraces the virtues of men, women, children, slaves, and old men; but when he is pressed to find a single virtue—the virtue common to all instances of virtue—his definition narrows to exclude all but the virtue associated with men,[9] namely, that of ruling others (*M.* 73c9–d1);[10] and in his final attempt to define virtue, he designates gold and silver, along with political honor and office, as the great goods that the man of virtue has the power to acquire (*M.* 78c7–8).

Is Meno a bad man? Or is Grote right to say that "there is nothing in the Platonic dialogue to mark that meanness and perfidy which the Xenophontic picture indicates"?[11] Are we to take seriously Socrates' charges, though made teasingly or by way of banter,[12] that Meno is a bully (*hubristēs, M.* 76a9), a scoundrel (*panourgos, M.* 80b8, 81e7), spoiled (*truphōn, M.* 76b8), and tyrannical (*turanneuōn, M.* 76b8)?

For the most part, to be sure, Meno is "deferential to Socrates";[13] he is "polite to Socrates . . . even when the argument turns against him."[14] His good manners even make Socrates' name-calling appear at times unwarranted and spiteful. When, for example, Meno asks Socrates to teach him what he means by his assertion that we do not learn but that all learning is recollection (*M.* 81e4–6), is it at all

Greek word *krisis,* "decision," and the *Crito* is the dialogue in which Socrates faces a life-and-death decision. And Polus is the impetuous *pōlos,* "colt," of *Gorg.* 463e.

9. Guthrie (1975), 242, n. 1, notes that at *Prot.* 325a there is a similar shift from virtue to manly virtue that passes without comment.

10. Cf. *Gorg.* 452d. Indeed, this definition of Meno's follows Socrates' instruction that Meno try to recollect what Gorgias says virtue is.

11. Grote (1888), II, 232. Klein (1965), 35–38, relying on his wealth of knowledge of history, portrays a Meno of rather dubious character. As Anastaplo (1975), 84, notes, however, "one must wonder whether Mr. Klein's considerable scholarship sometimes gets in the way of a direct confrontation with the text and especially with the character of Meno." Meno is in the *Meno* not yet a villain, even if he is not quite of pristine character.

12. Thompson (1901), xix–xx, says the charges are made "good-humoredly"; cf. Klein's (1965), 89, "jokingly." I would not wish to go quite that far. By the time Socrates makes such charges, he is no longer as well disposed toward Meno as he was at first. Socrates may not be ready yet to give up on Meno's improvement, but he is dismayed by his conduct.

13. Thompson (1901), xix.

14. Allen (1984), 134. I do not think, however, as Allen does, that Meno is polite "throughout."

reasonable for Socrates to accuse Meno of deliberately attempting to catch him in a contradiction (*M.* 82a2–3)? Is Meno not speaking the plain truth when he denies having had any such intention and explains that he spoke as he did merely by force of habit (*M.* 82a4–6)?[15]

In fact, however, Meno is not consistently polite. We may note in this regard the indelicacy of his comparison of Socrates to a stingray (*M.* 80a4–6). Although Meno calls it a joke (*M.* 80a5), it is a gratuitously offensive barb: not content to use it to allude to Socrates' penchant for "numbing" those he meets, Meno extends the analogy to the physical resemblance between Socrates and the ugly fish. Moreover, we must not forget that Meno—and not just Anytus—speaks threateningly to Socrates (*M.* 80b5–7): "I think you choose well not to travel abroad from here or live abroad; for if you did such things as a foreigner in another city, you might well be arrested as a wizard." Meno's good manners, it appears, vary directly with how well disposed he is at the moment toward Socrates: he starts off remarkably well mannered, but after Socrates repeatedly finds fault with his definitions of virtue, Meno's patience, and his veneer of gentility, begin to wear thin. It is when he falters badly that he suddenly remembers having heard that Socrates is a perplexed man who perplexes others.

As far as Socrates' manners are concerned, let us note that he hurls not a single nasty epithet at Meno until after *M.* 75c4–7, where Meno objects for no good reason to Socrates' proposed definition of shape as that which alone always accompanies color. From that point on, Meno is no longer, in Socrates' eyes, a merely misguided young man in need of direction. Meno is now a quite disagreeable young man—even more in need of direction.

ii. What Is Virtue? Round 1

Socrates disappoints Meno, too. Word of Socrates' wisdom having no doubt reached him, Meno expects Socrates to display his wisdom readily and to enlighten him with respect to how one comes to have virtue. Meno is quickly disabused of that naïvely optimistic expectation, as Socrates informs him that far from knowing what sort of

---

15. The *Meno* makes it seem not at all unlikely that Meno habitually asks those he encounters to teach him; that appears to be his way.

thing (*hopoion*) virtue is, he knows not at all (*to parapan*) what virtue is.[16] Indeed, Socrates insists that one cannot know what sort of thing something is unless one knows what it is: one who does not know at all (*to parapan*) who Meno is cannot know if he is handsome or wealthy or of noble birth.

Socrates' principle of the "priority of definition," as it has come to be known, makes rather frequent appearances within the Platonic corpus. In the *Gorgias*, for example, Socrates wants Polus to hold off on praising oratory until its nature has been clarified (448e), and he requires of himself that he define oratory before passing judgment on its worth (463c). At *Rep.* 1.354b–c, Socrates says that without knowing what justice is, he cannot know whether it is a virtue or a vice, wisdom or ignorance, or whether the just person is happy or unhappy.[17] Related, yet distinct, notions are found in the *Euthyphro* and in the *Hippias Major*. In the *Euthyphro* (7b–e), Socrates will not allow Euthyphro to judge a particular act holy (prosecuting his own father for murder), without first defining holiness. And in the *Hippias Major* (26c), Socrates reproaches himself for attempting, without knowing first what beauty and ugliness are, to pronounce certain aspects of certain poems ugly and others beautiful. (The distinction between the *Meno, Gorgias*, and *Rep* 1 cases, on the one hand,[18] and the *Euthyphro* and *Hippias Major* cases, on the other, is simply that whereas in the former it is the entity to which the quality is applied that is unknown, in the latter it is the quality itself that is unknown.)

In some of these instances, the *Meno*'s among them, there is an unmistakable pedagogical motivation behind Socrates' insistence on the priority of definition. Meno wants desperately to know how he can come to be counted among the virtuous. Although he is chasing after something he calls virtue, he has given no thought to what it means to be genuinely virtuous. Young Hippocrates in the *Protagoras*

16. *Hopoion* is used here to indicate the traits a thing possesses. It is used slightly differently in the slave-boy-demonstration, where the slave-boy is unable to calculate the (incalculable) length of the line upon which a double-size square is constructed but is eventually able to say what sort of line it is: a diagonal. *Hopoion* surfaces again when Socrates eventually agrees to consider with Meno what sort of thing virtue is without yet knowing what virtue is (*M.* 86e1–2).

17. Given the definitions of justice proposed in *Rep.* 1, one truly could not with confidence call it a virtue or know whether he who has it is happy or unhappy.

18. See also *Lach.* 190d: "Then, Laches, suppose we first set about determining the nature of courage, and in the second place proceed to inquire how the young men may attain this quality by the help of studies and pursuits" (trans. Jowett [1961]).

is equally eager to acquire virtue and equally unclear on exactly what it is. In these cases and others, Socrates seeks to teach an important lesson: one ought not to pursue something without considering its nature first; for how, otherwise, can one assess whether what one is pursuing is worthy of pursuit?

As important as it is to Socrates to prevent impetuous young men from doing themselves irreparable harm, his "priority of definition" principle is not invoked exclusively for this end. It is a principle with broad application that packs considerable epistemological and methodological punch. If one does not know at all who Meno is, one certainly should not comment on whether he is handsome, well-born, or wealthy. Indeed, on what grounds do people presume to make pronouncements about the features of things they know not at all? Later on in the dialogue, Socrates mockingly remarks that Anytus must be a prophet, since he claims to know, without having had any acquaintance with sophists at all, that they are bad (*M.* 92c). If, then, it would not be right for Socrates, in accordance with his principle, to venture to say how people come to have virtue if he knows not at all what virtue is, the inevitable question arises: is it true that Socrates knows not at all what virtue is? Since Socrates does not disavow knowledge of all things—he does not say, for example, as we shall soon see, that he knows not at all what shape is—what could he mean by saying of himself that he does not know virtue?

What Socrates must mean by disavowing all knowledge of virtue but not all knowledge of other things is that what he lacks, with respect to virtue but not with respect to all other things, is a level of understanding or skill that qualifies as knowledge; he must mean that despite all that he has thought, reasoned, and concluded about virtue, he cannot claim to know it. And, indeed, how could he possess moral knowledge? The knowledge of virtue is what he calls in the *Apology* "wisdom greater than human" (*Ap.* 20e1), the kind of wisdom that only the gods possess, the kind of wisdom that it is both foolish and impious for a human being to pretend to have. It is with respect to virtue that the chasm between gods and men yawns widest: the highest *human* wisdom is the kind that Socrates has, that is, the recognition of the limits of human wisdom.[19]

---

19. As Socrates recounts at *Ap.* 23a5–b4, he comes to understand the oracle to be saying that the height of human wisdom is Socratic wisdom, namely, the knowledge that one lacks wisdom concerning the most important things (*ta megista*): human virtue. The oracle, Socrates says, in proclaiming him wisest, uses the name "Socrates" as a mere place-holder; the oracle's intention is to designate as wisest that man, any

If no human being can know what virtue is, then surely none can know how it comes to be present in a human being. But one might well form opinions, even true opinions, both about the nature of virtue and about how virtue comes to those who have it. That is why Socrates undertakes to conduct a moral inquiry with Meno, asking first, as is proper, what virtue is. Throughout the investigation, however, Socrates fully recognizes that its result will not transcend opinion. He has vigorously conducted such investigations for a lifetime and still knows "not at all" what virtue is. Elenchus, the method he deems most appropriate to moral discourse, has not yielded and will not yield moral knowledge.[20]

Having disavowed knowledge of virtue, Socrates is in a position to ask Meno, who will find the question unproblematic, what he thinks virtue is or, what amounts to the same thing, what Gorgias says virtue is. What ensues is a struggle between Socrates and Meno over the definition of virtue.

At the heart of the struggle is the matter of whether virtue is defined by what is done (Meno's view) or by how it is done (Socrates' view). Socrates finds troubling not simply Meno's enumeration of different virtues for men, women, slaves, children, old men, and so on, but the implication of this enumeration, to wit, that virtue is a function of *what* is done and not of the manner in which it is done. The virtue of a man, Meno/Gorgias says, consists in taking part in the affairs of the city, helping friends and harming enemies, and protecting oneself; the virtue of a woman consists in managing the household well, looking after its contents, and being subject to her husband.[21] Socrates, by contrast, determines whether something

man, who knows that he does not know virtue. The oracle maintains, then, not that, as a matter of fact, no one is wiser than the man Socrates, but rather that the wisest of men, the man who is as wise as a man can be, knows, *like* Socrates, no more with respect to *ta megista* than that he does not know.

20. Contra Irwin (1977), 139–40, and Fine (1992), 208–9, both of whom think that Socrates in the *Meno* holds that true opinions about virtue's qualities can eventually lead to knowledge of virtue. For a view similar to mine, see Bedu-Addo (1984), 4: "Since the *Meno* distinguishes between knowledge and true opinion, to say we can't *know* anything about what x is like without knowing x is not to say that we can't have or say true things (true opinions) about x without knowing x's nature" (emphasis in original); and 5: "We do not know what virtue is, nor do we know what sort of thing it is, but we do have opinions about what sort of thing it is, by the consideration of which opinions we may attain true opinion about what virtue is."

21. In the case of masculine virtue, Meno speaks of having the *ability* to do rather than of actually doing (*M.* 71e3, 73c9). Meno, then, finds the virtue of a man in the skill he possesses but that of a woman in her actually doing what is expected of her.

counts as virtue by asking whether it is done "well," by which he means temperately and justly.[22] For Socrates, then, virtue functions adverbially, such that it can univocally modify very different activities. But for Meno, who thinks virtue is determined by what one does, it follows that insofar as different roles entail different virtues, there can be no one sense of virtue common to all.[23]

Socrates tries to help Meno find, even among his own disparate virtues, some common ground. He selects out of Meno's potpourri of virtues the virtue Meno calls "managing well," *eu dioikein,* a phrase that Meno actually uses in this form only in his description of the virtue of a woman. Socrates proposes for Meno's consideration that managing well might be something common to Meno's conception of both the virtue of a man and the virtue of a woman—though the man manages a city and the woman a household (*M.* 73a6–7). As immediately becomes clear, however, Socrates regards the managing aspect of "managing well" (that is, the activity performed) as merely incidental to this shared virtue, emphasizing instead the "well" (that is, the manner of its performance), which he forthwith interprets to mean temperately and justly. Indeed, as of *M.* 73b3, the "managing" element has altogether dropped out of Socrates' account of what the virtuous man and woman have in common, and Socrates speaks only of what both a man and a woman need "if they are going to be good." He thereby eases the transition to child and old man, neither of whom is a manager, yet who also need the very same qualities if they are to be good: "all human beings are thus good in the same way; for they come to be good by obtaining the same things" (*M.* 73c1–3).

When Meno, however, makes another attempt to identify what is common to all instances of virtue, he is drawn, despite Socrates' efforts, not to the "well," but to the "managing," in "managing well." Thus, when he casts about for a single common virtue, what he looks for is a single form of managing. Ironically, however, he comes up, not with a form of managing more inclusive than the previous one, but with a most exclusive one: the form of managing on which he

22. Socrates takes the "well" that Meno uses only in describing the womanly virtue of household management and extends it to the man's management of the city (*M.* 73a6–7). He then goes on to take "well" to mean temperately and justly (*M.* 73a7–9).

23. Meno agrees that health and strength mean the same for everyone (*M.* 72e2–3, e9) but balks when Socrates extends this idea to virtue (*M.* 73a4–5). Interlocutors raise similar challenges at *Charm.* 165e, *Rep.* 1.337c, *Euthyd.* 298c, *Cra.* 429a–b.

settles excludes not only children, slaves, and old men, as the previous one did, but women, too; he so narrows his definition of virtue that it applies to no one but men in their prime. Virtue is now, for Meno, nothing more than ruling others.[24]

Is Meno's failing in this early part of the dialogue an epistemological one or a moral one? Does he not know how to formulate an adequate definition or is he unable to appreciate the moral dimension of virtue? There can be no doubt that Meno is no whiz at definition: instead of a single virtue common to all kinds of virtue, he cites the various kinds; he cannot see (as Socrates can [*M.* 73d2–4]) that his "ruling others" definition is technically inferior to the earlier definition of "managing well"; and he fails to articulate in any way the difference he senses between the virtue case, in which he refuses to concede an unvarying essence that transcends variety in application (*M.* 73a4–5), and the case of health and strength, in which he does acknowledge such an essence (*M.* 72e2–3; e9). Nevertheless, his more disturbing and more serious defect is a moral one: Meno subscribes unthinkingly to the common view that one ought to help friends and harm enemies; he certainly does not appreciate, on his own, the importance of justice and the other virtues or parts of virtue to virtue; and even when Socrates does get him to see and to admit that managing "well" entails managing with justice and temperance, he is still unable to transfer that lesson to the new definition of virtue he proposes—the ability to rule others.

Were Meno's problem primarily an epistemological or logical one rather than a moral one, would he not have had just as much trouble recognizing that health and strength are the same in men and women as he does in recognizing that virtue is the same for everyone? The reason he has considerably more trouble in the latter case is, no doubt, because what he really believes is that only men have real virtue, and that real virtue, manly virtue, the virtue he craves, has little or nothing in common with what women and children and slaves and old men have that goes by the same name. When Socrates insists, then, that virtue, like health and strength, *is* the same for everyone, Socrates makes more than just a logical point. In effect, he democratizes *aretē.* If virtue is the same for everyone, then virtue cannot be a matter of one's social position. Moreover, if virtue is the

24. See n. 9. The term *archein,* "to rule," reappears at *M.* 86d6–8, where Socrates chides Meno for trying to rule only Socrates but not himself.

same for everyone, then anyone can be virtuous: all one need do is comport oneself justly and temperately.

And so, to drive home his moral point, Socrates presses on: "You say virtue is being able to rule? Shall we not add to that justly and not unjustly?" (*M.* 73d7–8). Meno concurs, asserting that "justice is virtue" (*M.* 73d9–10). Since, however, justice is, as Meno will soon agree (*M.* 73e7–74a6), but one virtue among many, justice cannot in itself constitute, after all, the sought-after definition of virtue.[25]

iii. What Is a Good Definition?

Since Meno is having difficulty producing an adequate definition of virtue, Socrates provides him with a model definition, a definition of "shape," *schēma*. Why does Socrates choose to define a geometrical term rather than some other? Vlastos (1991a), 120, has argued that by the time Plato composes the *Meno* he has become enamored of mathematics. Even if that is so, however, what is decisive for Socrates' choice of example is that Meno takes himself to be proficient in mathematics. As the dialogue will very soon reveal, Meno regards himself as Empedocles' student and prides himself on the learning he has acquired from him. Empedocles is himself, in turn, Pythagoras's student. Meno, then, is linked to Pythagoras through Empedocles, and this link provides a promising explanation for the pervasiveness of Pythagorean geometry, along with Empedoclean physics, in this dialogue.

The definition of shape that Socrates offers is as follows. Shape is that which, alone among the things that are, always accompanies color (*M.* 75b9–11). We note that Socrates proffers this definition,

---

25. Since there are other virtues besides justice—Meno lists courage, temperance, wisdom, and magnificence (*megaloprepeia*), among others (*M.* 74a4–5)—the problem of breaking the single whole, virtue, into a plurality of virtues surfaces once again as it did in Meno's first definition. The plurality problem here, however, arises, as Socrates says, "in a different way from that in which it happened just now" (*M.* 74a8). The most important difference surely is that whereas the virtues in the swarm of virtues that Meno identified for man, woman, slave, child, and old man, respectively, are not virtues at all, justice, temperance, and piety, insofar as they are ways in which things are done rather than things that are done, are at least really virtues. I shall discuss at the end of this chapter the plurality of virtue insofar as it has "parts"—justice, temperance, and piety—and the unique problem this sort of plurality occasions. I shall consider Meno's list of the other virtues in Chapter 4, when I discuss the passage *M.* 88a–c, in which Socrates and Meno enumerate the goods of the soul.

not as the unique or even as an especially good definition of shape, but rather as one that suffices for his present purposes, introducing it with the words "Let shape be *for us (hēmin)*" (*M.* 75b9–10). All Socrates needs is a definition on which Meno can pattern his definition of virtue: "For," says Socrates, "I would certainly be satisfied if you spoke similarly to me about virtue" (*M.* 75b11–c1). Thus, unless Meno finds fault with the definition, it will stand.

Alas, find fault he does. Meno's immediate response to Socrates' definition of shape is to call it *euēthes,* "simple" or "simpleminded" (*M.* 75c2). What does that mean? When asked by Socrates to say what it means, Meno responds, probably reproducing an eristic quibble he had encountered somewhere, perhaps through his association with Gorgias,[26] that the definition is useless to "someone"[27] who does not know color. But who, after all, is unfamiliar with color? Socrates had tried to offer a clear, nontechnical definition that could serve as a model for defining virtue. Why does Meno reject Socrates' definition out of hand?

Let us note that Meno's complaint that the definition Socrates proposes will fail for someone who does not know color is but his second thought on the matter, uttered in an attempt to assign content and meaning to his first, more visceral, objection. The very first thing that Meno says is that Socrates' definition is *euēthes,* "simple" or "simpleminded." Unlike the gloss of it that follows, which implies that for Meno the problem with Socrates' definition is that it might prove too difficult or too obscure for "someone," the *euēthes* objection implies, on the contrary, that the fault of the definition lies in its containing nothing sophisticated or esoteric or technical—indeed, nothing that the man in the street would not understand, nothing, that is, to distinguish the educated and cultured man from the boor. We may assume that Meno's immediate response to Socrates' definition—and not his subsequent commentary on it—betrays his true feelings: what he really finds repugnant is just how plain, how unpretentious, the definition is; what is distasteful to him is not that the definition does use terms that someone might not understand but that it does not.

Meno, as Socrates quickly realizes, prefers the high-flown, the *tragikē* (*M.* 76e3). The definition Meno favors is, therefore, one that

26. That Socrates suspects Meno of relying on a sophistic source might well underlie his speaking of the objector as "eristic." It is likely that Socrates suspects a similar source for Meno's paradox, which he also calls "eristic" (*M.* 80e2).

27. Not to him, of course.

contains the more technical term "effluences," *aporroai*. We note that Meno expresses with respect to "effluences" no worry such as the one he expressed with respect to "color"; yet is it not far more likely that someone might fail to know "effluences" than that someone might fail to know "color"?[28] Moreover, Meno is surprisingly unperturbed by the fact that if, as in his preferred definition, color is defined as an "effluence from shapes," *aporroē schēmatōn* (M. 76d4), the definition might be useless to someone who does not know shape.[29] By offering a definition of color that commits the same offense as the initial definition of shape does, Socrates is able to expose the disingenuousness and shallowness of Meno's objection to the definition of shape: despite what Meno says, he is not really bothered by the use of unknown terms; what offends him is the use of known terms, that is, of terms known to everyone. Meno does not like Socrates' definition because Meno is a snob. Socrates, however, clearly does like the original definition of shape that he offered. It has one merit that surely counts for much in his eyes: it is, as he says, "the truth," *talēthē* (M. 75c8, d5). What Socrates no longer likes is Meno.

Meno's response to Socrates' proposed definition of shape represents a turning point in the dialogue, the point at which Socrates sours on his interlocutor. Once Meno objects to Socrates' definition of shape as the only thing that always accompanies color (M. 75b9–11), Socrates sees Meno for "the clever and disputatious (*eristikon*) and contentious sort" (M. 75c9)[30] that he—and not just an anonymous "someone"—is.[31] From now on, although Socrates pretends that he and Meno are friends—"But if, just as you and I now, people, being friends were willing to converse with one another..." (M. 75d2–3)—it is just pretense. Socrates clearly finds Meno's reaction

28. Although the word *aporroē* is a perfectly ordinary Greek word, it takes on a technical and specialized meaning in Empedoclean perception theory, a meaning with which an ordinary Greek speaker would most likely be unfamiliar. "Effluence" is, in our context, technical jargon.

29. Davis (1988), 113, like me, finds it significant that the third definition defines color in terms of shape. Bluck (1961a), 243, however, dismisses the matter, saying that by this time an adequate definition of shape has been arrived at, presumably the definition of shape as the limit of a solid. Yet one may reasonably suppose that the terms in "limit of a solid" are no better known than "color." They may be known to Meno, but would they be better known to him than "color"?

30. This is the first of three occasions upon which Socrates associates Meno, or what Meno says, with eristic. The other two are at M. 80e2 and 81d6.

31. We can tell that Socrates resists Meno's "someone" ploy, since he makes a point in what follows of getting Meno to admit that the terms Socrates is now using are known to Meno.

to his straightforward and easily understood definition needlessly ob-structive,[32] as well as gratuitously snobbish.

We may note that Socrates' second definition of shape—"the limit of a solid"—is more acceptable to Meno than the first one was: its terms are at least technical; that is, they are not "simple" ones that everyone can understand.[33] They do not, however, begin to approach in degree of ostentation a term like "effluences," and for that reason, Meno's reception of the second definition of shape is tepid com-pared with the enthused reception he accords to the definition of color: "But I would stay, Socrates," Meno says with respect only to the "effluences" definition, "if you were to give me many answers like this" (M. 77a1–2). Not only does the arcane terminology of the definition of color greatly please Meno, but he has yet another cause for being pleased: Socrates' very act of providing a definition of color represents his yielding to Meno's authority. "Yes, gratify me," Meno commands (M. 76c3)—and Socrates complies. Meno is, as Socrates says, the handsome, spoiled bully who dares to issue commands to an old man, exploiting the old man's weakness for good looks. Soc-rates complies with Meno's order not only by formulating the de-sired definition but by doing so "in the style of Gorgias, in the way that you would most easily follow" (M. 76c4–5).[34]

Which definition is Socrates' favorite? There can be no doubt that Socrates prefers the first one, his definition of shape as the only thing that always accompanies color: (a) If he prefers some other, why is this the one he proposes? Indeed, he never would have of-fered another had Meno not rejected this one. (b) He says, twice, that it is "the truth" (M. 75c8, d5). (c) It is intended to serve as the

32. See Klein (1965), 62: "Whatever weight we might attach to Meno's dissatis-faction with Socrates' statement, it is hard not to suspect Meno of deliberately delaying his playing the part he had agreed to play. Such behavior may well be called dispu-tatious and one could accuse Meno of merely competing for some verbal victory with-out caring in the slightest about the matter under investigation. And could not Gor-gias' schooling be held responsible for this attitude?"

33. Davis (1988), 112, asks: "in what sense is solid more known than color? Meno accepts it [the second definition] because its mathematical form is familiar to him." I would argue that it is precisely because solid is generally less known than color that Meno prefers the second definition and is willing to accept it. We may note that Socrates checks to see that Meno is familiar with the term "solid" specifically as it is used in geometry.

34. Sternfeld and Zyskind (1978), 11, note that Socrates reaches "the limit of [his] adjustment to Meno . . . [as] indicated by his response; he says he cannot continue long in this style."

model for an acceptable definition of virtue. When Socrates says, then, at *M.* 76e6, "The other one was better," he surely refers to the original definition of *M.* 75b9–11.[35]

The features of this definition that recommend it to Socrates are, first, that it says something true; second, that it uses familiar terms, terms that are not needlessly technical and grandiose; and, third, that unlike the definition of color that, as Socrates points out, works equally well for sound, smell, and many other things of that sort (*M.* 76d9–e1), Socrates' first definition of shape identifies shape uniquely: shape is the *only* thing that always accompanies color.[36] (Meno, ever careless of such things, misses, in his paraphrase at *M.* 75c4–5 of Socrates' definition of shape, the uniqueness of shape's role vis-à-vis color: he omits the word "only," *monon.*) We shall see in the next section how these three admirable features of the first definition of shape, when reproduced in the dialogue's last definition of virtue, go quite a long way toward providing an adequate definition for virtue.

A long way, but certainly not the whole way. In truth, even in the matter of shape these features do not go the whole way. Socrates' favored definition of shape, despite exhibiting the three strengths mentioned, fails to get to the essence, to the *ousia,* of what shape is; at most, it picks out a trait that shape alone always instantiates.[37] It seeks to understand shape not as it is in itself but as it relates to something else: shape is, after all, on Socrates' "definition," no more than the only thing for which the presence of color is a sufficient condition. Socrates' definition of virtue, patterned as it is on his

35. Klein (1965), 70, believes, as I do, that Socrates' preferred definition is "the first—sober—one which, correlating 'surface' and 'color,' hinted at a possibly satisfactory answer about 'human excellence,' " rather than "the geometrical—narrow— one which was given in Meno's own terms." Bluck (1961a), 254, and Guthrie (1975), 249, n. 1, however, think Socrates prefers the second definition: they do not say why. If their reason is that since it comes later it is the more likely referent of "the other one" that Socrates at *M.* 76e6 says is better, we may counter that, even much later, at *M.* 79d1–2, where Socrates speaks of "the answer I just now gave you about shape," he is referring, this time quite unambiguously, to the first definition of shape, the one in terms of color.

36. It is clear, I think, that Socrates is no fan of the definition that Meno prefers.

37. Perhaps the notion that shape is the only thing that always accompanies color is not even true, let alone an adequate definition of shape. Yet Meno does not appear to doubt its truth. And we have no reason to suspect, at this early stage of the dialogue, that when Socrates says that something is true, he does not mean what he says. I admit to being sympathetic to the truth of Socrates' view, at least at the level of perception: if one sees something colored, one sees something shaped in some way.

definition of shape, is, as we shall see in Section iv, marred by the limitations of the definition of shape no less than it is graced by its merits.

Defining shape is a simpler task by far for Socrates than is defining virtue.[38] In no time at all Socrates produces two acceptable definitions of shape; he could, perhaps, produce others as well.

iv. What Is Virtue? Round 2

Now that Socrates has given Meno a definition of which he approves (M. 77a1–2), it is Meno's turn, in accordance with his and Socrates' agreement (M. 75b4–5), to venture once more to define virtue. Meno's new definition of virtue, borrowed from an unnamed poet, sees virtue as "to rejoice in fine things and to have power." In Meno's paraphrase, the definition becomes "Virtue is to desire fine things (kala) and to have the power to acquire them" (M. 77b2–5).

This definition, let us note, is not all bad. On the negative side, it shows just how intractable Meno's moral failings are: despite Socrates' efforts, Meno is as haughty as ever, and justice and temperance still find no place in his conception of virtue. On the positive side, however, Meno's new definition reflects in certain respects the perhaps unwitting progress he has made as a definer: the new definition neither breaks virtue into pieces nor uses unknown or technical terms; moreover, it picks out virtue uniquely.[39]

According to Meno's definition, there are two marks that distinguish the man of virtue, two criteria by which one man may be judged superior to his fellow: (1) a penchant for the fine and (2) power. Socrates considers, and discounts, each of these in turn. Let us begin by considering Socrates' response to Meno's first proposed indicator of virtue, "desiring fine things."

Socrates is occupied with this part of Meno's new definition from M. 77b6 to 78b2. It is his aim in this stretch of text to level all people with respect to what they want. We note his concluding words: "and in this respect [in respect of what people want], no one is better than another" (M. 78b5–6). He thereby discredits the foolish and

---

38. See Sharples (1985), 137.

39. As noted, the definition of color in terms of effluences does not pick out color uniquely; a definition along these lines would also serve to say "what sound is, and smell, and many other things of that sort" (M. 76d9–e1).

groundless elitism manifest in the first component of Meno's latest definition.

In order to accomplish his goal of having all people turn out to be the same with respect to their wants, Socrates employs two strategic moves: first, he reduces "fine things," *kala*, to "good things," *agatha*, and, second, he replaces "desiring," *epithumein*, with "wanting," *boulesthai*.[40] In order to understand Socrates' game plan, it is best first to try to determine how Socrates understands Meno's definition: what does Meno mean by proposing that those who have virtue desire fine things? As Socrates understands him, Meno, by saying that those who have virtue desire fine things, seeks to elevate those who have refined tastes above those whose pedestrian tastes mark them as hopelessly ordinary. Socrates' immediate substitution of *agatha* for *kala*—"Do you say that the one who desires fine things desires good things?" (*M.* 77b6–7)—is the first step toward eliminating such specious class distinctions: "good things" lacks the highbrow air of "fine things." Meno, unaware of the implications of this substitution,[41] readily assents to it;[42] he now finds himself committed to the proposition that some people, those who lack virtue, desire "bad things," *kaka*. Socrates accepts Meno's assertion but presses him further: do those who desire bad things think they are good, or do they desire bad things while recognizing them as bad? Meno insists that some people, probably those he disdains as crude or vulgar,

40. Similar moves appear in the *Gorgias*. For the move from fine to good, see the notorious argument at *Gorg.* 474–75; for the move from *epithumein* to *boulesthai*, see the argument at *Gorg.* 466–68, where, although the move Socrates makes is from *ha dokei*, "what seems good to one," to *boulesthai*, the same sort of point is being made.

41. It is possible that Meno understood Socrates to be asking whether *kala* constitute a (proper) subset of *agatha* rather than whether *agatha* can be substituted for *kala*.

42. Guthrie (1975), 247, n. 1, notes: "M. was really beaten when he lightly agreed to the substitution of *agatha* for *kala* at 77b7." Thompson (1901), 102, points out that as a result of the substitution, "any poetic tinsel attaching to the word *kala* is removed." It seems unlikely that what Socrates is determined to banish in urging the replacement of *kala* with *agatha* is the "moral flavor" (this is Guthrie's phrase) of *kala;* for it is difficult to see, on the one hand, what Socrates stands to gain by substituting a nonmoral term for a moral one or, on the other, what investment Meno has in the moral one. It is far more plausible to maintain that Socrates wishes to suppress that nuance of *kalon* that is important to Meno, the one that gives the term snob appeal. As Sharples (1985), 138, says: "the contrast Meno has in mind is that between those who have the correct, splendid ambitions for themselves and those who lack, as it were, proper aristocratic taste in matters of behaviour."

desire bad things while recognizing them as bad. Meno is no doubt thinking, not of *kaka,* "bad things," but still of *aischra,* "base things" or "crass things," things that are the opposites, not of *agatha,* "good things," but of his original *kala,* "fine things." Thus, what Meno must mean is that even though the masses recognize their tastes as low-brow, they persist in desiring what they desire: crab cakes, not caviar. But Socrates goes on: can such people desire to possess these things? And if they do, can they be thinking that bad things benefit their possessors or do they recognize that bad things harm their posses-sors? Meno, no doubt continuing to think of *aischra* rather than of *kaka,* declares that some people (presumably, those without "class") desire to possess bad things (by which he means vulgar or crass or base things) thinking they are beneficial: to common people, why would not at least some of the things that appeal to their humble tastes appear beneficial? As long as Meno has not yet, in his own mind, made the transition from the pair fine/crass to the pair good/ bad, he sees no absurdity in the claim that some people desire to possess bad (that is, crass) things thinking they are beneficial. But Socrates forces the point: if someone thinks bad things are benefi-cial, must he not fail to recognize that they are bad? In other words, would it not be absurd for people to think bad things beneficial— qua bad? Bad and beneficial are straightforwardly mutually exclusive in a way that vulgar, or base, and beneficial are not. Once Socrates gets Meno to see that if a thing is thought bad, it cannot, then, be thought beneficial, Meno must concede that those who desire to possess bad things thinking they are beneficial do not think the things they desire are bad. Insofar as they think these things bene-ficial, they think them good, and whereas they may desire things that are in fact bad, they desire them—since they are ignorant of these things' badness—as good. Hence, those who desire bad things thinking they are beneficial actually desire (to possess) good things.

Thus far, Socrates has considered only the first of two sets of peo-ple identified by Meno as desiring bad things: those who believe that the bad things they desire are beneficial. What he has shown with respect to this set of people who desire bad things is that they do not desire bad things after all: although the things they desire may be in fact bad, they desire (to possess) good things. The second set of people who desire bad things consists, according to Meno, of those who desire bad things while recognizing them as harmful. Soc-rates contends—and Meno agrees—that there is no one who wants (*bouletai*), to be harmed, because there is no one who wants (*bouletai*) to be wretched and unfortunate. Since bad things harm their possessor, there can be no one who wants (*bouletai*) bad things. Socrates concludes, therefore, that those who desire bad things thinking them harmful actually do not want (since no one wants) bad things.

If we attend carefully (as Meno does not) to this second stage of Socrates' argument, we note that although Socrates denies that anyone can *want* (*boulesthai*) bad things thinking them harmful, he does not deny that someone can desire (*epithumein*) them. Apparently, then, one *can*, as far as Socrates is concerned, desire bad things even while recognizing them as bad; what one cannot do is *want* them. Desire, brute appetitive craving (*epithumein*), for bad things is able to persist even in the face of one's recognition that the objects of one's desire can cause one harm. Desire can remain unaffected by judgment;[43] wanting (*boulesthai*), by contrast, takes as its object only things one judges to be good or beneficial.[44]

There is some scholarly dispute about how careful Socrates is to preserve fine distinctions between terms close in meaning. In the *Protagoras*, Socrates derides Prodicus for being obsessively fond of fine distinctions, making reference, at *Prot.* 340a8–b1, specifically to his distinction between *epithumein* and *boulesthai*. Nevertheless, Socrates himself does at times clearly distinguish between *epithumein* and *boulesthai*. Santas (1979), 315, n. 16, notes that for Plato, for example at *Lys.* 221a7–b3, "there are such things as bad desires (*kakai epithumiai*), whereas Plato never speaks, to my knowledge, of bad or harmful *boulēsis*." Moreover, in the *Charmides*, at 167e4–5, Socrates says fairly explicitly that the objects of *epithumein* are pleasures, the

---

43. If it is true that Socrates allows that an agent might desire (and pursue) bad things even while judging them harmful (although he surely does not allow that the agent might *want* them under such circumstances), then he ought not be charged, as he so often is, with overintellectualizing human choice, of making it always a function of one's rational determination of one's own good. Sharples (1985), 139, lodges the typical charge: "However, Socrates might justly be criticised, here as in the *Protagoras* (356ab), for simply assuming that human behaviour is too rational; it may be illogical to want something while knowing that it is bad for oneself, but that it is illogical does not mean it cannot happen." Whereas it is true that in the *Protagoras* Socrates portrays men as rational calculators of pleasure and pain, whose "salvation" lies in, of all things, a hedonic calculus (*Prot.* 356e5–6), this portrayal is, I believe, confined to the *Protagoras*, just as Socrates' advocacy of hedonism itself is. Both, in my view, are ironic. See Weiss (1990).

44. In the *Gorgias* argument at 466–68, there seems to be some equivocation on *boulesthai*, with its object being at first what is thought good and later shifting to what is really good. There is no comparable equivocation here. Socrates' point here is not that one cannot want (*boulesthai*) anything but what is in fact good; his point is simply that one cannot want (*boulesthai*) what one deems bad in the sense of harmful to oneself.

objects of *boulesthai*, goods. The truth of the matter, it seems to me, though perhaps it is an unsettling truth, is that Socrates is at times careless and at times overly fastidious about such distinctions.[45] It depends on what the situation calls for. In the *Lysis*, we may note, there *is* (contra Santas) an occasion upon which Socrates unmistakably uses *boulēsis* indistinguishably from *epithumia*. He says of Lysis's parents, who love their son, that they surely would want (*boulointo, Lys.* 207d7) or desire (*epithumoi, Lys.* 207e2) him to be happy and therefore would presumably allow him to do whatever he wants (*ha boulei, Lys.* 207e6) or whatever he desires (*hōn an epithumēis, Lys.* 207e7). In our *Meno* passage, however, it is clear that Socrates recognizes a distinction between *epithumein* and *boulesthai:* he shifts quite deliberately from *epithumein* to *boulesthai* in order to be able to make the claim that no people want what they recognize as harmful, a claim that would hardly be plausible if it spoke instead of what people *desire*. And although it may seem paradoxical to say that one may desire, but one cannot want, what one judges to be bad in the sense of harmful, Socrates' point is well taken: despite one's recognition that certain things are harmful, one may still be drawn to those things; yet insofar as no one wants to suffer and be wretched, no one really wants the bad things that one finds oneself at times helplessly attracted to or craving. To be wretched, then, Socrates concludes (in a "playful inversion" of Meno's definition of virtue),[46] is to desire (*epithumein*) bad things (that is, things one regards as harmful to oneself), which, as has been argued, remains possible for one to do, and to get them. The desire is itself an important source of wretchedness, because it is one's desires that impel one to pursue even things that one recognizes as being bad for oneself.

Meno, of course, fails to notice the shift from *epithumein* to *boulesthai*. He thinks, therefore, that by agreeing that "no one wants bad things" (*M.* 78b1–2), he has in effect admitted defeat: "You probably speak truly, Socrates" (*M.* 78a8–b1). Once it becomes clear that Meno has missed the distinction between "desire" and "want," Socrates can, without fear of detection, replace the "desire" in Meno's

---

45. Such inconsistency in the dialogues is not unusual: flute playing, for example, which quite frequently serves as a paradigmatic case of *technē*, is relegated in the *Gorgias* (at 501e) to a knack, an *empeiria*, something that aims at gratification rather than at some genuine good. For further discussion of *epithumein/boulesthai*, see McTighe (1984), 198, with n. 17, 215, 216, n. 53.

46. Sharples (1985), 139. Cf. Nakhnikian (1973), 5, who argues (too heavyhandedly) that there is a logical flaw here.

original definition with "want"—just as he earlier replaced "fine things," *kala,* with "good things," *agatha*—so that Meno's definition now reads: "Virtue is to *want good things* and to have the power to get them" (*M.* 78b3–4). Since, however, it has been shown that everyone wants good things (those who desire bad things while thinking them beneficial desire good things, since they do not know that the bad things are bad if they think them beneficial; and those who *desire* bad things while thinking them harmful nevertheless do not *want* them, since no one wishes to be harmed, wretched, and unfortunate), it follows that no person can be said to be superior to others with respect to his wants. But since Socrates does not make the claim that all men *desire* good things, that is, things they judge to be good or beneficial,[47] the possibility remains open that men might be distinguished from one another in terms of their respective desires, that is, in terms of the kinds of things that attract them and in terms of how tight the connection is between their desires and their rational judgments. The *Meno* certainly seems to imply that a man's desires can mark him as more wretched than his fellow, for the wretched are identified as being not only those who get (things they regard as) bad things but also as those who desire them.[48] Thus, even if, with respect to their wants, all men are equal, it need not be the case that all men are equal with respect to their desires.

47. *Rep.* 4.437b–439d is often cited as proof that Plato, in his middle period, abandons the Socratic view, a view widely believed to be affirmed in our *Meno* passage, that all desire is for good. As I understand the *Meno,* however, what it says is that all wanting (*boulesthai*) is for good, but desire need not be. This interpretation presupposes, of course, a quite restricted sense of "good," according to which it is equivalent to "beneficial." Were we to expand the range of "good" so that it comprised both what is judged beneficial and what appeals to the appetites, it would be (trivially) true that Socrates in the *Meno* believes all desire to be for good, for the person who craved and pursued what he judged harmful (and hence bad) would still desire it qua "good." As I understand the *Republic* passage, it broadens the scope of "good" in just this way and, therefore, although it maintains that thirst is for drink simpliciter, not for good drink, it regards this view as fully consonant with the view that all desire is for good. To appetite, drink simpliciter is good. To reason, only good drink is good. All desire, then, whether rational or not, is for good. Only rational desire, though, is for good in the sense of beneficial.

48. Socrates in the *Gorgias* (at 473e1) regards tyrants as the most wretched of men. Indeed, is it not true of them that they both desire bad things and have the power to acquire them? In the *Gorgias,* the tyrant is wretched because he gets what he mistakenly judges to be good (in the *Gorgias*'s terms, he gets what seems good to him but not what is good for him, when only the latter is what he truly wants); in the *Meno,* however, a person is wretched because he chooses to acquire things that he himself judges to be bad/harmful for himself. Meno is, of course, the tyrannical figure in this dialogue.

It is notable that Socrates does not argue here, as one would perhaps expect him to, that what sets the virtuous apart is that they pursue things worthy of pursuit, that is, things that are *in fact* good. Socrates fails to make this argument here because his current concern is to eliminate or greatly reduce Meno's groundless sense of his own superiority. Given that end, it is important that he prevent Meno from thinking that what men want constitutes the distinguishing mark of virtue: all men are the same, he argues, with respect to what they want. Since all men want what they think is good, Socrates argues, everyone wants, de dicto, the same thing (even though, of course, not everyone wants, de re, the same thing).

In context, then, when Socrates introduces the idea that all people want what they judge to be good or beneficial to themselves, he is spurred by a determination to rid Meno of his haughty airs. Whereas Meno wants to say that the virtuous, the refined, the excellent people have tastes superior to those of ordinary people, Socrates, by substituting *agatha* for *kala* and *boulesthai* for *epithumein*, gets him to admit that all men want good things and that, in terms of their wants, at any rate, no people are any better than others.

At the same time, however, that Socrates levels all people with respect to their wants, he implies something that is strikingly at odds with the view that is usually attributed to him, namely, the view that all people act on their wants, that is, on their assessment of what is best for them. For, he affirms quite plainly in our passage that people may desire, that is, have an appetite for (*epithumein*), and acquire (*ktasthai, M.* 78a8), presumably propelled by their desire, what they themselves judge to be bad. Such people are the ones Socrates calls wretched (*M.* 78a7–8). These wretched ones display the classic symptoms of incontinent action: though not wanting the things they judge to be bad (after all, no one does), they nevertheless do desire them and act on that desire to acquire them. The case of cigarette smoking, which is so frequently invoked to discredit the Socratic denial of incontinence,[49] in fact fits perfectly the model of the wretched set forth in the *Meno*. Why could one not say, on the *Meno*'s model, without its even sounding particularly odd, that a person is wretched if he (a) recognizes smoking's harmful effects, (b) does not want to be harmed, (c) does not, therefore, want to smoke but nevertheless (d) desires to smoke, and (e) consequently smokes?[50]

---

49. See, for example, Nakhnikian (1973), 10.

50. Although this is not the appropriate occasion for a full-scale discussion of the

Let us turn now, as Socrates does, to the second element in Meno's definition, to the power to get what one wants. If virtue, as has been shown, cannot be found in men's wants, might it perhaps be found in their power to get what they want? And if so, what are the good things that men want? Socrates proposes as the likely candidates for "good things" such things as health and wealth (*M.* 78c6–7). Meno says, however, that what he calls good things is the acquiring both of gold and silver and of political honors and offices; indeed, the good things are all and only such things as these (*M.* 78c7–d1).[51] What is Socrates to think but that these things—gold, silver, political honors and offices—are the things that Meno had in mind earlier when he spoke of *kala*, the finer things, which, on his view, only the virtuous desire? Indeed, what else can Socrates think but that it is on account of his desire for such things that Meno thinks himself superior to the common run of men? With derisive sarcasm, therefore, Socrates proclaims: "Well, so procuring gold and silver is virtue, as Meno, the hereditary guest friend of the great king of Persia, says" (*M.* 78d1–3). It has come to this.

The struggle between Meno and Socrates that began in the opening pages of the dialogue now resumes, with Meno's attention focused once again on a type of activity, and Socrates', on how the activity is done. Is it, Socrates asks, the acquisition itself of gold and silver that is virtue, or does it matter whether or not the acquisition is done justly and piously? Meno, not one to spurn conventional virtue outright, concedes to Socrates that it does matter, that if the acquisition is accomplished unjustly, it ceases to be virtue but becomes "badness," *kakia* (*M.* 78d7). But Socrates goes further—much

---

alleged Socratic denial of incontinence, I believe it is important to recognize that in interpreting Plato it is not necessarily fruitful to conflate all similar-sounding ideas on the assumption that they must be the same idea. As I show in n. 44, what Socrates says about *boulesthai* here is not the same as what he says in the *Gorgias* at 466–68. In the *Gorgias*, the object of *boulesthai* is eventually restricted to what is truly good. Here the object of *boulesthai* is what is judged good. In the *Gorgias*, Socrates' point is that one who commits injustice has not done what he wants because (a) what he has done is in fact bad for him (though he may not judge it so) and (b) no one wants what is bad for oneself. Here the point is, more simply, that no one wants things that one takes to be bad for oneself.

51. Meno does not quite acknowledge that health is a good thing. In speaking for himself, he says that the good things are the acquisition of gold, silver, and political office (*M.* 78c7–8). Might health be too commonplace a want, such that one's wanting it does not strike Meno as a mark of distinction? Perhaps Meno thinks that whereas undistinguished men do want health, they do not aspire to such *kala* as wealth and political office. Let us recall that in the *Hippias Major*, Hippias defines "the beautiful," *to kalon*, as nothing other than gold (*HMa.* 289e2–4).

further. He elicits Meno's assent, not only to the idea that if an act of acquisition is performed without justice, temperance, and piety, it cannot be virtue, but to the far more radical notion that on those occasions when acquisition cannot be accomplished without injustice, then "nonacquisition," *aporia*, is virtue (*M.* 78e6).[52] Meno's assent to this last, distinctly *un*conventional notion represents, for Socrates, a crowning achievement: he has moved Meno from locating virtue in what one does to locating it in how one does *whatever* one does. Even nonacquisition can be virtue if only this—and not acquisition—can be done justly, temperately, and so on. "So, the acquisition of good things," Socrates concludes, "will no more be virtue than their nonacquisition, but, as it seems, *whatever* comes to be with justice is virtue and whatever comes to be without all such things is badness (*kakia*)" (*M.* 78e6–79a1).[53]

At this point, Meno's definition of virtue lies in ruins. Socrates has shown, first, that since all men want good things, virtue cannot be a function of what a man wants. And he has also shown that virtue cannot be a matter of the power to acquire good things, because it is not the acquisition of good things that determines the presence

52. Bluck (1961a), 263, notes the play on words on *aporia*. In this context, *aporia* means nonacquisition, an alpha-privative having been annexed to *poros*, "acquisition." But *aporia* also means "poverty." Amazingly, then, what Socrates gets Meno to admit is that poverty can be virtue! Sharples (1985), 140, points out that besides these two meanings of *aporia*, namely, "nonacquisition" and "poverty," there is yet a third, "perplexity," which is just what Meno is about to be reduced to.

Wealth and poverty are an important theme in the *Meno* from its beginning. The Thessalians, who were renowned for horsemanship and wealth, are also now reputed to be wise, wisdom (in the person of Gorgias) having departed from Athens to Thessaly. The Athenians, including Socrates, are therefore in dire poverty with respect to knowledge of virtue. There is also the matter of Meno's wealth and his desire to be richer. In addition, as we shall see in the next chapter, Socrates describes himself as being *aporōn*, "without means," as opposed to *euporōn*, "well-supplied" or "rich," with respect to being able to answer the questions he asks (*M.* 80c–d). Also discussed in the dialogue (at *M.* 90a) is the wealth of Anthemion, Anytus's father.

53. See Adkins (1960), 228–29: Meno "is prepared to admit that justice and self-restraint are necessary to this desired end [of running his city and having his house run well, in the sense of efficiently], and hence that those qualities are desirable in a derivative sense . . . but . . . there is no doubt in Meno's mind which is the end and which is the means." In light of Adkins's insight, let us take due measure of Socrates' extraordinary accomplishment at *M.* 78c4–79a2: Socrates gets Meno to be less sure about which is the end and which is the means. See also Bluck (1961a), 202: "Plato (and his Socrates) sought to attach the co-operative, 'quiet' virtues to the concept of *aretē* inseparably—to combine the two sets of values. But the Meno of our dialogue holds the usual view of *aretē* as practical efficiency in public and private life." It is precisely this usual view from which Socrates is able to wrench him, at least for the moment.

or absence of virtue but rather the way in which *whatever* is done—whether acquisition, nonacquisition, or, indeed, anything else—is done. Socrates does not tolerate Meno's baseless elitism (let us not forget how appallingly coarse Meno's idea of the finer things is: gold, silver, and political prominence), nor does he relent until Meno acknowledges virtue to be a function, not of what one's affairs are, but of how one conducts them, whatever they are, that is, with justice, temperance, and piety. And Meno does come around: by the time this argument has ended, Meno has conceded that what sets the virtuous individual apart, what makes one man better than another, is not what he wants, and not what he has the power to get, but his choosing *not* to acquire what he both wants and has the power to get when to do so would be unjust, intemperate, or impious. What Meno has granted, in effect, is that the measure of virtue in a man is his assigning priority to justice, temperance, and piety over the acquisition of "good things."

We may note that the *Meno* passage, 78b3–79a2, with which we have just dealt, actually tends to undermine rather than to support the stock characterization of Socrates as a psychological or an ethical egoist.[54] (A psychological egoist affirms that it is psychologically impossible for one to act in opposition to what one determines to be in one's own self-interest; an ethical egoist affirms that what one *ought* to pursue is what one determines to be in one's own self-interest.) In this passage, Meno is helped to see that the acquisition of good things, that is, of things one judges to be good for oneself, is not virtue, that, indeed, on those occasions when acquisition of good things requires that one act unjustly, intemperately, or impiously, it is the nonacquisition of good things rather than their acquisition that is virtue. To generalize: according to this passage, if one judges *x* to be good for oneself, that is, to be beneficial and happiness producing for oneself, but one recognizes that *x* cannot

---

54. I think there are many reasons to think that Socrates is not an egoist of either kind, among them that he favors punishment for those who do wrong and lays blame for malicious intent on those who have it. (I direct the reader's attention to *Ap.* 26a, where Socrates states what would be the appropriate way to deal with him if he corrupted the young intentionally; and to *Ap.* 41d–e, where he says that although he is not angry at his accusers and at those jurors who condemned him, nevertheless they are blameworthy for meaning to harm him.) Kahn is one scholar who disputes the prevalent view that Socrates is a psychological egoist. See Kahn (1983), 101, n. 48, where he argues that psychological egoism is not entailed by the Socratic view that one who aims at the good is in fact pursuing his own best interest: "self interest can be used to justify or motivate, but not to define, the pursuit of what is good."

be secured without injustice, intemperance, or impiety, then, if one is virtuous, one will forgo *x*, choosing just, temperate, or pious conduct over the acquisition of *x*. This passage implies both that one's choices *can*, psychologically speaking, oppose one's determination that *x* is good/best for one and that, on occasion, one's choices *ought*, morally speaking, to do so. Hence, Socrates is here neither a psychological egoist nor an ethical egoist. Moreover, Socrates does not, in this passage, recommend justice, temperance, and piety on the grounds that they are ultimately to the agent's advantage and thus what he genuinely wants. On the contrary, this passage contends that virtuous people simply relinquish what they want for the sake of the right. They can do so; they ought to do so; and this is what they do in fact do.[55]

Socrates, then, sees (at *M.* 77b–79a) two ways in which a person might act in opposition to what he wants, that is, in opposition to his judgment of what is most advantageous to himself. A person might, on the one hand, yield to his desires for bad things even in the face of his recognition that they are bad for him (such a person is wretched: he desires bad things and gets them); a person might, on the other hand, neglect, for the sake of justice, temperance, and piety, that is, for the sake of the noble and right, the course that he regards as serving his interests. On either end of the spectrum, then, that is, to satisfy either what is most base in oneself or what is most noble, one may act against what one wants or against what one determines is to one's advantage. In both cases, of course, one indeed chooses something that appeals to one—to one's appetites in the one case, to one's nobility in the other; otherwise, one would not choose it. But in neither case does one choose what one "wants": in the first case, one does instead what one "desires"; in the second, one chooses instead what is just, temperate, or pious.

Socrates ought to be well pleased at the turn his and Meno's discussion has taken. Meno has been made to abandon his merely parroted answers and to acknowledge that virtue lies not in what one does, gets, and is able to do and get but in the just, temperate, and pious way in which one does whatever one does.[56] Moreover,

---

55. Socrates is not unaware of the difficulties of living justly, especially for those who have the freedom to do wrong with impunity. See *Gorg.* 526a, where he praises those among the powerful, like Aristides, who choose to live justly though they could easily live unjustly.

56. We note the glaring absence of the cardinal virtues of wisdom and courage in Socrates' discussion. Yet given Socrates' determination to temper Meno's ambition

not only has Meno come a long way from his initial views and his misplaced confidence in them, but he has, under Socrates' tutelage, reached a definition of virtue that closely resembles Socrates' model definition of shape. Shape, Socrates had proposed, is the one thing that always accompanies color. In other words, whenever something is colored, the only other feature that it will always reliably have is shape. Virtue, as we now see, is the one thing that always accompanies things done with justice, temperance, or piety, for "whatever comes about with justice [and other such things] is virtue" (*M.* 78e8–79a1). Whereas the good things that some hope to acquire—wealth, reputation, social standing, political office—might or might not be present when things are done with justice, temperance, or piety, virtue always is.[57] In other words, the presence of justice, temperance, or piety is a sufficient condition for the presence of virtue and of virtue alone, as the presence of color is a sufficient condition for the presence of shape and of shape alone. Should Meno define virtue as the only thing that always accompanies justice, temperance, and piety, he would, it seems, meet all the criteria that Socrates had set for himself in defining shape: he would be using no esoteric or technical terminology; his definition would be picking out uniquely the thing he seeks to define; moreover, he would be saying something that is true. To be sure, the definition of virtue as the only thing that always accompanies justice, temperance, and piety is not explicit. Yet if there can be no virtue without justice, temperance, or piety, as Socrates has been urging from the start, and furthermore,

and to encourage him to associate virtue not with greatness and distinction but with those qualities of soul that even a woman or slave can cultivate, it is not surprising that the virtues he champions are the humbler and more pedestrian justice, temperance, and piety rather than the bolder and rarer courage and wisdom (see n. 53). Meno does list courage and wisdom among the virtues, along with temperance and magnificence (*M.* 74a4–6). Of course, only courage, wisdom, and magnificence are Meno's original contribution; temperance is just a holdover from Socrates' discourse. Piety, which Socrates does not mention at first but introduces at *M.* 78d4, never makes it onto Meno's list.

57. Socrates might well say that wealth, reputation, social standing, and political office accompany, not virtue, but the appearance of virtue. In *Rep.* 2, Glaucon challenges Socrates to defend the idea that the just man is the happy man even if he not only reaps none of the rewards of appearing just—neither wealth nor good reputation nor honor—but is also subjected to painful and unfair treatment at the hands of others because he is *thought* unjust. Of course, Socrates is the man who perfectly fits Glaucon's description: although he is the most just of all men, he is reputed to be and is believed to be an impious corrupter of the young and is therefore publicly humiliated and executed. But is not Socrates, still and all, the happiest of men? And does he not, therefore, constitute in himself, the strongest argument for justice?

if the presence of justice, temperance, or piety guarantees the presence of virtue but not the presence of other "goods"—indeed, all good things but virtue might have to be sacrificed for the sake of preserving justice, temperance, and piety—then the presence of justice, temperance, or piety is necessary and sufficient for virtue and for no other good. Virtue, then, is the only thing whose presence is ensured by acts of justice, temperance, or piety, just as shape is the only thing whose presence is guaranteed by the presence of color.

What, then, is the cause of Socrates' discontent with the new definition of virtue? Why does he proceed now to undercut his own painstaking efforts on behalf of this definition, a definition for which he has labored from the dialogue's very inception? Why, too, does Socrates appear vexed and annoyed at Meno, as if Meno has done something wrong? What, after all, has Meno done but gone docilely along with everything Socrates has said? Furthermore, the definition for which Socrates berates Meno is not even his—it is Socrates'. Why, we must wonder, does Socrates pretend that his definition is Meno's[58] and then complain that Meno is toying with him, is teasing him (*paizeis, M.* 79a7) with it?

A partial answer is that Meno has fallen irretrievably from grace: Socrates will no longer conduct with him the gentle sort of exchange that is suited to conversation between friends. Indeed, no matter how polite, pliable, and agreeable Meno is, Socrates lets him know at every turn that things are not as they once were between them.[59] But this answer hardly explains Socrates' objections to "Meno's" latest definition. Are we to believe that his scolding of Meno bears no relation to real difficulties that he finds in this definition of virtue?

Socrates does indeed identify two serious flaws in the definition of virtue as the only thing that always accompanies justice, temperance, and piety. Insofar as this definition is, after all, his own and not Meno's, his objections to it can only reflect his frustration with his own inability to provide an adequate definition for virtue. Al-

---

58. Even though Socrates recognizes that Meno is really just "agreeing" with him, *homologeis* (*M.* 79b4), he attributes the definition to Meno: "*You* tell me that virtue is being able to acquire good things with justice" (*M.* 79a11). And further: "And this, *you* say, is a part of virtue" (*M.* 79b2). What Meno had actually said is: "It seems to me that it is necessarily as you say" (*M.* 79a2).

59. We may compare Socrates' unfriendly manner here, where Meno is actually agreeing with him, with his much gentler and more indulgent tone earlier—that is, before Meno's rejection of Socrates' initial definition of shape—even when Meno resisted Socrates' views or was unable to grasp his meaning or ventured an answer of his own that was rather wide of the mark (*M.* 72a–c; 73d–e).

though neither criticism, as we shall see, actually threatens the "truth" of the definition, both expose the limitations of its explanatory power. Moreover, because of these limitations, Socrates' inquiry is far from complete. Despite the enormous progress he has made in divesting Meno of his hopelessly wrongheaded views and in moving him closer to Socrates' far better one, Socrates does not himself believe—nor does he want Meno to believe—that he and Meno are ready to move on.

Let us look at the first objection, which accuses the definition of breaking virtue into pieces. How decisive an objection is this? One could say, on the one hand, that defining virtue in terms of its parts does not necessarily break virtue itself into parts, that it does not necessarily make virtue many. In other words, one could maintain that virtue as an unbroken whole, as a unit and unity, is present whenever an act is performed with one of its parts, that is, justly, temperately, or piously.[60] Yet one could also say, on the other hand, that such a claim is hardly perspicuous. What does it mean to say that virtue maintains its integrity even as it accompanies a manifestation of just one of its parts? How, indeed, does it do so? The problem of the whole/part relationship in virtue, a relationship not so different from the notorious "one over many" problem that plagues Plato's Theory of Forms (as in the *Parmenides*, at 131a–e), is not solved by the mere insistence that virtue remains whole even as it accompanies each of its distinct parts.[61]

According to the second objection, the new definition fails because it proceeds in the very way that Socrates and Meno earlier deemed illegitimate; that is, "it attempts to answer by way of things still being searched for and not yet agreed to" (*M.* 79d2–4). Meno is so quick to defend his earlier objection to Socrates' initial definition of shape (he hastens to say, "And we did right to reject it, Socrates" [*M.* 79d5])[62] that he fails to notice an important difference between that objection and Socrates' current one. Whereas Socrates worries that justice, temperance, and piety are unknown because, as parts of virtue, they cannot be known apart from the as-yet-

60. However Socrates' "doctrine" of the unity of the virtues is conceived, it precludes the possibility that an act or a person is, say, genuinely just but also impious or intemperate. At the very least, when something manifests one of the virtues *really*, it cannot at the same time manifest any of the vices.

61. For excellent discussions of the "parts of virtue" problem in Plato, see Penner (1973); Woodruff (1976); and Ferejohn (1982).

62. Despite Socrates' own use of "we," it was, of course, not "we" who "rejected that sort of answer" (*M.* 79d2) but Meno alone.

undefined virtue, there is no comparable obstacle to knowing color: color is not a part of shape such that it cannot be known apart from it.[63] But even if Socrates' objection is not identical to Meno's, it raises thorny problems of its own: not only can a proper definition of virtue not avoid making reference to its parts, but a proper definition of virtue's parts cannot avoid making reference to virtue. In Socrates' struggle with Meno over the definition of virtue, it is consistently Meno who defines virtue independently of justice, temperance, and piety, and it is consistently Socrates who inserts these parts of virtue into the proposed definition. For Socrates, then, circularity and self-referentiality, which are features of definition to be generally avoided, turn out to be ineluctable characteristics of any true definition of virtue.[64] Whereas Socrates himself steers clear of circularity and self-referentiality in both of his definitions of shape—neither the definition of shape in terms of color nor the definition of it as the limit of a solid makes any reference to shape's "parts," that is, to roundness, squareness, and so on—nevertheless, when Socrates comes to virtue, he refuses to permit either (a) virtue to be defined other than in terms of its parts (justice, temperance, and piety) or (b) virtue's parts to be defined other than in terms of it. This refusal by Socrates constitutes in itself an eloquent expression of his conviction that there is no extramoral domain to which one can go to find a true and adequate definition of virtue:[65] virtue will be present whenever things are done well, that is, justly, temperately, or piously; and there is no nonmoral state of affairs with which the presence of virtue will always reliably correlate.[66] This is a lesson that Meno certainly needs to learn, for he conceives of virtue in starkly nonmoral terms—as a matter of one's social role, as ruling, as manifest in one's refined taste, as power, and, especially, as the acquisition of gold, silver, and political prominence. Indeed, until Socrates pointed out

63. Ironically, as was pointed out in n. 29, the definition of color that Meno prefers, "Color is an effluence from shapes that is commensurate with sight and perceptible" (*M.* 76d4–5), does not define color independently of shape.

64. This is the case, at least, until Plato introduces the Forms. The "vision" of the Form of the Good constitutes the escape from the circle.

65. Plato, of course, devotes many dialogues to the definition of individual virtues apart from virtue. It is by no means certain, however, that Socrates can or even aspires to keep the individual virtues definable apart from one another and from virtue itself. He often starts off ostensibly seeking to define a single virtue independent of the others and of virtue itself, only to "discover" that this cannot be done.

66. This circularity is understood to be a feature of virtue rather than a problem with it. In the *Crito*, for example, Socrates states, as if there is no difficulty about it, that "[living] well and [living] nobly and justly are the same" (*Crito.* 48b8).

to Meno that the virtues are parts or pieces of virtue, parts that are integral to it, Meno never thought of virtue in that way. For him, Socrates' view that anything that manifests virtue will have been done well, and that anything done well will have been done with justice, temperance, or piety, is new.[67]

Socrates' definition of virtue, like his definition of shape, is, in the final analysis, inadequate: it defines virtue relationally without attending to what it is in essence. Just as shape is understood to be the only thing for which color is a sufficient condition, so is virtue conceived as the only thing for which its parts are (each) a sufficient condition. Although both definitions are flawed, and in the same way, it is in the case of virtue alone that the imperfection in its definition constitutes its strength. For, in the Cave, where human beings lack the greater-than-human understanding of virtue needed in order to break out of the circle of opinion, it is far better to define virtue in relation to its parts, that is, with reference to justice, temperance, and piety, than to attempt the reduction of a moral term to nonmoral ones.

Having found no way to define virtue without reference to its parts or to explain how virtue might remain unbroken even as it accompanies its parts, Socrates proposes that Meno revisit the question of the nature of virtue; he must, as Socrates says three times, raise it anew (*M.* 79c3–4, c7–8, e1–2).

---

67. The circularity that characterizes good definitions of virtue surfaces again in the notion of virtue defined as "guiding aright," *orthōs hēgeisthai* (*M.* 88e1, e3). Indeed, *orthōs hēgeisthai* is essentially just a paraphrase of the earlier "managing well," *eu dioikein* (*M.* 73a6–7, 8), which was immediately glossed by Socrates as "managing with justice and temperance."

2

Impasse, Paradox, and the Myth of
Learning by Recollection

Yet still when the human mind has once dis-
paraged of finding truth, its interest in all
things grows fainter; and the result is that
men turn aside to pleasant disputations and
discourses and roam as it were from object
to object, rather than keep on a course of
severe inquisition.

Francis Bacon, *Novum Organum,*
Aphorism LXVII

i. Impasse

Three times Socrates impresses upon Meno that he needs to start
over, that he must raise anew the question of what virtue is: (1) "So
you need to start again with the same question, as it seems to me,
my dear Meno: What is virtue?" (*M.* 79c3–5); (2) "Or do you not
think that the same question is again necessary?" (*M.* 79c7–8); (3)
"But [you should think] that the same question is again needed:
What is the virtue about which you say what you say?" (*M.* 79e1–2).
Meno may agree in principle that reconsideration of the question
of the nature of virtue is warranted (*M.* 79e4), but he wants no part
of it. He suddenly remembers having heard that Socrates is a perplexed man who perplexes others.[1] Socrates, then, must be to blame
for his utter failure (*M.* 80a4).[2] Like the stingray, whom Socrates

---

1. Meno must surely have heard good things as well about Socrates: does he not
seek Socrates' guidance on a question vital to him, how virtue is acquired? Moreover,
he is surprised by Socrates' protestations that he does not know what virtue is (*M.*
71b9–c1), and he seems to think word of Socrates' ignorance would be news back
home (*M.* 71c1–2). Only now, in his humiliation, does he remember a disparaging
report.

2. We may note the *to parapan* in Meno's declaration that he now cannot say "at

resembles both in appearance and in other ways, Socrates has rendered him numb in mind and tongue and unable to answer,[3] even though, before Socrates cast his spell, he was, he thought,[4] perfectly able to speak very well on countless occasions to many people about virtue. A frustrated Meno, having seen each of his proposed definitions of virtue defeated at Socrates' hand and having watched Socrates demolish even his own proposed definition, has finally had enough. Surely this nightmare will end, Meno must be thinking, once Socrates recognizes the fittingness of the stingray simile,[5] and

all" what virtue is (*M.* 80b4–5). *To parapan* figured earlier in Socrates' total disavowal of knowledge of what virtue is (*M.* 71b3, b5) and will figure again in Meno's characterization of Socrates' ignorance with respect to virtue (*M.* 80d6).

3. Benson (1989), 597, 598 with n. 16, takes note of an interesting difference between Euthyphro and Meno: Euthyphro says (*Euthyph.* 11b) that he cannot *tell* Socrates what he has in mind (because whatever answer he suggests fails to stay in place), but he never says he cannot *think;* Meno, by contrast, says that he has been numbed both in mind and in tongue (*M.* 80b1). Benson concludes from the difference between the two remarks that Meno, unlike Euthyphro, admits that he does not know. I think, however, that there is less here than meets the eye. As I see it, neither Euthyphro nor Meno thinks he does not know the answer; both think that Socrates has (temporarily) made them unable to speak what they know. Meno, it is true, says he cannot answer because Socrates has numbed both his mind and his tongue, but then again Meno does not distinguish between the ability to think and the ability to speak (see Chap. 1, nn. 2 and 7). Since what Meno regards as thinking is repeating what he has heard, then for him, having a numb tongue means having a numb mind; he believes that, were it not for Socrates' numbing effect, he could answer—and thus think—well. (That Euthyphro blames Socrates for his present inability to answer properly leads Benson to conclude that Euthyphro does not really admit his ignorance; curiously, however, Benson fails to draw the same inference in Meno's case.) Benson argues, too, that since in the upcoming slave-boy-demonstration, the slave-boy is truly perplexed and admits that he does not know, and since the slave-boy-demonstration is meant to parallel in its early stages the progress of the elenctic exchange that has taken place thus far between Meno and Socrates, it follows that as far as Socrates is concerned Meno, too, truly recognizes his own ignorance. I find myself also unable to agree with this point of Benson's. Socrates' intention in setting up the parallel between Meno and the slave-boy is to have the slave-boy serve as an example to Meno of how Meno ought to have conducted himself: like the slave-boy, Meno, too, should have admitted gracefully that he does not know, for as he can surely see now, there is no shame in such an admission, nor has the slave-boy been harmed—on the contrary, he has benefited—by his admission. The clear implication is that Meno should have, but did not, comport himself as well as the slave-boy does, because Meno should have, but did not, admit his ignorance, as the slave-boy does.

4. When Meno remarks that he did in the past speak very well on the subject of virtue on numerous occasions, "as, at least, it seemed to me," it is unlikely that there is in his qualifier "as, at least, it seemed to me" (*M.* 80b4) any irony or second-guessing of himself. Surely all he means is that maybe Socrates would not have agreed. See Ebert (1973), 171, who agrees that Meno's remark "does *not* imply a self-criticism . . . ; it is rather intended to remind his listeners of how unnatural the situation is into which he has been brought by Socrates' tricky questions" (emphasis in original).

5. Socrates accuses Meno of comparing him to a stingray in order to receive in

accepts its implication that he is a man at a loss, *aporōn,* who impoverishes (causes perplexity in) others, *poiō aporein* (*M.* 80c8).[6] Little does Meno realize that from Socrates' perspective the fact that it is now evident that neither he nor Meno knows what virtue is makes this a most opportune time for them to resume their joint investigation into the nature of virtue.[7] As Meno sees it, Socrates' utter ignorance of virtue (*M.* 80d5–6), coupled with his admission of utter ignorance,[8] poses an insurmountable obstacle to the search for virtue: how can someone in such a sorry epistemic state hope to conduct a successful investigation? Let us be clear that Meno's resistance to Socrates' ongoing investigation has nothing to do with any aversion on Meno's part to learning. On the contrary, Meno is glad to learn as long as he learns from someone who teaches. He has learned from Gorgias; he is eager, both at the *Meno*'s beginning and in its middle (*M.* 86c8–d2), to have Socrates teach him. Yet since he is unable to imagine what an investigation might yield in which there is no teaching and being taught,[9] and since it is becoming progressively more certain that Socrates is neither willing nor able

return the sort of flattering comparison that handsome people are accustomed to. But could this really have been Meno's intention? Socrates, as was explained in Chapter 1, begins imputing to Meno malicious intentions that he clearly does not have only in the aftermath of the incident in which Meno rejects without warrant Socrates' definition of shape. It is no wonder that Nehamas (1985), 8, calls Meno, on this occasion, "the much-maligned Meno."

6. The punning here on *euporōn,* "well-supplied" or "wealthy," on *aporōn,* "without means" or "at a loss," and on *aporein,* "to be without resources," "perplexed," or "at a loss," is reminiscent of the earlier pun on *aporia* (*M.* 78e6), which meant, in context, "nonacquisition" but also means "poverty" and "perplexity." See Chapter 1, n. 52.

7. Socrates hints here that investigation is appropriate only in the event that neither party to the investigation has knowledge, so that unless Meno were now at least "*like* someone who does not know" (*M.* 80d3), there could be no inquiry. We may note that Socrates, in saying of Meno that he is now "*like* someone who does not know," refrains from saying about Meno things Meno is not willing to concede about himself. Meno recognizes that he has conducted himself thus far in the inquiry *like* someone who does not know but, nevertheless, is not ready to admit that he is actually ignorant concerning the matter at hand.

8. Meno speaks only of Socrates' ignorance, not admitting his own. That he fails to concede his own ignorance also argues against Benson's position as discussed in n. 3. Meno's unwillingness to acknowledge his own ignorance is, furthermore, consistent with his having objected to Socrates' first definition of shape by suggesting, not that he does not know what color is, but that "someone"—someone *else*—might not know.

9. One wonders if Meno even understands what Socrates means when he says, "I want to consider (*skepsasthai*) with you" (*M.* 80d3–4). We note that later on in the dialogue (*M.* 86c8–d2), Meno too easily passes from "consider" to "hear": "I should most like," he says, "to consider and to hear," *skepsaimēn kai akousaimi* (*M.* 86c9–10).

to serve as his instructor, Meno resents being conscripted into yet another round of inquiry that is, from the start, doomed to failure.

ii. Meno's Paradox

Meno's objection is to elenchus. Elenchus, as he sees it, goes nowhere. It achieves nothing. The person who "conducts" it says he knows nothing at all about the matter under investigation. The other participant does his best to produce answers, only to have them shot down seriatim by the know-nothing leader. Meno lashes out. His only weapon is the captious double-talk he has picked up through his association with Gorgias.[10] He finds the relevant "argument" and launches it, in a somewhat garbled form,[11] at Socrates: "And in what way will you search, Socrates, for this thing of which you do not know at all what it is? For, of the things that you do not know, just what sort of thing will you search for on the supposition that it is that one? Or even if you do happen upon it, how will you know that this is the thing that you did not know?" (M. 80d5–8).

The paradox is an attack on Socrates. It is no accident that it is framed in the second person.[12] Meno has no interest in theoretical questions about how knowledge is acquired; he knows the answer: one goes to a teacher. But Socrates is no teacher. The paradox challenges Socrates to defend his practice.[13]

---

10. Gorgias is notorious for skeptical arguments such as this. See his *On Nature or the Non-Existent* (DK 82B3). It is noteworthy that Meno's paradox, like everything else he says, does not originate with him.

11. Socrates will set it right in his reformulation of it at *M*. 80e2–6.

12. Moline (1969), 155–57, detects sarcasm in Meno's use of the second person and in his use of the word *poion*. He thinks Meno questions Socrates' "good faith" inasmuch as Socrates plans to proceed to inquire even though he is purportedly "numb." Guthrie (1975), 238–39, n. 1, disagrees with Moline, seeing no sarcasm in Meno's paradox: there is no evidence, he claims, that Meno doubts Socrates' good faith. It seems to me that surely the stingray simile provides some evidence for Meno's distrust of Socrates; moreover, *poios* does indeed have a sarcastic edge when it is used in repartee, especially when the words the previous speaker has just uttered are repeated (see Thompson [1901], 116–17; Bluck [1961a], 272; Liddell, Scott, and Jones [1966]). (I render *poion* as "just what sort of thing" in an attempt to capture its sarcasm.) Sharples (1985), 144, prefers to call what motivates Meno's paradox "bewildered exasperation" rather than, as Moline thinks, a suspicion of bad faith.

13. There are no grounds for regarding the paradox itself as restricted in scope in any way, as, for example, Fine (1992), 219, does: "The paradox does not ask whether, in general, one can acquire knowledge; it asks only whether one can come

Meno's paradox actually contains two separate paradoxes, identified by Scott (1995), 29, as (1) the paradox of inquiry and (2) the paradox of discovery. The first of these, the paradox of inquiry, asks how one can search for what one does not know. It is this paradox that Socrates will soon expose and dismiss as a stock "eristic argument" (*M.* 80e2).

The second paradox is probably not best called a "paradox of discovery," for Meno is not asking, although he is generally thought to be asking, how new discoveries can be made; he is asking how new discoveries are verified. What drives Meno to his second paradox is not that the inquiry in which he and Socrates were engaged made no discoveries—it did in fact yield several answers to the question of the nature of virtue—but that there seemed to be no way of knowing if any of the answers produced was the right one even if it was. The challenge to Socrates posed by Meno's second paradox is, therefore: how can one (you) *know* that what one has happened upon, what one has discovered, is what one was looking for—even if it is? I rename the second paradox "the paradox of knowing."[14]

Scholars, no doubt taking their cue from Socrates (*M.* 80e1–2), tend to regard Meno's paradox with disdain.[15] To be sure, Meno has little interest in the theoretical epistemological questions the paradox raises. For him, the paradox merely represents his best hope of being rid of the unrelenting Socratic nuisance that is elenctic examination: if it really is necessary that one know in advance of inquiry what one is looking for, both in order to look for it and in order to know that one has found it, Socratic-style inquiry is indeed

to know things like virtue through inquiry." Even though the paradox is animated by Meno's disgust with virtue inquiry specifically, it is itself quite general (see Rohatyn [1980], 69–70). Socrates exploits the paradox's generality in his responses to it, referring in the recollection myth to all things, *panta chrēmata* (*M.* 81c6–7), and in the slave-boy-demonstration to all of geometry and to all other subjects, *pasēs geōmetrias tauta panta, kai tōn allōn mathēmatōn hapantōn* (*M* 85e2–3). Once Socrates can show one instance of learning by question-and-answer, namely, the slave-boy's learning how to double a square, he "refutes" the paradox for all things—including virtue.

14. Note that Meno does not use the word "discover," *heuriskein.*

15. Shorey (1933), 157: "a lazy and eristic argument"; Taylor (1948), 135: Meno "tries to run off on an irrelevant puzzle"; Guthrie (1956), 107: "a sophistic dilemma about knowledge"; Bluck (1961a), 8: "a convenient dodge," "an eristic trick." Contrast Nehamas (1985), 8: "Given the situation [namely, that both Socrates and Meno are presumably devoid of knowledge of virtue], and far from being a contentious move, Meno's raising of the paradox of enquiry is natural and well-motivated."

useless. But apart from the matter of what less-than-noble motives Meno might have in posing the paradox, there are the questions of whether the paradox itself has philosophical merit and whether Socrates in the *Meno* thinks it does.[16] Taking individually, then, the two paradoxes contained in Meno's challenge to Socrates—the paradox of inquiry and the paradox of knowing—let us ask with respect to each what its philosophical worth is and how Socrates assesses its merit.

The paradox of inquiry rests, it seems, on a mere verbal quibble. It is this paradox, therefore, that Socrates calls, aptly, eristic (*M.* 80e2): it has no philosophical bite. It exemplifies the sort of argument that Socrates easily dispenses with in the *Euthydemus*.[17] A fairly simple solution to it is suggested by Ryle (1976), 7–9, who seeks to disarm the paradox by way of a distinction between what he calls the adjectival and interrogative senses of "what one is looking for." One might know, Ryle explains, in the adjectival sense, that is, by description, what the object of one's search is without knowing in the interrogative sense what actual thing answers to that description.[18] Ryle thinks that this distinction is unavailable to Plato, who, he avers, neither had the vocabulary with which to express it nor actually recognized it, for if he did, he would have shown it in some way. Yet

16. Phillips (1965), 78, for one, takes the paradox seriously even while regarding it as "merely a dodge" from Meno's point of view. See also Klein (1965), 91–92.

17. See Nehamas (1985), 9, who notes that an argument very much like the paradox of inquiry is easily solved in the *Euthydemus*—where it is introduced as a purely contentious argument—by exposing the equivocation on *manthanein*, "to learn" (Bluck [1961a], 272, makes the same point). Since Nehamas does not pull apart the two paradoxes contained in Meno's paradox, he concludes that the paradox as a whole is taken quite seriously in the *Meno*, seriously enough to warrant the development of the recollection thesis. "At the very least, he [Plato] does not think that the paradox to which he can also supply a merely verbal solution has merely verbal force." See also Sharples (1985), 143, who contends that, unlike in the *Euthydemus*, "the issue here is a serious one."

18. On a certain model of inquiry, one we might call the "template model," even the paradox of inquiry would have force: if what one does in inquiry is match an object to a template, the object would indeed have to be known at the start of the inquiry. (Perhaps it is a model of this sort that White [1974–1975], 290–91, has in mind in speaking of the "attempt to *find* a thing and *recognize* it as what we were searching for" [emphasis in original] or of getting "the object somehow into one's 'ken' or mental 'view.' ") It is, I think, just this sort of model that the paradox is able to exploit by not specifying what sort of model for inquiry it does have in mind: in sophistry, ambiguity is the great facilitator. Inquiry, however, is, for Socrates, the attempt to solve a problem—virtually any sort of problem—to which the answer is *not* already known. It is the looking into a matter rather than the narrower looking for a thing. And insofar as it is the looking into a matter, it need not exclude problems concerned with how to do or to accomplish some task.

the way in which Plato has Socrates proceed in the *Meno* to address Meno's paradox does, I would argue, show, in fact, that he appreciates—even if he does not articulate—Ryle's distinction: the two geometry questions that Socrates will soon pose are models of how one can inquire into something when the solution is not already known. The first of these geometry questions is the one that is addressed in the slave-boy-demonstration. The solution to this question is, of course, known to Socrates, but even the slave-boy, who clearly does not know (interrogatively) what the solution is, nevertheless still knows (adjectivally) what is being sought. The second question is the one Socrates uses to illustrate how hypothetical method works (at *M.* 87a–b). In this case, the geometer knows what he needs to discover (in the adjectival sense), although he does not as yet know the solution (in the interrogative sense). He even has a means (the hypothetical method) for proceeding to find what he is looking for.

The matter of beginning an inquiry when one does not already know what one is looking for may, admittedly, be somewhat more complex when what one is looking for is not the solution to a math problem but the nature of virtue or one of its parts. In the case of virtue and its parts, it is not immediately obvious that one *can* know in the adjectival sense what one does not know in the interrogative sense. Does one truly understand (adjectivally) what one is looking for when one is engaged in a search for what virtue is if one has, let us say, vulgar ideas about morality (as Meno does)? In Plato's dialogues, of course, Socrates conducts his moral inquiries with interlocutors who harbor crude and sometimes even odious moral views; yet the fact that Socrates' immediate associations with the virtue terms are very different from those his interlocutors have never prevents inquiry from getting off the ground. Socrates, it would appear, regards any term that people use in common as a legitimate object for inquiry—even if, or especially if, the term's meaning is (or ought to be) in doubt or a matter of controversy. It suffices for beginning an investigation that people have opinions—not that they have the right opinions or, a fortiori, knowledge—about the meaning of the terms they regularly use: if they have opinions, they understand the question well enough. Since Meno quite confidently holds beliefs about virtue, Socrates can—and does—undertake to investigate with him the what-is-virtue question. Indeed, given the brute fact that such an investigation has just been conducted, is it any wonder that Socrates denounces as "eristic" the paradox that would deny its very possibility?

Many commentators on Meno's paradox of inquiry think it founders on the all-or-nothing character it assigns to knowledge.[19] For
them, the *to parapan* in Meno's formulation—"And in what way will
you search for this, Socrates, if you do not know at all (*to parapan*)
what it is?" (*M.* 80d5–6)—is, therefore, the prime offender.[20] But it
is not as if the *to parapan* is Meno's invention. It is Socrates who says
of himself early on that he does not know "at all," *to parapan*, what
virtue is. And there is no reason to think that Socrates no longer
stands by his earlier declaration; he neither does nor says anything
that could be construed as a recanting of it. Meno is, to be sure,
irked by what he perceives as the audacity of a man who, on the one
hand, virtually boasts that he knows *not at all* what virtue is but, on
the other, presumes to conduct, at Meno's expense, a seemingly
endless inquiry into it. Nevertheless, Socrates means what he says.
For him, knowledge *is* an all-or-nothing affair, and he insists that he
has no knowledge with respect to virtue. That he believes himself to
be completely lacking in knowledge of this matter does not, of
course, mean that he claims to hold no opinions about it, or even
that he claims to hold no true opinions about it; what it does mean,
however, is that he regards himself as *knowing* not "at all," *to parapan*,
what virtue is.[21] If Socrates truly believes that he knows not at all
what virtue is but wishes nevertheless to proceed with his inquiry
into the nature of virtue, it seems rather unlikely that *he,* at any rate,
could think that the solution to the paradox lies in removing the *to
parapan* and grounding the possibility of inquiry in the inquirer's
beginning with some knowledge. What seems more likely is that Socrates believes (as is implicit in the way in which he always conducts
his *elenchoi,* including, of course, the elenchus concerning the nature
of virtue with which the *Meno* begins) that inquiry into what one
does not know at all is not only possible but necessary. It is possible
because one can raise a question without knowing its answer; it is
necessary because one does not as yet know the answer. Just as in

---

19. See Cornford (1971), 124–35; Moravcsik (1971), 57; Calvert (1974), 147;
Scolnicov (1976), 52–53; Thomas (1980), 123, 128–29.

20. For the view that *to parapan* plays no important role, see Nehamas (1985), 10.

21. Cornford (1971), 124–25, regards beliefs as "degrees of knowledge intermediate between complete knowledge and blank ignorance." Yet beliefs are not, for
Socrates/Plato, "degrees of knowledge" at all. It is useful to bear in mind in this regard
that it is in the *Meno* that Socrates both draws the distinction between knowledge and
true opinion and claims to *know* that there is such a distinction to be drawn (*M.* 98b3–
5).

the *Euthydemus*, so here, the paradox of inquiry is for Socrates no stimulus to serious reflection. It is a mere sophistry, fueled by a simple equivocation. It is not surprising, therefore, that neither the myth of recollection nor the slave-boy-demonstration addresses this paradox.[22]

But what of the paradox of knowing? If it is easy for Socrates to dismiss the paradox of inquiry's claim that the one who lacks prior knowledge of something cannot begin to seek it, is it equally easy for him to dismiss this paradox's claim that one who lacks knowledge cannot know he has found what he is looking for even if he has? Does not the fact that that the myth of recollection and the slave-boy-demonstration seem to attempt to address the paradox of knowing suggest that Socrates indeed takes this paradox (if not the paradox of inquiry) quite seriously? Let us look, therefore, to the text itself to see if, perchance, it contains some indication that Socrates regards the paradox of knowing as posing a more formidable challenge to elenctic investigation than the paradox of inquiry does.

iii. Socrates' Paradox

There is indeed one remarkable feature in the text that may well suggest that Socrates feels more acutely the sting of the paradox of knowing than that of the paradox of inquiry. It is a feature that, though certainly glaring, has somehow gone unnoticed by most commentators (Meno does no better) and has been critically underinterpreted by the few who have noticed it. I refer to the fact that in Socrates' reformulation of Meno's paradox, there simply is no counterpart to the paradox of knowing that figures so centrally in

---

22. Irwin (1977), 139, thinks that in both the myth and slave-boy-demonstration, Socrates does indeed address the paradox of *inquiry*. According to Irwin, Socrates' solution to the paradox is that all that is needed for inquiry into x is "enough true beliefs about x to fix the reference of the term 'x.'" But both recollection theory and the slave-boy-demonstration show how one can find the answer to the question one poses—not how one can pose the question. Certainly in the slave-boy-demonstration, the question is immediately understood by the slave-boy; what the slave-boy does not know is the answer. Moreover, at the end of the demonstration, it is not about the question but about the answer that the slave-boy is said to have already had true opinions in his soul. Nehamas (1985), 17, also disagrees with Irwin on this point.

Meno's version.[23] To see that this is so, let us compare Meno's paradox with Socrates' restatement of it.

Meno's paradox runs as follows:

(a) And in what way will you search, Socrates, for this thing of which you do not know at all what it is? (b) For, of the things that you do not know, just what sort of thing will you search for on the assumption that it is that one? (c) Or even if you do happen upon it, how will you know that this is the thing that you did not know? (*M.* 80d5–8)

Here is Socrates' reformulation of it:

(a') It is not possible for a man to search either for what he knows or for what he does not know. (b') For he would not search for what he knows, for he knows it, and there is no need to search for such a thing; nor for what he does not know, for he does not even know what he will search for. (*M.* 80e2–6)

Both versions of the paradox begin with an introduction, (a) and (a'), respectively. Following the introduction, Meno's version proceeds to give two reasons, (b) and (c), for its claim that Socrates cannot search for what he does not know: (b) that he will not know what to look for, and (c) that, even if he happens upon what he is looking for, he will not know it. But, whereas Socrates' version contains something, (b'), that, though fuller than (b), does correspond to it, it contains nothing at all, no (c'), that corresponds to (c).

Although this striking difference between Meno's formulation of the paradox and Socrates' reformulation of it has not attracted much attention, three other differences have. The first is that Meno's paradox is stated in the second person and Socrates' version of it in the third. Moline (1969), 160, places great emphasis on this difference; he sees Socrates' revision of the paradox as his attempt to turn Meno's sarcastic tirade against him into a depersonalized, dispassionate statement of a real philosophical problem. The second is that

23. Among the more prominent commentators on the *Meno* who make no mention at all of this difference are Bluck (1961a), Vlastos (1965) and (1991), and Klein (1965). Klein (1965), 91, speaks of "Socrates' (amplifying as well as simplifying) recapitulation" of Meno's paradox, but he does not spell out what constitutes the amplification or the simplification. It seems to me, that to leave out the paradox of knowing is not just to simplify.

the phrase *to parapan*, "at all," is present in Meno's formulation but absent from Socrates'; on this matter, see Section ii, above.[24] For those who regard this difference as the crucial one, the solution to the paradox lies in the recognition that attainment of new knowledge begins not from blank ignorance but from some measure of knowledge, however small. Let us note, however, that Socrates' formulation of the paradox, even without the *to parapan*, can hardly be construed as allowing for degrees of knowledge: in Socrates' version of the paradox, one either knows or does not know; these are exhaustive alternatives; there is no middle ground. The third difference is that Meno's formulation is inelegant and fails to take the classic form of a dilemma, but Socrates' formulation is an elegantly stated, classic dilemma. Among those who see this as the primary difference between Meno's and Socrates' paradoxes are Phillips (1965), 77; White (1975), 290, n. 4; and Seeskin (1987), 113, n. 1. It would seem, however, that there is nothing at stake philosophically in this change.

Indeed, none of these differences—is the paradox stated in the second person or the third; is it expressed extravagantly or moderately, that is, with or without the phrase *to parapan*; is it elegantly or awkwardly articulated, posed as a classic dilemma or not?—is much more than cosmetic. Moreover, these differences that have so exercised scholars can be easily accounted for: on the assumption that Socrates wishes to reconstruct the stock eristic argument from which Meno's paradox derives, he would quite naturally (a) remove from it its highly personal nature (as indicated by the second-person singular), (b) state it in the form of a dilemma (to the effect that it is impossible to search either for what one does know or for what one does not know), and (c) leave out the *to parapan*, which disturbs the perfect symmetry of the dilemma.

In what comparably tidy way can Socrates' unceremonious excision of the paradox of knowing from his version of the paradox be accounted for? Is there an equally simple explanation for Socrates' utter neglect of part (c) of Meno's paradox, the part I have called the paradox of knowing, the challenge Meno poses to Socrates at *M.* 80d7–8: "Or even if you do happen upon it, how will you know that this is the thing that you did not know?" Surely in comparison

---

24. Fine (1992), 222, n. 29, points out that "Plato is cavalier in his use of *to parapan* elsewhere too: Despite its occurrence in 71a7 and b3, 5, it is omitted . . . at 71b3–4."

with the three largely stylistic differences that scholars have emphasized, this difference stands out as one of far greater substance.[25]
How odd, then, that even those scholars who do notice it dismiss it
as unimportant.[26] Moravcsik (1971), 57, for example, brushes this
difference aside, saying: "If one understands what one investigates,
then one will know whether an answer is given to the original question." Scolnicov (1976), 53, takes a similar line, in reverse: "unless
you have an inkling of what the solution may be, you don't have a
question to start with." Scott (1995), 31, who is to be credited with
identifying the two distinct paradoxes within Meno's paradox, thinks
that Socrates intended to state the paradox of knowing in his reformulation but that "there is merely a slight inaccuracy in the formulation at 80e3 and . . . the word 'discover' (*heuriskein*) would have
been more appropriate than 'inquire' (*zētein*)." Yet for a reader who
is not prepared, on the one hand, simply to bury, as do Moravcsik
and Scolnicov, the difference between the paradox of inquiry and
the paradox of knowing as if the distinct issues they raise can be
collapsed into one another or, on the other hand, to presume, with
Scott, that when Socrates reformulates Meno's paradox using *zētein*
and not *heuriskein*, he has simply blundered,[27] the pressing question

25. Guthrie (1956) translates the *ē*, "or," that introduces this second paradox as
"To put it another way," thereby thoroughly assimilating the second paradox to the
first. In context, however, the "or" indicates that even if Socrates could somehow
overcome the first hurdle of getting the inquiry off the ground, there would still be
a second to overcome: "If you do not know at all the thing you are searching for, how
would you search for it, *or* even if you could search for it, how would you know that
what you happened upon is the thing you were looking for?" For the identical construction, see *M.* 96d2–4: "And so I really wonder, Socrates, whether there perhaps
are no good men at all, or what the manner of becoming [good] is of those who
become good." The *ē*, "or", here functions in precisely the same way as the *ē* in Meno's
paradox. It certainly cannot be translated "or in other words." The passage must be
rendered "or [if there are good men, then] what the manner of [their] becoming
[good] is. . . ."

26. Fine (1992), 219, n. 21, notices this difference but offers no explanation for
it. See also Sharples (1985), 143.

27. In his 1991 article, Scott argues, as I do here, that Socrates' purpose in developing a recollection thesis is to provide Meno with an incentive to inquire. Scott
maintained there, as I do here, that since recollection addresses, if anything, the
second paradox but (a) seems in the dialogue to be intended to respond to the
frivolous paradox of inquiry, which alone appears in Socrates' version of the paradox,
and (b) in fact has nothing to say to that paradox, then recollection must have only
a motivational function. In his 1995 book, however, Scott abandons his earlier view,
contending that Socrates meant for his version of the paradox to contain the second
paradox (the one Scott calls the paradox of discovery and I call the paradox of knowing), and that it was only because of an infelicitous choice of words, the use of *zētein*
instead of *heuriskein*, that he seems to end up doing nothing more than restating

remains: why does Socrates cause the paradox of knowing to vanish? What does he see in it that makes him pretend not to have seen it at all?[28]

As we attempt to discern Socrates' view of the paradox of knowing, it is instructive to bear in mind that Socrates, in effect, withholds from *it* the label "eristic argument." Whereas Socrates attaches this label to his reformulated version of Meno's paradox, his reformulation, as we have seen, preserves only the paradox of inquiry. If, as has been argued, Socrates indeed regards the paradox of inquiry as but a specious bit of sophistry that hardly merits a second thought, it stands to reason that he would refer to it disparagingly as an eristic argument.[29] Might it be that Socrates omits the paradox of knowing from his restatement of Meno's paradox in part in order to indicate that he does not regard *it* as similarly "eristic"? If Socrates' way of showing his disdain for the paradox of inquiry is first to pronounce it an eristic argument, next to denounce it outright as not a good argument (*M*. 81a3), and finally to ignore it for the duration of the dialogue, what attitude of his does he mean to convey by silently dropping the paradox of knowing? Could it be that Socrates hints thereby that he recognizes its power and knows he cannot refute it?

I propose that Socrates deletes the paradox of knowing from his restatement of Meno's paradox precisely because he recognizes that *with respect to the issue of virtue* he cannot answer it: it is in virtue inquiry that one will indeed not *know* that one has found the answer one seeks even if one does happen upon it; it is here that the need to go on testing and examining one's answers is never fully exhausted. Elenchus, Socrates knows, will not end the search.

Meno's paradox of inquiry. I find most implausible the idea that Socrates uses *zētein* instead of *heuriskein* by mistake.

28. White (1975), 290, n. 4, refuses to recognize any such difference between Meno's and Socrates' formulation of the paradox on the grounds that "this supposition leaves it quite unexplained why he [Plato] never mentions the fact, and thenceforth acts as though he has only one difficulty to face." Surely, however, Plato often sets his readers the task of both noticing and seeking to explain such difficulties.

29. White (1974–5), 289, n. 1, contends that by *eristikon*, here rendered "eristic," Socrates means not sophistical but only contentious or obstructionist, and that therefore the reader ought not to conclude that Plato does not take the argument seriously. Yet for Socrates to call the paradox even contentious or obstructionist constitutes a rebuke to Meno; if he thought the argument a fine and appropriate one, he would hardly reprimand Meno for raising it. Moreover, Socrates unmistakably impugns the argument's worth when he responds "no" at *M*. 81a3 to Meno's question "Well, does this argument not appear to you beautifully spoken, Socrates?" (*M*. 81a1–2).

What Socrates believes to be true of virtue, however, he simply does not believe to be true of other areas of investigation. Whereas he surely accepts, on the one hand, that in all matters that are subjects for inquiry, including virtue, it is impossible to search for what is already known, because it is already known,[30] and it is both possible and necessary to search for what is unknown,[31] he clearly believes, on the other, that in all subject matters *but* virtue, inquiry into the unknown frequently culminates in new knowledge. For Socrates, mathematics is a prime example of a subject matter in which inquiry leads to discovery in the form of knowledge (witness the geometry example at *M.* 86e–87b); but mathematics is, therefore, for him in this respect *un*like virtue; it is in this respect like all the other disciplines, the *mathēmata*, whose status as kinds of *technē* distinguishes them from virtue, at least in the Cave. Craftsmen, from physicians to shoemakers, no less than mathematicians, can make new discoveries that Socrates counts as knowledge. In all of these areas there are "objective" tests: in mathematics there are incontrovertible proofs (there is, for example, in the slave-boy-demonstration, the counting of equal half-squares);[32] in crafts there is the eating that is the proof of the pudding (shoes that are comfortable and hold up well, the trireme that proves effective in battle, the treatment or drug that cures disease or illness or repairs physical deformity).[33] It is virtue for which, as Socrates is well aware, there is in the Cave no objective test; it is in moral questions, questions of the best way for human beings to live, that there is in the Cave no clear-cut way of securing the answers one finds. In the Cave, therefore, the only thing one can do (and, from Socrates' point of view, the thing one consequently must do) is pit one opinion against another to see which coheres best with the deepest of human strivings and beliefs.

---

30. See Aristotle, *Eth. Nic.* 6.9.1142a27–b11: "for men do not inquire about the things they know about."

31. White (1976), 42, thinks that Plato believes just the opposite, namely, that we cannot inquire into what we do not know and can inquire only into what we already do know. I would argue that for Socrates inquiry begins with the recognition that one lacks knowledge—not with the recognition that one already has it. Generally speaking, Socrates' view is that the obstacle to inquiry is not lack of knowledge but the mistaken belief that one has knowledge. We may note what Socrates says to Meno in commenting on the slave-boy's progress: "Then, do you think he would have tried to inquire or learn what he thought he knew, though he did not, before he fell into perplexity, realizing that he did not know, and longed for knowledge?" (*M.* 84c4–7).

32. See *Euthyph.* 7b–c.

33. See *Lach.* 184e–186b and *Gorg.* 514a–e. Also see *Theaet.* 201b, where witnessing something with one's own eyes constitutes grounds for claiming to know.

Meno has no interest in inquiry that will not yield knowledge; yet it is precisely in such inquiry that Socrates wants him to engage. Meno believes that the only way to learn is to be taught; Socratic inquiry is a way to learn without being taught—though also without attaining knowledge. The predicament, therefore, in which Socrates now finds himself is that although he wishes to persuade Meno to persist in elenctic inquiry and would like, in addition, to combat Meno's belief that the only way to learn is to be taught, he can assure Meno neither that elenctic inquiry will yield knowledge nor that through it Meno will come to learn—that is, will come to have *knowledge*—without a teacher. If he admits outright, on the one hand, that elenctic inquiry into virtue will not yield knowledge, Meno will hardly have incentive enough to persevere; but if he maintains, on the other, that elenctic inquiry into virtue will yield knowledge, how long would that falsehood survive? Faced, then, with two impracticable choices, Socrates has recourse to a third, practicable one. He does what he so often does when he finds himself in a bind: he takes refuge in myth.[34]

iv. The Myth of Learning by Recollection

The myth to which Socrates now has recourse begins with an account of the fate of souls that he claims to have heard from priests and priestesses and that, in addition, garners support from Pindar, among other poets. According to the account-cum-poem, souls are immortal and undergo repeated rebirths; they ought, therefore, to strive to live as righteously as possible in order that they may be reborn as noble kings or as beings "swift in strength and great in wisdom." Tacked onto this account and its moral lesson is the added idea that all learning is recollection.

Does Socrates in the *Meno* believe that the soul is immortal, that it migrates from life to life, that it learns by recollecting what it once

---

34. It is important to recognize that Meno's paradox has backed Socrates into a corner and that although he believes that the answer to the virtue question will indeed not be known by ordinary mortals, he nevertheless must say *something* if he is to keep Meno inquiring. To the contention of scholars, then, that Socrates would surely not have taken the trouble to develop the myth of recollection in the *Meno* unless he believed it or something like it, the appropriate answer is that his alternative is to say nothing and to allow Meno to quit the inquiry believing himself to have triumphed. I shall argue in Chapter 4 that recollection, though not the myth of recollection, plays an important part in Socrates' defense of moral inquiry in the form of elenchus.

knew? Or are these "doctrines" only a rhetorical device for inducing Meno to go on with the inquiry into virtue? I shall argue for the duration of this chapter and in Chapter 3 that neither the recollection thesis, as a general account of how knowledge is acquired, nor the metaphysical notions that undergird it are Socrates' own beliefs, but that his development of, first, the myth and, then, the slave-boy-demonstration constitutes his fight "in word and deed" (*M.* 86c2–3) for the value of moral inquiry. As Socrates makes clear, what recommends the view that all knowledge comes by recollection is that *it* makes good men of its adherents, whereas the alternative view, Meno's paradox, makes bad men of those who subscribe to *it.* Although it is generally supposed that the purpose of the myth is to answer, to solve, or to refute Meno's paradox, and although this is surely what Socrates would like Meno to believe it does, the recollection thesis is needed neither to dispose of the trivial and sophistic paradox of inquiry, to which it is irrelevant, nor to refute the paradox of knowing as it applies to subjects other than virtue where verification is unproblematic; moreover, it is, as Socrates is well aware, woefully inadequate for solving the paradox of knowing as it applies to virtue. Since, in the Cave, no satisfactory response to the paradox of knowing as it applies to virtue is forthcoming, the purpose of Socrates' recollection thesis can only be to distract Meno from it in order that he not abandon the inquiry into the nature of virtue. A little inventiveness in service of this all-important end is, Socrates must think, surely not out of line.[35]

What indications are there that Socrates does not take the myth seriously? First, there is the sheer fact that he presents a myth, as opposed to a reasoned *logos,* in response to Meno's paradox.[36] Critical reflection, it is clear, plays no part either in the myth itself or in Socrates' discovery of it or in his apparent endorsement of it:[37] it

35. See Robinson (1953), 11: "Socrates seems prepared to employ any kind of deception in order to get people into the elenchus."

36. According to Ebert (1973), 177, the myth must be ironical because it is "delivered in lieu of an answer to a short and meaningful question." Rohatyn (1980), 71, speaks of the myth's "grossly unsatisfactory character as an explanation of how knowledge is possible. . . . Socrates in effect admits he has no answer but only a myth." Ryle (1976), 9, asks: "Why does Plato let the Socrates of our *Meno* so un-Socratically erect upon a poem and a fairy-story a self-demolishing epistemology?" Brumbaugh (1990), 300, views the myth as "an odd way for Plato to introduce an intended new doctrine."

37. Vlastos (1965), 165–66, argues that despite Plato's probably having heard about reincarnation from the Pythagoreans, he attributes it to priests and priestesses. By doing so, Plato means to indicate, according to Vlastos, that reincarnation is for him a matter of religious faith and not a doctrine he arrived at by way of theoretical

is, he says, something he has "heard" that strikes him as true and fine. What aspect of what he has heard so strikes him? He does not explicitly say. Perhaps he means to restrict judgment "true and fine" to the moral lesson that follows from the immortality and rebirth of the soul: "it is required, therefore, to live out one's life as piously as possible" (*M.* 81b6–7).[38] For, first, by the time Socrates has finished his account of the myth and of its associated doctrine of recollection, it is not on the grounds of its truth that he recommends the thesis to Meno; he extols instead its practical value in shaping the character of those who embrace it. Second, by presenting the myth as something he has heard,[39] Socrates packages it to appeal to Meno, who regularly quotes approvingly the words of others. We may note in this regard how Meno with eager impatience interrupts Socrates midsentence the moment he realizes that Socrates is about to reproduce the words of another: "Saying what saying?" he asks (*M.* 81a7). Third, Socrates hints at the self-serving motive of those from whom he has heard it: the priests and priestesses who are its source

speculation. In my view, by having Socrates cite priests and priestesses as his source, Plato emphasizes the doctrine's extrarational character and indicates thereby the *improbability* that Socrates endorses it.

38. The truthfulness that Socrates claims for his myth at the end of the *Gorgias*, in which he speaks of the fate that awaits souls upon their descent to Hades—the souls of those who have lived justly during their lifetimes, of those who have lived unjustly but not irredeemably so, and of those who have lived irreparably viciously— is surely not factual truth but moral truth. When Socrates says (*Gorg.* 523a) that Callicles no doubt will regard the story that Socrates is about to tell him as just a story whereas he himself regards it as a *logos* that he tells Callicles as something true, what he means is that whereas for Callicles the moral of the story will not be one that he feels he need take seriously with regard to how to lead his life, it is one that Socrates takes most seriously. We may note that Socrates tempers his endorsement of the details of the tale he has heard about the afterlife by saying such things as that "something like this" will occur (*Gorg.* 524b). In other words, whether the details of the story are true or not, it remains true that there is a noble and good way for human beings to live: justly and righteously. Here, too, then, when Socrates asks Meno to consider whether he finds true what the priests and priestesses say (*M.* 81b3), what he surely cares about is whether Meno believes, as he does, that one ought to live one's life as righteously as possible. Socrates, as we shall see, has good reason to think that Meno, because of his connection to Pythagoreanism via Gorgias and Empedocles, does indeed embrace the notions of immortality and transmigration of the soul; what is in question is whether he draws from these ideas the appropriate moral conclusion.

39. Vlastos (1983), 56–57, suggests that Plato puts "that wildest of Plato's metaphysical flights, that ultra-speculative theory that all learning is recollecting," into Socrates' mouth because it is "an answer to a problem in Socratic elenchus." Yet Plato, in fact, keeps this doctrine out of Socrates' mouth by having Socrates attribute it to priests, priestesses, and poets rather than present it as a reasoned account of his own as he does, by contrast, in the *Phaedo.*

endorse the myth so as to be able to give an account of their piety business.[40] Fourth, it is unlikely that Socrates thinks he has solid grounds for accepting the myth as true. In the *Apology*, he makes quite a point of saying that he does not know—and, moreover, that no one knows—what happens to human beings after death (*Ap.* 29a–b); indeed, he regards it as the height of hubristic impiety to suppose that one does know such things (*Ap.* 29b). Socrates, then, might well be convinced of nothing more than that lives ought to be lived as piously as possible. But this is a truth of *this* world. What Socrates denies to all human beings, as he denies to himself, is any right or warrant to embrace as factually or literally true the necessarily fanciful speculations about the fate that awaits our souls after death.[41]

What Socrates looks to the myth to provide, then, is not an accurate account of what our souls have experienced and will experience when not in their current bodies but a story that will convince Meno to live courageously, pursuing even inquiry that seems hopeless to him. In fashioning the myth, Socrates will therefore draw upon ideas currently in circulation, ideas that are familiar to Meno and to which Meno may be presumed to be sympathetic; he will also play, strategically, upon Meno's vanity. In these ways, Socrates will use the myth not to solve Meno's paradox but to break down Meno's resistance to continued inquiry: as Socrates says, Meno's paradox has the effect of making those who subscribe to it lazy and is pleasing to those who are soft, but the belief in recollection makes those who adopt it active searchers (*M.* 81d5–e2).

40. Is this too cynical a reading of Socrates' intention in speaking of "priests and priestesses who make it their business to be able to give reason for the rites they perform" (trans. Vlastos [1965], 165)? In light of *Rep.* 2.364b–365a, it hardly seems so. In this *Republic* passage, Adeimantus describes how "beggar priests and diviners go to the doors of the rich man and persuade him that the gods have provided them with a power based on sacrifices and incantations. If he himself, or his ancestors, has committed some injustice, they can heal it with pleasures and feasts" (*Rep.* 2.364b–c). At *Rep.* 2.364e–365a: "They persuade not only private persons, but cities as well, that through sacrifices and pleasurable games there are, after all, deliverances and purifications from unjust deeds for those still living. And there are also rites for those who are dead; while, for those who did not sacrifice, terrible things are waiting" (trans. Bloom [1968]). Socrates' wry criticism of the priests and priestesses who are the source of the *Meno* myth is barely perceptible; indeed, the ability to "give an account," *logon didonai*, is for Plato usually the mark of wisdom. That Socrates would no more than hint at his disdain for the source of the myth is, however, hardly surprising in light of his interest in selling Meno on it.

41. Socrates' description of life after death in the *Apology* is not put forward as literally true but as what can reasonably be hoped for (*Ap.* 40c, 41c).

The themes in the myth with which Meno is likely to be familiar are Pythagorean in origin.[42] They are as follows: (a) life continues for souls after their current bodies expire; (b) the souls that will go on living after their bodies' death also preexisted their current bodies; (c) souls transmigrate from one body to another (metempsychosis); and (d) all nature is akin. We know from Meno's approval earlier of the Empedoclean definition of color that he is a proud disciple of the flashy Empedocles. Empedocles, moreover, is a follower of Pythagoras and is known to have subscribed to such Pythagorean notions as the soul's surviving death and its entering into and passing out of a succession of bodies. There can be little doubt, then, that the concepts of the survival of the soul after the body's death and its relocation from one body to another are notions with which Meno feels at home and to which he is therefore likely to be receptive.[43]

What Meno is probably unfamiliar with, because it is a Socratic innovation, is the concept that learning takes place by way of recollection. Although recollection does play a role in the Pythagorean belief in metempsychosis, the role it plays is a restricted one: it seems to extend no farther than the crediting to Pythagoras himself—and perhaps to a handful of select others[44]—the power to recover knowledge of his own previous incarnations (DK 21B7, 31B129). In other words, Pythagorean doctrine limits to a few extraordinary souls the wondrous ability to remember their former lives; it certainly does not suggest that recollection of previous existences is a way for ordinary people to come to learn what they do

42. As Guthrie (1975), 249, notes: "the doctrines of immortality, reincarnation, remembrance of former lives and the kinship of nature are to be found in earlier Pythagoreanism and its sympathizers like Empedocles." Thompson (1901), 286–87, points to the probable Orphic origins of the Pythagorean transmigration doctrine but notes its centrality to the Pythagoreans. I think it likely that, as scholars generally believe, the *Meno* was written just after Plato's trip to Sicily, where he was exposed to Pythagorean ideas such as immortality and transmigration. Exposure to ideas, however, does not entail acceptance of them.

43. Socrates speaks of the soul as being "immortal," *athanatos* (*M.* 80c5), although it seems, according to Diogenes Laertius's account of Pythagoras (DK 14, 8), that transmigration was the gift Pythagoras's former self, Heraclides of Pontus, was granted *in place of* the immortality that was forbidden to him. Apparently, then, the immortality that was withheld from Heraclides was not the eternal existence of his soul but his perpetual existence as Heraclides.

44. Empedocles, for example, claimed to know the nature of his own previous existences (DK 31B117): "For by now I have been born a boy, girl, plant, and dumb sea-fish."

not know.[45] By refashioning ideas that Meno is comfortable with, however, Socrates seeks to assure Meno that effort expended on inquiry is not wasted effort.

Socrates employs a similar strategy when he includes in his presentation of learning as recollection the notion that "all nature is akin": "For since all nature is akin, and the soul has learned all things, nothing prevents it, if it has recollected one thing—what men call 'learning'—from discovering all other things if one is courageous and does not tire of searching" (M. 81c9–d4). The Pythagorean precursor of this notion is that "all things that come to be alive must be thought akin" (DK 14, 8a). The kinship that Pythagoras recognizes among all living things hardly supports Socrates' stipulation that all things, insofar as they are related by nature, are also connected, or can be connected, by thought. Nevertheless, Socrates uses it to draw the conclusion he wants: if all nature is akin, then Meno, having learned one thing, will be able to learn all other things by himself, that is, without consulting a teacher who already knows.

Finally, Meno, as we have seen, glories in his ability to give good answers and to make impressive speeches; indeed, the pride he takes in his answers and speeches is not in the least diminished by their being but rehearsals of what he recalls of the words of others. Socrates calls attention repeatedly throughout the dialogue's beginning to Meno's heavy reliance on his memory and on his skill at recollecting the words of others and to the contrast between Meno's prodigious memory and his own purportedly poor one. At M. 71c–d, Socrates is presumably unable to remember, because of his poor memory (*mnēmōn*), if he thought Gorgias knew what virtue is when he met him. He asks Meno to remind (*anamnēson*) him what Gorgias had said. At M. 73c, when Meno is apparently unable to appreciate Socrates' point that all instances of virtue have in common the presence of justice and temperance, Socrates tells him to try to *recollect* (*anamnēsthēnai*) what Gorgias said—as if Gorgias were ever asked this question! At M. 76a–b, when Meno presses Socrates to supply him with a definition of color, Socrates upbraids Meno as follows: "But you yourself are not willing to *recollect* (*anamnēstheis*) and tell me what Gorgias says virtue is." And when at M. 79d1 Meno has given Socrates a definition of virtue in terms of its parts, Socrates says to Meno: "If you *remember* (*memnēsai*), when I was answering you just now about

45. A useful discussion of recollection in Pythagorean doctrine compared with recollection in the *Meno* may be found in Bluck (1961a), 62–71.

shape. . . ." Five times in the space of just eight Stephanus pages, Socrates makes reference to memory, reminding, recollecting, or remembering. And Meno in these few pages manages to quote not only Gorgias but a poet as well (*M.* 77b2–3)[46] in attempting to respond to Socrates' demand for a definition of virtue. Even though none of the reminding, recollecting, or remembering in the *Meno*'s opening sections has anything to do with recollecting prenatal knowledge, nevertheless Meno, the rememberer par excellence, is sure to warm to any notion of learning that connects it to recollection.[47]

The *Meno*'s thesis that all learning is recollection need not, then, be read as Socratic or Platonic dogma. It is, as we shall see, sloppily and hastily assembled from the jumble of just-discussed Pythagorean-like ideas. Moreover, and most important, the conclusion that Socrates derives from his recollection myth is the moral lesson that belief in learning as recollection will have a salutary effect on human character (it will make men active and ready to search), whereas belief in the alternative, that is, in Meno's "eristic" paradox, will have a deleterious one (it will make men lazy and is the sort of thing that men who are "soft," *malakoi* [*M.* 80d7], find pleasant to hear).[48] Socrates "puts trust," *pisteuōn* (*M.* 81e2), in his thesis's truth but does not affirm its intrinsic merit.[49]

Let us focus our attention now directly on the myth and the recollection thesis it contains. Socrates speeds through the following

---

46. Although the poet's identity is uncertain, it has been argued (see Thompson [1901], 100) that the poet may well be Simonides, who has a Thessalian connection and whose poem on a similar topic is discussed in the *Protagoras* at 339a–347b.

47. See Klein (1965), 97: "Is not the assertion that what is called learning is but 'recollection' (*anamnēsis*) an echo of his own experience, his own 'memorizing'?"

48. See Rohatyn (1980), 71, who notes that Socrates, by presenting a myth "whose point or outcome is a regulative principle of sorts," in effect admits that he has no answer to the question of how knowledge is possible.

49. We may note how much weaker Socrates' commitment to recollection is at the conclusion of his presentation of the myth—he only "trusts" in its truth—than it was at its start, where he asserts that what he has heard from priests, priestesses, and poets seems to him true and fine (*M.* 81a8). (As was argued earlier, however, even the stronger assertion probably applies only to the moral lesson included in what the priests, priestesses, and poets say, namely, that one must live one's whole life as piously as possible.) Socrates' declaration that he "trusts," *pisteuōn* (*M.* 81e2), in the recollection thesis and his imploring of Meno not to be "persuaded," *peithesthai* (*M.* 81d6), by the eristic argument are reminiscent of the *Gorgias*'s discussion at 454c–455a of the relationship between persuasion and the two ways in which a person may come to be persuaded, namely, by "having learned," *memathēkenai*, and by "having come to trust," *pepisteukenai*.

ideas in succession: the soul is immortal and never perishes; the soul has been born many times; the soul has seen all things (both those here on earth and those in Hades); there is nothing the soul has not learned; there is nothing surprising in the soul's being able to recollect about virtue and other things those things, at any rate, that it, indeed, knew before; all nature is akin; nothing prevents the soul that has recollected one thing from discovering all other things if one is courageous and does not tire of searching; the whole of searching and learning is recollection.

Socrates does not elaborate on any of these points. Although he says twice that the soul is immortal and that it experiences rebirth, he offers nothing by way of explanation and amplification, leaving readers—and Meno—to make of it what they will. Moreover, the frenetic pace of his discourse makes it impossible—no doubt deliberately so—to think along with it and evaluate its cogency as it proceeds. We note that Socrates does not pause after each point, as he does in elenchus, for a response from his interlocutor.

Here are some difficulties that go unaddressed: (a) How do we know how many births any particular soul has already experienced such that we can say with confidence of every soul that it has seen all things? (b) What does it mean to say that the soul has "seen," *eōrakuia*, all things? Is this "seeing" of the ordinary sort or is it extraordinary in some way? (c) Why does Socrates specify, as the places where all things were seen by the soul, here and Hades? (d) What are the things the soul has seen? Do these include Forms? (e) What is meant by the soul's having "learned," *memathēken*, all things. What is the relationship between its having seen, its having learned, and its having recollected? (f) Surely the soul cannot "recollect" all the way down; it must learn something in some other way (by seeing?) that it can then "recollect."[50] But if all learning is recollecting, then there is, presumably, no other way of learning, and everything the soul has come to know it has to have recollected. (g) What is the force of the qualification "those things, at any rate, that it, indeed, knew before," *ha ge kai proteron ēpistato* (*M.* 81c9), if there is, in fact, nothing the soul has not seen or learned? (h) Why should the kinship of all of nature ensure that the discovery of one thing will lead to the discovery of all others? (i) Are we really to believe

---

50. Several scholars have noticed this difficulty. See Ryle (1976), 4: "retrieval cannot, in logic, be the origin of knowledge—any more than Proudhon's 'Property is theft' can, in logic, cover all ownerships." See also Thomas (1980), 143; and Davis (1988), 125.

that courage and perseverance will suffice for the discovery of all things once one thing has been recollected?

If, as has been argued, Socrates has no intention of providing a clear and thoroughly thought-through account of recollection as the way in which learning occurs because he does not himself credit the thesis that all learning is recollection with being an adequate response to Meno's paradox of knowing, his slipshod presentation of the myth and of the support it provides for the notion that learning is recollection is understandable. He neither explains that notion nor argues for it nor develops it nor earnestly probes it nor takes credit for it—because it is not a theory to which he subscribes. Indeed, the very extravagance of the claim that *all* learning is recollection renders it suspect. Since all Socrates intends to do is to provide Meno with a story that he will like, a story that pleasantly recalls to his mind notions with which he is familiar and that are the exclusive province of an elite group (we recall how pleased Meno was at the mention of "effluences," a technical term with which he—but not everyone!—is familiar), a story that will make him proud of his expertise at remembering, all in order to encourage him to continue with the inquiry and to open him up to the possibility that there is learning without teaching, why would Socrates trouble himself about getting the points he makes to cohere with one another and to stand up to scrutiny when considered by themselves? Socrates has little reason to fuss over such matters as how many lives a particular soul has already lived, how recollection could be the way in which the soul learned its very first truths, or how the notion of the kinship of nature can ensure that recollection will proceed smoothly from one recollected thing to every other when he himself is not convinced that all souls live many lives, that all learning is recollection, or that the kinship of nature is a kinship of all forms of knowledge. One might well argue that the evident incompleteness and sketchiness of Socrates' presentation are weaknesses Plato implants by design, their purpose being to alert the reader to the low esteem in which Socrates holds the recollection thesis that he himself proposes.

Besides these instances of (deliberate) inattentiveness to detail, however, there is one point with respect to which Socrates takes particular care. He begins with the notion that the soul has "seen" all things. Left unelaborated, this term suggests no more than the ordinary perception of which ordinary people are capable.[51] Soc-

---

51. Mugler (1948), 369, thinks this is seeing through the senses.

rates then stipulates that the soul has seen what it has seen "both here and in Hades," implying that the soul's sojourns are confined to just these two places.[52] Finally, Socrates asserts that the soul has seen "all things," suggesting that there are no other things for the soul to see but those it has seen here and in Hades.[53] If we put together the ideas that (a) the soul "sees" in an ordinary way, (b) it has been only here and in Hades, and (c) it has seen "all things," we realize that the soul Socrates envisions is limited in its powers and its range; in particular, although it descends periodically below the earth, it experiences no ascent "above" it.[54]

We may well wonder how the soul can actually have seen all there is to see when confined to just earth and Hades. For no matter how many times it goes around, it continues to cover the same ground.[55] Might Socrates recognize that for the soul that he describes, a soul whose powers are restricted to ordinary perception and whose geographical range is limited to earth and to Hades, there may be

52. Hackforth (1955), 74, Klein (1965), 96, and others have assumed that "seen" must be nonliteral, since there can be no literal seeing for disembodied souls in Hades. In the myths in the *Apology* and *Gorgias*, however, souls not only see but converse: they meet each other in Hades, witness each other's punishments, commiserate with each other, and even talk about virtue. Unless one assumes from the start that the Theory of Recollection in the *Meno* involves the recollection of supersensible Forms, there is no reason to rule out something very much like literal seeing here.

53. The clause containing this idea is not altogether perspicuous, because the word *kai*, "and," that appears in it is itself ambiguous. The Greek is *kai eōrakuia kai ta enthade kai ta en Haidou kai panta chrēmata*. Rendered literally, this reads "and it has seen both those here and those in Hades and all things." It is the last "and" that is problematic. Are the things referred to as "all things" to be taken to be things other than the things both here and in Hades or, taking *kai* epexegetically, are these things to be regarded as identical to the things both here and in Hades? If we choose the former interpretation, we must conclude that Socrates means to hint that the soul has actually seen things outside here and Hades; if we choose the latter, we conclude that all the things the soul has seen, it has seen here and in Hades. I favor the latter interpretation because Socrates' myth suggests an endless cycle of birth, descent to Hades, birth, descent to Hades, and on and on. How, within that scheme, could the soul have seen other things, elsewhere? The point of Socrates' insistence that the things here and in Hades are indeed "all things" is to ensure that the current soul will be able now to learn all things by recollection: if it had not seen "all things" in its previous lives, how could it recover them all now? See Verdenius (1957), 294, who renders *kai* "and generally."

54. The Hades in the *Meno* really is the Underworld, unlike the "Hades" in the *Phaedo*, which is the realm of the "unseen," in the sense of beyond sense perception (through a pun on *Haidēs*, "Hades," and *aides*, "unseen"). In the *Phaedo*, Socrates makes sure to say "Hades, in the true sense" (*Phd.* 80d6–7), to distinguish the Hades to which he refers from the Underworld. See Appendix I.

55. In the *Phaedo*, by contrast, some souls are said to be freed from the cycle of rebirth, and there is talk of ascent—not just of descent. See Appendix I.

knowledge that is beyond its reach? He provides one subtle indication that he does. Having said that "there is nothing that it [the soul] has not learned" (*M.* 81c7), Socrates goes on to say: "So there is nothing surprising in its being possible for it [the soul] to recollect, about virtue and other things, *those things, at any rate, that it, indeed,*[56] *knew before*" (*M.* 81c7–9). Coming on the heels of the unqualified pronouncement that there is *nothing* that the soul has not learned, the proviso "those things, at any rate, that it, indeed, knew before" can only be understood as hedging: it suggests that there are, after all, things the soul did not know before.[57]

What might these things be? What would Socrates think it likely that the soul, despite its many incarnations and innumerable turns at life both here and in Hades, did not know before? The most obvious candidate is virtue: virtue, we note, is the only thing Socrates identifies by name ("about virtue," *peri aretēs,* "and other things," he says at *M.* 81c8) when he hints that there might be things that our souls did not know before. It certainly stands to reason that the very thing that eludes our souls in this life (it is "about virtue," *peri aretēs,* that Socrates says that neither he [*M.* 71b3] nor anyone he has ever met [*M.* 71c3–4] knows anything at all) is what has eluded all souls in all previous lives—whether on earth or in Hades.[58] Indeed, if we look at the end of the *Apology,* we find Socrates expecting to do in Hades precisely what he did in Athens (though perhaps with a better clientele): search for somebody wise and examine people's views about virtue (*Ap.* 41b–c). Moreover, since these activities will constitute for him, as he says, "inconceivable happiness" (*Ap.* 41c3–4), it is apparent that he envisions having in Hades no greater access to *knowledge* of virtue than he does on earth.

If recollection, then, cannot help us to come to know virtue—since we never knew it before, neither here nor in Hades—might it not, perhaps, prove useful in accounting for our coming to know

---

56. The *kai* must be emphatic. "Also" is not a possible translation, because the assumption of the sentence is that the soul does not yet know in the present what it is recollecting from the past.

57. Perhaps in order to avoid the apparent contradiction between the soul's having learned all things and its being able to recollect those things, "at any rate," that it knew previously, Sharples (1985) (mis)translates this clause: "seeing that it knew these before also."

58. Gulley (1954), 196, contends that "the argument of the *Meno* . . . clearly envisages a previous experience different *in kind* from the experience of present life" (emphasis in original). How can that be so, however, when the present life is but one in a series of lives lived by the soul, some in Hades but some, too, here on earth?

other things? The truth is that in the case of other things knowledge is attained without recollection. Either there is someone else who knows and can be consulted (a teacher or an expert) or, alternatively, there is a way to arrive by oneself—if one is persistent—at a verifiably satisfactory answer: one might devise a proof in mathematics; in the arts, one might figure out how to remove a technical difficulty or how to improve a product or service and test one's results. In all such cases, it is the proof or the testing that enables one to know one's discovery to be true.[59]

The myth pretends that virtue, like other things, can come to be known by recollection of what was prenatally known. In fact, however, things other than virtue do not need to be recollected in order to be known, and virtue cannot be recollected, because it was never known. Knowledge of virtue, it seems, requires ascent—beyond the world of moral opinion, beyond the Cave.

We are now in a position to enter the raging controversy over whether there is implicit in the *Meno*'s recollection myth a Theory of Forms. The majority of scholars believe that the *Meno*'s myth presupposes the Theory of Forms; they believe that what Socrates holds is that the soul learns, in this lifetime, by recollecting the Forms it had apprehended before this lifetime. Among those most confident of the presence of Forms are Taylor (1948), 130, who says, "as no one denies, the whole characteristic metaphysics of the *Phaedo*, the theory of forms and the doctrine of 'reminiscence,' are explicitly taught in the *Meno*"; Guthrie (1975), 253–54, who would find it "incredible" if there were not a belief in transcendent forms in the *Meno*: "if a moral quality existing outside the sensible world and seen by bodiless souls is not a Form or Platonic Idea, it is difficult to see what is"; and Gulley (1954), 195, who argues that the opposition between knowledge and true opinion as outlined at *M.* 98a, taken together with the preexistence of souls, "clearly implies not only that the reality known is other than anything which the experience of the present life can in itself afford but that it is superior to it."[60]

---

59. Recollection alone, even if there were such a thing, would not guarantee truth. We might easily misremember, or mistakenly believe we remember, things we knew in an earlier existence. Pace Gulley (1954), 194, who contends that recollection enables the person who recollects to *know* that a proposition is true, that it takes him beyond mere true belief. See also Allen (1959), 165, and Bluck (1961a), 318, who agree with Gulley.

60. Other staunch supporters of Forms in the *Meno* include Cherniss (1936); Levinson (1953); Hackforth (1955), 74; Gould (1955), 130; and Bluck (1961a).

Several scholars, however, resist the temptation to read the Theory of Forms into the *Meno*. Prominent among them are Ross (1951), 18, n. 3, and 22, who declares that there is "no reference, explicit or implicit, to the Ideas in the passage dealing with *anamnesis*"; Sharples (1985), 14; and Ebert (1973), 180, n. 2.

Whereas Ross is certainly right to insist flatly that the *Meno*'s recollection passage contains no explicit reference to Forms, his assertion that it also contains no implicit reference to them could, perhaps, use some support. What supports his view are the limitations that Socrates imposes on the souls he describes: he confines them to the earthly realm and to Hades, in effect barring their entry into any exalted realm beyond the reach of the senses.[61] The tale he tells is of souls that, as embodied, live an earthly existence and, when disembodied, live presumably as shadows below; it is a tale of souls that have inhabited human bodies and, as seems likely, lower forms of life as well, that is, animal and vegetable. Certainly, the things the soul has seen while incarnate and on earth are material and sensible things. And if all the things the soul has seen are akin by nature to each other, would they not all have to occupy the same ontological realm,[62] the realm of sensibles—not of Forms? If souls do nothing but descend and return, descend and return, how and when and where will they have glimpsed the pure and perfect intelligibles that Plato calls Forms?

To conclude: I have argued in this chapter that the myth of recollection in the *Meno* is driven by Meno's paradox—in particular, by that part of the paradox that I call the "paradox of knowing." Socrates brushes aside the challenge represented by the paradox of knowing (since he cannot successfully meet it when it is applied to virtue) with a quick story about transmigration and recollection, a story likely both to please and to flatter Meno. I have argued, further, that Socrates does not endorse the myth he presses on Meno, that he neither believes it nor believes that it constitutes a real solution to the most troubling truth about virtue inquiry, namely, that it does not yield knowledge. In closing this chapter, I offer one last point in support of this contention.

61. The *Meno*'s myth, by depriving the soul of ascent, in effect denies the reader the warrant to "look ahead," so to speak, to "Platonic" dialogues; it compels the reader to look to the Socratic dialogues for descriptions of Hades, in none of which do we transcend our merely human nature.

62. Tigner (1970), 4, contends that if from recollecting one thing one can go on to discover all, then all things learned must be "of the same ontological family."

Socrates encourages Meno to believe, on the basis of the myth of recollection, that as long as one is courageous and does not tire of searching, nothing prevents the soul from discovering all things, once it has recollected just one (*M.* 81d2–4). Yet has there ever been anyone braver, more energetic, and more tireless in the pursuit of virtue than Socrates? And where have his relentless efforts led him? After a lifetime of devoted investigation and examination, he is the first to admit that he knows not at all what virtue is. Socrates sees all too clearly that something more than, something altogether different from, determination and perseverance in "recollection" is needed if the inquirer into virtue is to achieve success in inquiry— when, that is, success in inquiry is measured, as Meno would have it measured, by knowledge attained.[63] Socrates stands as crushing proof that no soul, no matter how sedulously and persistently it searches, no matter how courageously and unflaggingly it investigates, will come to know *all* things once "it has recollected one." Virtue is resistant to our most dogged efforts: so long as we are in the Cave, our souls will not come to know what no human soul has ever known, here or in Hades.

63. According to a literal interpretation of what Socrates says, he ought to be able, given his recollection thesis and the thesis of the kinship of all nature, to begin with some piece of knowledge that he has learned (that is, "recollected"), say, that a square double the size of an original square is constructed on the diagonal of that square, and proceed from there to discover, with the proper diligence and assiduousness, of course, what virtue is. Are we really to believe that Socrates thinks it possible to learn moral truths from mathematical ones?

3

The Slave-Boy

Learning by Demonstration

> We come into the world without any innate
> conception of a right triangle or a half-tone
> interval, but from some sort of specialized
> instruction we learn each of these things. . . .
> But as for good and bad and fine and
> shameful and fitting and unfitting, and the
> flourishing life (*eudaimonia*) and what is
> proper and incumbent on us and what we
> must do and what not—who was not born
> with an innate conception of these things?
>
> Epictetus, *Discourses* 2.11.2–4

At the end of his mythical presentation, Socrates is ready to move on. Meno, however, is intrigued by the notion that learning is recollection and is eager to hear more about it: "But what do you mean by this, that we do not learn but that what we call learning is recollection? Can you teach me how this is so?"(*M.* 81e4–6). What Meno wants now is to see how—and if—recollection works. What Socrates wants, of course, is to return with Meno to the elenchus. If he is to have any hope at all of holding on to Meno, he must somehow find a way to tie recollection to elenchus and to show that elenchus works.[1] Thus is the slave-boy-demonstration born.

The slave-boy-demonstration is nothing but an elenchus that succeeds—except for one thing: real *elenchoi* do not succeed, for real *elenchoi* do not result in knowledge. Socrates cannot afford to demonstrate a real elenchus because, as he is well aware, any real elenchus will necessarily resemble the one he conducted with Meno at the beginning of the dialogue. And that elenchus is what triggered

---

1. This is no easy task, as Socrates says at *M.* 82a7.

Meno's paradox in the first place. The slave-boy-demonstration is not, then, after all, an elenchus that succeeds. It succeeds, but it is not an elenchus. It only looks like one.

Would Socrates knowingly serve up a fake elenchus? The exchange that takes place between Socrates and Meno immediately preceding the slave-boy-demonstration certainly suggests that he would. Wholly without warrant, Socrates calls Meno a "scoundrel," *panourgos* (*M.* 81e7), accusing him of a scheme that he plainly lacks the cleverness to devise.[2] Socrates is the clever one who has been up to no good; he betrays his own lack of innocence by putting a blameless Meno on the defensive. It should come as no surprise, then, if the slave-boy-demonstration that Socrates designs to bolster his dubious recollection thesis is itself not quite on the level.

The introductory exchange also tells us something about Meno. It shows just how entrenched in Meno is the belief that the only way to learn is to be taught. For Meno ascribes to Socrates not only the view that "what we call learning is recollection" (*M.* 81e5) but also the position that "we do not learn" (*M.* 81e4–5)—and this despite his purported expertise at repetition![3] For Meno, to say that men learn in any way other than by being taught is tantamount to saying that they do not learn. What Socrates maintains is, of course, that we do learn (how, otherwise, could he have just said that "there is nothing that it [the soul] has not learned" [*M.* 81c7]) but that the process by which we learn is recollection (*M.* 81d2–3).[4] Unless Socrates can, through the slave-boy-demonstration, divest Meno of his

2. There is little reason to suspect that Meno has any intention of catching Socrates in a contradiction, as Socrates charges (*M.* 82a2–3). See Klein (1965), 96: "Meno candidly swears that nothing was farther from his mind." Indeed, poor Meno protests his innocence, attributing the unfortunate phrasing of his question to habit; moreover, he immediately rephrases it, substituting "show" for "teach": "if you are able somehow to show me (*endeixasthai*) that it is as you say, show me (*endeixai*)" (*M.* 82a5–6).

3. Recall that in the case of Meno's paradox, Socrates assumes that Meno quotes inaccurately an eristic paradox that he had heard. See *M.* 80e1–2.

4. Even in his opening question at *M.* 70a1–4 concerning how virtue is acquired, Meno simply equates the option that virtue is taught (*didakton*) with the option that virtue is learned (*mathēton*). He asks, "Can you tell me, Socrates, whether virtue is taught (*didakton*); or is it not taught but a matter of practice (*askēton*); or is it neither a matter of practice nor is it learned (*mathēton*) but comes to men by nature or in some other way?" Moreover, it is likely that at least in part it is Meno's conflation of learning with being taught that gives rise to his paradox: what Meno cannot grasp is how Socrates, a putative nonknower, together with himself, another putative nonknower, can come to learn something through inquiry; where is the teacher who will certify the truth of their answers?

association of learning exclusively with teaching,[5] the nonknowing, nonteaching Socrates will never persuade Meno to take up with him, once again, the inquiry into virtue.

i. Geometry and Virtue

The slave-boy-demonstration is an exercise in geometrical problem solving. There is no reason to think, nor does Socrates give us any reason to think, that geometry and virtue are relevantly similar.[6] It was argued in Chapter 2 that for Socrates geometry, like mathematics generally, is a *mathēma,* a teachable and learnable subject in which there are recognized experts and final proofs. As such, geometry resembles all other *mathēmata,* including crafts, in which it is possible to learn from another or, on occasion, even by oneself because there are unambiguous tests or standards not open to question against which one's achievements can be measured.[7] In the *Gorgias* at 451a–b

5. As we shall see in Section iii, it is not teaching and learning that are mutually entailing; rather, it is teaching and learning *from someone* that are. Since learning simpliciter does not imply teaching, learning by elenchus remains possible. In a dispute between Hoerber (1960), 89, and Bluck (1961b), 95, Hoerber contends that *mathēton* and *didakton* refer to very different modes of education, namely, to inward learning and to transmission from one person to another, respectively, whereas Bluck argues that the two terms are "on a par." Since in my view it is not learning simpliciter but rather learning from someone that is on a par with teaching, learning simpliciter— though, obviously, not learning from another—is possible without a teacher.

6. Those who, like Allen (1959), 167, think Socrates' argument, and his recollection thesis in particular, pertain only to geometry (and other a priori sciences) and to virtue, and that "recollection" is, therefore, just another name for "inference," would need to say why we should think that virtue is like geometry—why, that is, virtue should be thought to be either an a priori science or something learned by inference. As is explained in what follows, Socrates' strategy is to argue from what is true of geometry to what is true of all disciplines (the slave-boy, he says, will "do the same" in all *mathēmata* [*M.* 85e1–2]) and then from what is true of all disciplines to what is true, therefore, of virtue as well. There is, moreover, no emphasis in the demonstration on the a priori nature of geometry. (We note that flute playing, hardly an a priori science, counts as a *mathēma* at *M.* 90e6.) Some scholars think that what the slave-boy comes to know about is the geometer's abstract diagonal, since he seems to be able to universalize from the drawn diagonal to all diagonals. Yet even when one learns to tie one's shoelaces or to bake an apple pie, one universalizes to all shoelaces and to all apple pies. Has one, in these cases, come to know about the abstract shoelace or apple pie?

7. See Ryle (1971), 254–55: "Learning how to do new and therefore more or less difficult things does indeed require trying things out for oneself, but if this trying-out is not controlled by any testing or making sure, then its adventurousness is reckless-ness—not enterprise."

and 453e, arithmetic is one *technē* among many others. In the *Euthyphro* at 7b–d, Socrates designates calculation as that which easily resolves disputes about number; measuring, as that which lays to rest differences about greater and less; and weighing, as that which silences disagreements about heavier and lighter. It is only in matters of virtue (that is, in matters concerning just and unjust, noble and base, and good and bad) that enmities arise and quarrels cannot be ended simply.[8] In the *Gorgias* at 514a–e, Socrates makes clear just how different crafts are from virtue: in crafts, unlike in virtue, one must be able to point either to a teacher or to an undisputed achievement before claiming to be, and before being reputed to be, an expert; one who claims expertise but can point to neither is mocked. Similarly in the *Laches* at 185–86, having had good teachers or having produced excellent works suffices to establish one's legitimacy as an expert. Indeed, in the *Meno* itself, objective criteria for excellence in *technai* are recognized: Phidias is able to earn a living as a sculptor because of the undisputed excellence of the works he produces; and a shoemaker or clothes mender who returns products in worse condition than they were in when received quickly starves to death (*M.* 91d-e).[9] Not so with teachers of virtue, whether professional or lay: for until the criteria for an excellent human being are as clear and unproblematic as are the criteria for a fine pair of shoes, how can the quality and effectiveness of "instruction" in virtue be assessed? So unclear is it who teaches virtue and who does not that Socrates is forced to conclude, in the latter half of the *Meno*, that virtue, unlike the various *mathēmata*, has no teacher. Indeed, it is particularly with respect to virtue that people are prone to exaggerate their wisdom (*Ap.* 21b–22e):[10] in the absence of undisputed

---

8. See Nussbaum (1979), 69: "From the earliest texts (and fifth-century texts are fully consistent with these) we see the use of *arithmos* to mean that which is counted, and a close association [exists] between . . . numerability and knowability." A comic version of this point is found at *Euthyd.* 294c, where Ctesippus will not accept Dionysodorus's claim to know everything until Dionysodorus says how many teeth his brother Euthydemus has and a count of them is taken.

9. Even if a purported expert is able to fool the people, even if he is able to fool them for a very long time, that does not alter the fact that in disciplines other than virtue we know who counts as an expert and what counts as a test of expertise. If an automobile mechanic deceives people and deceives them for a long time, not really fixing their cars but only making their cars appear fixed, people still understand both what it means to be an expert auto mechanic and what tests in principle demonstrate whether someone does or does not qualify as one.

10. Socrates, as we know, sees himself distinguished from others by his recognition and admission that he lacks knowledge of the most important matters, moral ones

criteria and recognized experts, how can any claim to wisdom be discredited?[11] It seems, then, that it is in the matter of virtue alone that there are no clear standards: it is not known who improves and who ruins character, whether sophists should be driven out of town or flocked to, if Socrates is the most virtuous of men or a man of impiety who exerts a corruptive influence on the young. It is virtue, then, that is different; for in the case of virtue, not only are there no teachers or experts, but the reason there are no teachers or experts is that there is no sure method of verifying the truth of one's beliefs.[12]

Intuitively, then, virtue is not like geometry. Moreover, were it not for the prima facie uniqueness of virtue, the very question that prompts this dialogue would not arise: would Meno ask how excellence in carpentry or geometry or medicine is acquired? Would Socrates deny on behalf of himself and Athenians generally all knowledge of what the various *technai* are? It is virtue, it is always virtue, that presents a problem.[13]

Socrates, it seems, has two choices. He can either expose or obscure virtue's anomalousness. There can be little doubt, of course, that if he exposes it, Meno will become more reluctant than ever to pursue moral inquiry. His only hope, then, is to obscure it. And so, in the myth, Socrates quietly puts virtue together with "other things"; and in the slave-boy-demonstration, he allows virtue to slip unnoticed into the class of all *mathēmata*. His strategy in the slave-boy-

(*Ap.* 21b). In the *Gorgias*, Socrates is able to catch Gorgias in a contradiction when Gorgias will not admit that he neither knows justice nor teaches it to those of his pupils who come to him lacking this knowledge. Polus, in looking back on the predicament in which Gorgias finds himself as a result of his conversation with Socrates, asks Socrates: "Who do you think would deny that he himself knows what is just and would teach it to others?" (*Gorg.* 461c). The obvious answer to Polus's question is, of course, Socrates. Later on in the *Meno*, Anytus makes the claim that any *kalos kagathos*, any Athenian gentleman, can teach virtue (*M.* 92e). We may note, too, that in the *Protagoras*, Protagoras defends his profession of teaching virtue by saying only that he does so a little better than others: everyone teaches everyone virtue; indeed, everyone in lawful and humane societies is a veritable expert (*dēmiourgos*) at virtue (*Prot.* 327c–d).

11. The most Socrates can do is show people the inconsistency in their beliefs about virtue; but they can always say in their defense that Socrates has confused them with his verbal tricks. What comparable defense is open to a shoemaker when the shoes he purportedly repaired fall apart?

12. Socrates, it seems, takes as dim a view of the prospect of human beings' achieving knowledge only with respect to one other subject: death. See *Ap.* 28e–29b.

13. See Kraut (1984), 204–5: "True, a slave can learn geometry, but that hardly shows that he can acquire a knowledge of virtue, justice, the good, etc."

demonstration is to contend that since what is true of geometry, namely, that it can be learned by "recollection," is likewise true of all *mathēmata*, there is every reason to continue the elenctic investigation into virtue.

There are many good reasons, reasons that have nothing to do with any putative resemblance between geometry and virtue, for Socrates to have chosen for his demonstration of recollection a problem in geometry.[14] First, as we have seen (in Chap. 1, Sect. iii), Meno has an interest in geometry and, as Empedocles' and, by extension, Pythagoras's pupil, no doubt prides himself on his astuteness in geometry. When the slave-boy goes wrong in the slave-boy-demonstration, venturing the incorrect answer "double," and Socrates asks Meno if the slave-boy knows the answer, Meno promptly shoots back, "Certainly not," *ou dēta* (*M.* 82e9). It is, indeed, because of his knowledge of geometry that Meno is able to gauge the slave-boy's progress. Second, Meno is only taken with the grand, the *tragikē*: the slave's mastery of anything less intellectually challenging than a theorem in geometry would leave Meno unimpressed. Third, Meno is likely to be shocked, and most unpleasantly so, by how quickly an ignorant slave masters the Pythagorean theorem—and just by being asked questions at that! The expected benefits of this shock are both that Meno will be humbled and that he will be left with no excuse for abandoning the inquiry: if even his slave-boy can succeed, on what grounds can he refuse to continue? And, finally, Socrates needs to choose for his experiment a discipline in which the answer can be arrived at quickly; otherwise, he will fail to make his point that inquiry is worthwhile and will consequently fail to persuade Meno to revive their languishing inquiry into the nature of virtue.

Socrates counts on Meno to be taken in by his little display, but the reader must steadfastly resist its seduction. For what the slave-boy-demonstration shows is how someone who does not know the solution to a particular geometrical problem can be taught to solve that problem by someone who knows both the solution and its proof, someone who has the requisite knowledge probably because he, in turn, has learned the solution and the proof from a teacher of geometry. Of what relevance is such a demonstration to the inquiry Socrates proposes to conduct with Meno, when that inquiry poses a

---

14. None of these reasons has anything to do with the supposed a priori status common to geometry and virtue. See n.6.

question whose answer, not only Meno, but Socrates himself does not know, a question that is, moreover, not susceptible to "proof," a question affiliated with a discipline in which there are no teachers from whom Socrates, or anyone else, could have learned?[15]

The slave-boy-demonstration makes a mockery of Meno's challenge. What Meno wants to know is how the blind can lead the blind; what Socrates shows him is how the sighted can lead the blind.[16] What Meno wants to know is how an ignorant Socrates dares propose to lead an inquiry ("And how are you going to search for this, Socrates, when you know not at all what it is?" [M. 80d5–6]); what Socrates shows him is how a knowing Socrates dares do so. What Meno wants to know is how one will ever be sure that the answer one happens upon is the answer one was looking for; what Socrates shows him is a problem whose solution is backed by nothing short of an incontrovertible proof. There is considerable impertinence in Socrates' flagrant disregard of Meno's concerns: rather than acknowledge or express regret that the slave-boy-demonstration does not quite reproduce those features of virtue inquiry that are the source of Meno's skepticism, Socrates pretends instead that the slave-boy-demonstration squarely addresses Meno's paradox. Socrates thus attempts to fool Meno. If we, the dialogue's readers, are to avoid being fooled, we will have to be smarter and less gullible than Meno.[17]

15. See Klein (1965), 107: "Throughout the exhibition, Socrates seems to know all about the 'double square,' and it is this knowledge of his which enables him to play his role as teacher. We are not certain, though, whether this situation will still prevail when, in his conversation with Meno, the problem of 'human excellence' will be taken up again."

16. Many scholars believe that the fact that Socrates knows the answer to the question he poses to the slave-boy is of no consequence: insofar as the slave-boy, as they contend, draws the truth out from within his own soul, the teacher's knowledge is merely incidental to the slave-boy's accomplishment. I will argue in Section iii that it is no insignificant and negligible feature of the demonstration that Socrates knows how to solve the geometry problem it raises: if Socrates knows the solution, then the solution *can* be known; and if it can be known, it can be taught to another; and if geometry can be known and taught, geometry is unlike virtue. For now, however, what I wish to stress is the irrelevance of the slave-boy-demonstration to Meno's paradox: if Socrates knows the answer in the slave-boy-demonstration, the demonstration fails to address the paradox's central concern of how someone who does not know can conduct an inquiry. Indeed, if the slave-boy-demonstration is to address Meno's challenge adequately, it is not sufficient that the slave-boy not know. Meno never doubts that a nonknower can come to know by learning from a knower who both poses the problem and teaches him the solution to it. What Meno doubts is that a nonknower can successfully conduct an inquiry (by himself or in company with other nonknowers) into something he does not know at all.

17. See Burger (1984), 2–3: "But should one assume that Plato, in fabricating this

ii. The Diagram

In the slave-boy-demonstration, Socrates teaches the slave-boy how to double the size of a given square. Socrates is able to teach the slave-boy because Socrates has the requisite knowledge; he has knowledge because someone has taught him; someone has been able to teach him because geometry is teachable; and geometry is teachable because the solutions to geometrical problems are objectively testable. The slave-boy, in turn, is able to learn from Socrates because he has already acquired the concepts and skills needed for doubling a square: he understands such notions as larger, smaller, equal, square, and triangle; he knows how to count, add, and multiply.

Socrates' most important pedagogic tool is the diagram he draws in the sand. This visual aid enables the slave-boy to see—even as he thinks—why his wrong answers are wrong and why the right answer is right. Because of how central the diagram is to the slave-boy-demonstration, and because my interpretation of it differs in two critical ways from standard interpretations, I digress now to focus directly on the diagram.

My view of the diagram deviates from traditional ones in two ways. (1) On traditional interpretations, the two equal lines that go through the center of the original square are transversals that bisect the sides of the square (some scholars call these lines "mid-parallels" to capture their location at the midpoint of the square's sides; for convenience, however, I will simply call them "transversals"). On my view, the equal lines that go through the center of the square are diagonals.[18] (2) On traditional interpretations, Socrates draws a new

image of Socratic conversation, intends to present to his readers no more, and no less, than Socrates appears to address to his interlocutors? To make this assumption would be to ignore the very character of the dialogue as a dialogue, which more often than not displays the intellectual limitations of the characters it represents. If Socrates is indeed the Platonic spokesman, it is only to the extent that he speaks over the heads of his interlocutors, whose very partial understanding of his speeches affects the direction in which the conversation develops."

18. The tradition so heavily favors midpoint transversals that, at first, I believed myself to stand alone in holding the view that the lines Socrates draws through the center of the square are diagonals. My research, however, turned up three and a half predecessors in the diagonals view. The three are Mugler (1948), 388; Ebert (1973), 181, n.17; and Boter (1988). The "half" refers to Aristippus, in whose twelfth-century Latin translation of the *Meno* there appears, following the translation of *M.* 82c2–3, "And does it not also have these here through the center?" a square containing *both* midpoint transversals and diagonals. Most scholars never consider the possibility that the lines might be diagonals. Of those who do, Cherniss (1951), 406, n.32, dismisses Mugler's view without argument; Sharples (1989) seeks to refute Boter but concedes

square in the final stage of the demonstration. On my view, he returns to the original square with its original diagonals.[19]

I commence by simply stating my view. Its defense immediately
follows. Socrates begins by drawing a square (M. 82b9–10); it is
clear, I think, that Socrates means *tetragōnon* to denote a square.[20]
Let us call the square ABCD. Socrates then proceeds to highlight
the features of the square, namely, equal sides and equal diagonals,
the things that make the square a square as opposed to some other
four-sided figure.[21] As a square, the figure ABCD has four equal sides
(M. 82b10–c2); it is thus distinguished from a rectangle with unequal sides. As a square, it also has two equal lines (that Socrates now
draws) through the center, namely, the diagonals (M. 82c2–3); it is
thus distinguished from a rhombus, which has equal sides but not
equal diagonals. Although Socrates does not say he is drawing diagonals, it seems reasonable to assume that this is what he draws.[22]
Socrates next ascertains—no doubt because he is about to ask about
the length of the side of a square that is twice as large as the one
he has drawn (M. 82c4–5)—that the slave-boy knows that squares
can be of any size, larger than this one or smaller. He then assigns

that Boter might be right; Fowler (1990), 176—with Cherniss and Sharples—strongly
inclines toward transversals but admits that "it may not be possible to settle the matter
definitively."

19. As far as I know, my interpretation of how Socrates proceeds in this final stage
is both original and unique.

20. Boter (1988), 212, n.9, thinks that the technical term for a square is *tetragōnon*,
so that the slave-boy, not being technically adept in geometry, would understand by
tetragōnon just a four-sided figure. As best I can determine, however, in both its technical and common sense *tetragōnon* designates a square. On this point, see Sharples
(1989), 222, n.6. As Heath (1925), I, 188, observes, the Pythagoreans used the term
tetragōnon to denote a square (see Aristotle, *Metaph.* 1.5.986a26), although it was also
used at times to denote any quadrilateral (as it does elsewhere in Aristotle).

21. It is the view of Ebert (1973), 181, n. 17, and Boter (1988), 210–12, that
Socrates is gradually defining a square: having started with an indeterminate four-
sided figure, he builds up to a square. In my view, however, Socrates starts with a
square and then reviews for the slave-boy those features of a square that set it apart
from other four-sided figures. As Sharples (1989), 223, n. 7, points out, unless *tetra-
gōnos* meant "square," it would hardly be right for the slave-boy to answer "Certainly"
to the question "Is a *tetragōnon* figure one that has all four sides equal?"

22. I find it surprising that nearly all readers of the *Meno* take the lines that Socrates draws to be transversals that bisect the sides of the square. Transversals are hardly
a natural feature of squares the way diagonals are. Moreover, the diagonals are the
most easily constructed of equal lines through the center. I am inclined to believe
that, were it not for the fact that the diagrams that accompany translations of and
commentaries on the *Meno* invariably contain transversals, the average reader would
suppose that Socrates intends diagonals by the expression "these equal ones through
the center."

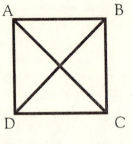

Figure 3.1

lengths of 2 ft. to each of the sides of the square he has drawn and asks the slave-boy how big the whole square is—that is, what its area is. Before pressing him for the answer, however, Socrates sees to it that the slave-boy knows that to calculate area one multiplies the length of one side by the length of the adjacent side (*M.* 82c6–d5): Socrates offers him the hypothetical case in which one side of the figure is, as was stipulated, 2 ft. but the other is not the stipulated 2 ft. but 1 ft. The boy recognizes that the area of this hypothetical figure is 2 × 1. Having determined that the slave-boy knows how to calculate area, Socrates has him calculate the area of the original square, whose assigned dimensions are 2 ft. × 2 ft. The boy calculates, correctly, 4. The first diagram that Socrates draws is represented in figure 3.1.

The slave-boy, then, knows the area of Socrates' square to be 4 sq. ft. To Socrates' question of how big a square would be that is twice as big as this one, the boy readily answers, correctly, 8 sq. ft. What he does not know is the length of the line that will produce an 8 sq. ft. square, and he supposes that a line of double the length of the original line will do so: if the 4 sq. ft. square has a side of 2 ft., the 8 sq. ft. square, he reasons, will have a side of 4 ft. Socrates now doubles the sides of the original square (see fig. 3.2): he adds CE, equal to DC, to generate the line DE, which will be twice as long as DC; he then adds EF, FG, and GA so that there are four equal sides in the new square GFED, each side of the new square being twice the length of the corresponding side of the original square.[23]

23. As Bluck (1961a), 298, reasonably argues, the line, DE, that is double the length of DC is not drawn until *M.* 83b1–2, where Socrates says: "Well, let us draw four equal lines." The passage, then, is best interpreted as follows. Socrates asks (*M.* 83a5–6): "Well, does not this line [the already drawn DC] become double [itself] if we add a second line of the same length [the not-yet-drawn CE] to it?" The slave-boy

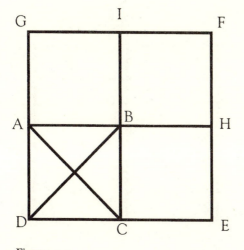

Figure 3.2

He also completes the three internal squares equal in size to ABCD by adding BH and BI. Since four squares of the same size are not double but quadruple just one of those squares, the slave-boy recognizes that his answer, DE, is incorrect (*M.* 83b3–c2). But as Socrates quickly points out, the reason doubling the length of the side yields not a double- but a quadruple-size square is that 4 ft. × 4 ft. is 16 sq. ft. and not 8 sq. ft. (*M.* 83c2–3).

Under Socrates' guidance, the slave-boy next ventures the answer 3 ft.: since a side of 2 ft. generates a 4 sq. ft. square, which is too small, and a side of 4 ft. generates a 16 sq. ft. square, which is too large, the right length will have to be between 2 ft. and 4 ft.; hence, 3 ft. To show the slave-boy that this answer, too, is incorrect, Socrates (see fig. 3.3) takes half of DC (1 ft.) and adds it to DC to generate the line DJ, which is 3 ft. (2 ft. + 1 ft. = 3 ft.). Socrates then completes the square with sides of 3 ft., generating the new square LKJD. Since, however, 3 ft. × 3 ft. is 9 sq. ft., not 8 sq. ft., 3 ft. cannot be the correct answer either.

agrees. Socrates continues (*M.* 83a6–b1): "And from this [the line just referred to, the doubled DC], you say, will come the figure of 8 sq. ft. if there come to be four lines of this length?" The slave-boy again agrees. Then Socrates says (*M.* 83b1–2): "Well, let us draw four equal lines from it [that is, from the doubled DC—not yet drawn]." Socrates now draws four equal lines, beginning by extending the already drawn DC: he adds to it CE, which, like DC, is also 2 ft. long, thereby generating DE; he then continues to draw EF and FG; finally, he draws GA, to complete the fourth equal line, GD.

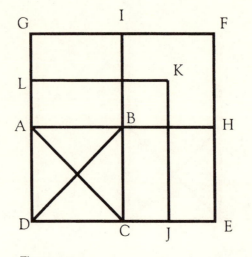

Figure 3.3

What Socrates wants to get the slave-boy eventually to see is that the double-size square is constructed on the diagonal AC. Whether AC has, as on the proposed reading, been in the diagram all along, just waiting to be discovered by the slave-boy or whether it needs, as the standard view would have it, to be drawn now, Socrates must return to the original diagram, ABCD, in order to construct the double-size square on its diagonal, AC.

On the standard view, Socrates cannot, however, simply return to the square ABCD. For not only does the original figure ABCD have lines extending from it to form (a) a 16 sq. ft. square and (b) a 9 sq. ft. square, but it also contains (c) transversals that are likely to prove confusing to the slave-boy when Socrates asks him, at the end of the demonstration, to count the half-squares on either side of the newly inserted diagonal AC. Proponents of the standard view, therefore, assume that Socrates now draws a new square, one just like the original square, ABCD, but with no additional lines either appended to it on the outside or cluttering it on the inside. Interestingly, even Boter, who argues most elegantly for Socrates' having inserted at the outset diagonals rather than transversals into the original square, joins the advocates of transversals in supposing that Socrates starts all over, replicating the original square and not inserting the diagonal into the new square until M. 84e4. Boter thereby forfeits, it seems to me, the clear advantage of the diagonals view, namely, that only on that view does the diagonal that constitutes the solution to the geometrical problem of the slave-boy-demonstration remain a steadfast presence—from beginning to end—in the diagram.

As I see it, Socrates does not draw a new diagram. And so when he asks the slave-boy at *M.* 84d3–4, "Is this not our figure of 4 sq. ft.? Do you understand?" he can actually mean what he says; for the figure to which he refers is indeed their figure of 4 sq. ft.: the original square ABCD.[24] But if, as I maintain, Socrates does use the original diagram, how can he rid it of the lines that are now most inconveniently protruding from it, the lines that he added to it in constructing the 16 sq. ft. and then the 9 sq. ft. squares?[25] Is drawing a brand new 4 sq. ft. square the only way to eliminate these nuisances? There is, surely, another option: Socrates can simply *erase* the unwelcome appendages that form the 16 sq. ft. and 9 sq. ft. figures. All Socrates need do is smooth out the indentations made in the sand by the lines he added, and he is back to his original square ABCD, the one that already contains, on my view, the diagonals AC and BD.[26]

If my view is correct, it is to the old square that Socrates now proceeds to add (see fig. 3.4) CM, MN, and NB, to complete the second square; then NO, OP, and PB, to complete the third; and, finally, PQ and QA, to "fill in this one in the corner" (*M.* 84d6–7). And as his last step, Socrates reflects the diagonal AC in each of the three new squares: "Well," he asks the slave-boy, "is there this line (*hautē grammē*), from corner to corner [referring to the diagonal AC] that cuts each of these figures in two?" (*M.* 84e4–85a1).[27] As Socrates

24. We may note that Socrates does not say, "Is this not just like our figure of 4 sq. ft?" or even, "Is this not the same as our figure of 4 sq. ft.?" He says, "Is this not our figure of 4 sq. ft.?"

25. The 16 sq. ft square is particularly unwelcome, for how can Socrates draw a new 16 sq. ft. square when one is already in place?

26. That Socrates might simply erase the unwanted lines in the sand is the innovative aspect of my interpretation to which I referred in n. 19. Erasing added lines is surely the most efficient way to return to "our figure of 4 sq. ft." (*M.* 84d3–4).

27. It is evident that when Socrates says, "Is there this line (*hautē grammē*) from corner to corner?" he points to an already existing line, the diagonal AC. Whenever Socrates refers to a line or figure that is not yet drawn but is in the process of being drawn, he uses, not the simple demonstrative, "this," *houtos,* but one of the available emphatic demonstratives—either the simple demonstrative *houtos* to which is attached the deictic suffix, *i,* or *hode,* both meaning "this here." (I apologize for the awkwardness in English of "this/these here.") That this is so may be seen most clearly in those cases in which Socrates contrasts an already drawn line or figure with one now being drawn. Consider: (a) "So a square figure is one that has all these (*tautas*), lines equal" (*M.* 82b10–c2), referring to the sides of the already drawn square, ABCD. "And it is one that has these here (*tautasi*), equal ones through the center?" (*M.* 82c3–4), re-

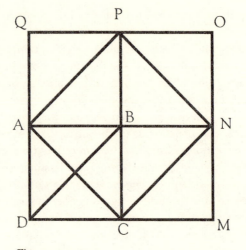

Figure 3.4

sees it, each of the squares has, as it were, its own AC that cuts it in half.[28] He goes on, then, to draw the other "AC's": CN, NP, and PA. The diagram is now complete (fig. 3.4).

What remains is for me to defend the diagonals view.[29] There are, it seems, four main grounds for the view that the two equal lines through the center are transversals. The first is that Socrates asks if the slave-boy is aware that there are larger and smaller squares; with transversals in the diagram, the slave-boy could easily answer this

ferring to the diagonals (or, on the standard view, the transversals) now being added. (b) "Then, in it there are these here (*tauti*), four figures [those now being drawn], each of which is equal to this (*toutōi*), 4 sq. ft. square [the already drawn square, ABCD]" (*M*. 83b3–4). (c) "Is this (*touto*) not our figure of 4 sq. ft.?" (*M*. 84d3–4), referring to the original square, ABCD. "And could we add this here other one (*touti*) equal to it?" (*M*. 84d4–5), referring to the square now being drawn, BNMC. (The other emphatic demonstrative, *tode*, replaces the *touti* in the case of the third and fourth squares that are added [*M*. 84d6, d7].) I conclude, then, that had Socrates been drawing the diagonal now, as opposed to pointing to the old AC already present, he would no doubt have said not "this line," *hautē grammē*, but "this here line," *hē grammē hautēi*. (On occasion, Socrates uses the emphatic demonstrative to refer to an already drawn line when he wants to contrast it with another already drawn line or to single it out from among other drawn lines; what he never does, however, is use the unemphatic form of the demonstrative to refer to a new line that he is in the process of drawing.)

28. If, as the standard view maintains, Socrates in fact draws all four diagonals now, why does he not say, "Are there *these here four lines* from corner to corner cutting each of these figures in half?" The privileging of AC suggests that it is already in place.

29. Some of what I say in defense of the diagonals view may be found as well in Boter (1988).

question, for the effect of transversals is to create smaller squares within the larger one. The second is that Socrates asks the slave-boy what the area would be of a figure 2 ft. × 1 ft.; if transversals were drawn, he would be looking at a 2 ft. × 1 ft. figure within the larger 2 ft. × 2 ft. square. The third is that in ancient Greece the area of a given figure is calculated by counting figures internal to it—not by multiplying the lengths of the sides; transversals would enable the slave-boy to calculate, by counting internal squares, the area of both the 2 ft. × 1 ft. rectangle and the 2 ft. × 2 ft. square. The fourth is that transversals are needed to help the slave-boy discount the answer 3: only with the transversals in place will the slave-boy be able to count nine 1 sq. ft. squares and recognize that since he should be counting only eight such squares, his answer is wrong.[30]

To the first reason it may be said that had Socrates actually drawn smaller and larger squares, he surely would have called the slave-boy's attention to them. Yet the only drawn figure he speaks of is the original drawn square: "Well, could there be both a larger figure of this sort [referring to the drawn square] and a smaller?" (M. 82c3–4). His use of the potential optative ("could there be") only serves to emphasize the theoretical nature of this question—there are no such squares literally before them.

Against the second reason it may again be said that Socrates would surely have referred to the 2 ft. × 1 ft. figure he just drew had he just drawn one rather than ask abstractly what the area of the 2 ft. × 2 ft. drawn figure would be if *it* were, counterfactually, 2 ft. × 1 ft. Here, too, the potential optative is used (M. 82c5–8).

With regard to the third reason, it seems clear that regardless of how area was normally figured in classical Greece, in the *Meno* it is calculated by multiplying the lengths of the figure's sides. Only once, in the case of the slave-boy's answer 4 ft., does Socrates have him count squares: he counts four 4 sq. ft. squares (fig. 3.2) when there should have been only two. Perhaps Socrates believes that the slave-boy will be better able to appreciate the untenability of his answer if given graphic proof of it. But even in this case, Socrates immediately returns to multiplication of lengths of sides as the surest proof: doubling the side gives us not a double but a quadruple figure, Socrates says, "for 4 × 4 is 16" (M. 83c2–3). Socrates consistently relies on multiplication to determine the area of whatever figure is in question, asking how much 2 is taken once, how much 2 is taken twice,

---

30. See Bluck (1961a), 294, 301–2.

how much 4 is taken 4 times, how much 3 is taken thrice. Only at the end of the dialogue does Socrates again resort to counting figures; but there he has no alternative. By what other method could he establish that the square constructed on the diagonal of the original 4 sq. ft. square is one whose area is 8 sq. ft.?[31]

With respect to the fourth reason, we note that the answer 3 is discounted *not* by the counting of squares but explicitly by multiplication of the lengths of the sides: 3 ft. × 3 ft. is 9 sq. ft. (*M.* 83e8–9). In this way, it differs from how the answer 4 is discounted: although 4 is also ultimately discounted by multiplying, it is first discounted by counting the four 4 sq. ft. squares within the newly constructed 16 sq. ft. square. We may observe, however, that transversals are not needed for counting *those* squares: in the case of 4, the squares to be counted are the original square ABCD plus three additional new ones of the same size. One might even argue that the reason the counting of squares is, in the case of the answer 4, supplemented by multiplication of the lengths of the sides is to ensure that when the next answer, 3, is suggested, the slave-boy will be able to discount it just by multiplication. For if the diagonals view is correct, this is the only way the slave-boy could discredit the answer 3: without transversals in the original square ABCD, there are no squares to be counted! There is, moreover, no indication whatever in the text that Socrates constructs any of the lines inside the 9 sq. ft. square needed to form the nine putative smaller squares; the text tells us only that Socrates adds to the original square, ABCD, the lines needed to make each side of the new square 3 ft. long—and nothing more.

The diagonals view has several clear advantages over the transversals view. First, as was noted earlier, diagonals, unlike transversals, differentiate the square from the rhombus, a figure that, like the square, has not only four equal sides but also equal transversals—though not equal diagonals. If the equal lines through the center are diagonals, then Socrates may be seen to be alerting the slave-boy to the features distinctive of a square: four equal sides and two equal diagonals.

Second, diagonals—but not transversals—will play an important role in the solution of the geometrical problem at hand. Indeed, as has been argued, if Socrates prefers that the slave-boy calculate the

---

31. Both Klein (1965), 100–101, and Fowler (1990), 178, I believe, rely too much on their expertise in ancient Greek geometry in interpreting this passage. See Chapter 1, n. 11. The text makes clear that multiplication of (lengths of) sides is involved rather than the counting of figures.

area of a figure, not by counting its internal squares, but by multi-plying the lengths of its adjacent sides, transversals turn out to be utterly useless even in the earlier stages of the demonstration. The diagonals, by contrast, are indispensable: they contain the answer the slave-boy seeks.

A third point in favor of the diagonals view is that Socrates, at *M.* 84a1–2, tells the slave-boy that if he does not wish to reckon (*arith-mein*), he should show or point out (*deixon*) what line the 8 sq. ft. square is from; yet only on the diagonals view is the line actually there for the boy to point to.[32] Now that the slave-boy has ruled out every integer that might reasonably be thought to constitute the nu-merical length of the line and realizes that he cannot answer by assigning the line a length, Socrates offers him as an alternative something that he can do, something that he will eventually do (at *M.* 85b2), namely, show, or point to, the appropriate line.[33] If, then,

32. Boter (1988), 212, starts out making this point but does not hold fast to it. He says at first: "I would suggest that the wording of 83e11–84a1 [corresponding to *M.* 84a1–2 in Sharples] may provide an indication that the diagonals have already been drawn: Socrates asks the slave to point out (*deixon*) the line which forms the base of the square with an area of 8 sq. ft. if he feels unable to calculate the length of that line." But Boter then retreats from that position, conceding that "it is possible that Socrates invites the slave to point out where the line should be drawn." Although the text does not require that we take Socrates to be asking the boy to point to a line that is already there rather than to indicate where the line should be, nevertheless let us recognize how unreasonable it would be for Socrates to ask the boy, who is looking according to the transversals view not at a blank square but at a square that contains transversals, to "show" or "point out" where the line should be. Since, moreover, there are (at least) two other reasons to favor the diagonals view, this passage, I think, is best construed as offering a third.

33. Socrates, of course, knows that the diagonal is irrational. See *Rep.* 7.534d: "Then, as for those children of yours whom you are rearing and educating in speech, if you ever rear them in deed, I don't suppose that while they are as irrational as lines (*alogous ontas hōsper grammas*, 534d5) you would let them rule in the city and be the sovereign of the greatest things" (trans. Bloom [1968]). It is precisely because irra-tional lines cannot be numerically expressed that Socrates, from the very start, pro-vides the diagonals that can be pointed to, calling the slave-boy's attention to them as he draws them (*M.* 82c2–3). We may note that Socrates speaks as early as *M.* 82e5, and again at 83c3, of what sort of line, *poia* or *hopoia*, as opposed to how long a line, *posē* or *pēlikē*, the double-size square is constructed on. So the notion of "sort of line" is not a new one when Socrates offers the slave-boy the option, at *M.* 84a1, of pointing to—instead of reckoning—the sort of line on which the double square is constructed. That "the diagonal" is the right answer to the *poia* question may be clearly seen at *M.* 85b2, where the slave-boy finally points to it; his pointing to the diagonal and saying, "From this one," *apo tautēs*, constitutes the correct response to the question "From what sort of line?" *apo poias grammēs;* (*M.* 85b1–2). Brown (1971), 206–8, is to be credited with noting that a *poia* question calls for a geometric, as opposed to an arithmetical, answer.

the slave-boy does not yet know what to point to, it is not because all he sees before him is a square that contains transversals.

Why does Plato have Socrates draw, at the very beginning of the demonstration, the diagonals to which the slave-boy nevertheless does not point, and cannot point, until its very end? As will be argued, the slave-boy-demonstration is, on its face, a farce; and this is its best gag. If learning were recollection, then surely the drawn diagonal would have jogged the boy's memory.[34] Yet the slave-boy looks at it and looks at it and . . . looks at it; nothing happens. The fact that the diagonal is before him for the entire demonstration but means nothing to him until the demonstration's end is the clearest indication that it is, alas, not by recollection but by teaching that the slave-boy learns how to double a square.

iii. The Demonstration

Something comic and something serious occur simultaneously in the slave-boy-demonstration. On the surface, something comic occurs: Socrates pretends that the slave-boy is "recollecting" how to double a square, that he is not being taught something new but recovering something old. Beneath the surface, however, something quite serious occurs: Socrates is explaining how and why elenchus works, to the extent that it does, and why it is of value—not, to be sure, in the matter of geometry (and all other knowable and, therefore, teachable subjects) but in the matter of virtue.

The rest of this section will be devoted to the farcical side of the demonstration and the "recollection" thesis it advances. It will contend that Socrates conducts what is, despite its question-and-answer format, clearly just a geometry lesson; that he teaches the boy something he never knew before, something fairly challenging, namely, how to double a square; that there is nothing that the boy does in the demonstration that even remotely resembles what the myth describes as the calling up of latent knowledge, whether acquired in past lives or otherwise lodged in the soul; that, instead, Socrates twice steers the boy off course, only, finally, to construct a proof that the boy is able to follow: he leads the boy to water, and the boy drinks.

---

34. Let us recall that in the *Phaedo* a prime example of recollection is that of one's being reminded by a drawn Simmias of the real one. For discussion of recollection in the *Phaedo*, see Appendix I.

Section iv will consider the serious underside of the slave-boy-demonstration and the very different recollection thesis it promotes. We shall see that the two summaries that Socrates provides, the one in the demonstration's middle (*M.* 84a4–c10), the other upon its conclusion (*M.* 85b8–86b5), offer an account of the nature of elenchus, of what it can do, and of why it is beneficial. As we shall see, the two recapitulations fit, not what has taken place at the surface level of the slave-boy-demonstration, but what would have taken place had the subject been virtue, and the interlocutor, someone like Meno.[35]

Let us turn, then, to the subject of this section, the slave-boy-demonstration—on its surface. Perhaps the most difficult thing to prove, to those who do not see it, is that something is a farce. Yet there are clues. Socrates indicates, both before and after the demonstration, that the worth of the recollection thesis lies, not in itself, but in the way it benefits its adherents (*M.* 81e1–2, 86b7–c3). His questions are, for the most part, so leading as to be but statements with question marks affixed to their ends.[36] Not only is the entire process called "recollection," but Socrates seems to associate with "recollection" everything the boy does along the way and beyond—whether it is the boy's producing wrong answers (*M.* 82e12–13), acknowledging his ignorance (*M.* 84a4–5), or recovering (in the future) knowledge out of himself by himself (*M.* 85d6–7). And most important, Socrates knows from the start the answer to his question. The strained attempts of scholars to deny that the slave-boy is being taught by Socrates and to affirm that the boy does, in some sense, have inside himself the answer that Socrates simply draws out are motivated in part by a refusal to believe that Socrates might just be pulling Meno's leg. Nevertheless, pulling Meno's leg is precisely what Socrates is doing—on the surface.

Among the grounds upon which scholars stake their denial that Socrates teaches are the following:[37] (a) the slave-boy is expected to

35. Socrates employs, as we shall see in Chapter 4, a similar strategy at *M.* 90a1–e1, when he speaks, at the surface level, of how Anthemion, Anytus's father, came by his wealth. There can be no doubt, however, that beneath the surface he is addressing the question of how, not wealth, but virtue comes to men.

36. See Anderson (1993), 135: "Each step is thinly disguised by a question mark at the end—which functions not to indicate that the slave recalls or believes what Sokrates has said, but rather functions only to elicit from the slave a confirmation that he understands what Sokrates has said."

37. It is worth noting in this connection a passage in the *Republic* often cited by scholars to bolster Socrates' denial of teaching in the *Meno*. The passage is *Rep.*

understand what he hears;[38] (b) the slave-boy is not supposed to take what Socrates says "on authority";[39] (c) Socrates does not quite feed the slave-boy the answers;[40] (d) Socrates leads the slave-boy to false answers as well as to true, so it is left up to the slave-boy to discriminate between right and wrong answers;[41] and (e) the boy is told to answer only what he believes.[42]

None of these grounds, however, counters successfully the plain reality that Socrates teaches the slave-boy how to double a square. After all, should a pupil who is taught be expected *not* to understand what he is taught? Why should it be a requirement for teaching that the lesson be absorbed passively? Indeed, why would a pupil who has been completely passive be said to have learned? Furthermore, only very rarely is learning from someone a matter of taking what is said "on authority": an authority who *teaches* gives his students a reason to accept what he says. Even in crafts, the pupil may be shown *why* it is appropriate to produce an artifact in a particular way rather than in another.[43] That Socrates expects the boy to understand him and not just to imbibe his words or take them "on authority" is a sign that Socrates *does* teach the slave-boy—not that he does not.

Yet Socrates' teaching of the slave-boy is hardly just a matter of the slave-boy's being expected to understand what he is being

---

7.518b–c, in which Socrates says that education is not, as is frequently asserted, a matter of pouring into the soul knowledge that is not in it, as though one were "putting sight into blind eyes," but rather a matter of turning the power through which one learns together with one's whole soul away from "becoming" and toward the light of "being." Let us note, however, that Socrates in this passage is hardly describing ordinary education. Yet even ordinary education is, to be sure, unlike putting sight into blind eyes; for no education presupposes that the teacher's task is to put into a student who is unable to learn ($\approx$ blind) the ability to learn ($\approx$ sight). A teacher's task is to help a student grasp something new that he is quite capable of grasping.

38. Bluck (1961a), 13; Guthrie (1975), 255.

39. Vlastos (1965), 158–59; Bluck (1961a), 296.

40. Bluck (1961a), 13; Devereux (1978), 119; Desjardins (1985), 276; Fine (1992), 210.

41. Vlastos (1965), 159; Moravcsik (1971), 65; Devereux (1978), 125, n. 5; Sharples (1985), 8; Fine (1992), 210.

42. Nehamas (1985), 19.

43. Several commentators regard the sophistic method of teaching, in which, presumably, the pupil simply memorizes what he is told, as the "teaching" from which Socrates means to distance himself. See, for example, Bluck (1961a), 13; Devereux (1978), 120; Desjardins (1985), 276. But could this be what Socrates means, say, in the *Apology* when he says he does not teach? Does he not mean, at least in large measure, that he does not know and, therefore, cannot teach? Why should we think that here, in the *Meno*, all he means by denying that he teaches is that he does not have his students memorize what he says?

taught. It must be acknowledged that Socrates comes perilously close to actually telling the slave-boy what to think, that he does, indeed, feed the slave-boy the answers. Let us consider, for example, the following exchange (*M.* 83d4–e2): "Then the line that produces the 8 sq. ft. figure must be greater than this 2 ft. one but less than the 4 ft. one?" "It must." "Then try to tell me how long you say it is." "3 ft." What answer but 3 ft. could the slave-boy have offered at this point? Moreover, the feeding is even more transparent in the diagram's final stage, where, as Vlastos (1991a), 119, puts it: "Extending the diagram, he [Socrates] plants into it the line that opens sesame, and *then* the boy 'recollects' that the side of a square whose area is twice that of a given square is the diagonal of the given square" (emphasis in original).

Finally, neither that the slave-boy is led to wrong answers just as he is led to correct ones, nor that he is not told outright what to answer but is told rather to answer as seems right to him (*M.* 83d2), means in the least that Socrates encourages the slave-boy's indepen-dent thinking. By leading the slave-boy to wrong answers, Socrates actually discourages the slave-boy from thinking for himself. Even though the boy has the ability to avoid on his own the wrong answers to Socrates' questions—he knows even at the time of his first wrong answer, "double" (*M.* 82e3), that the area of a square is determined by multiplying the lengths of two of its sides and he knows how to multiply—Socrates, instead of encouraging the slave-boy to use his skills, encourages him to follow slavishly wherever Socrates leads. And the point at which Socrates commends the slave-boy for having answered "what seems right to you," *to gar soi dokoun* (*M.* 83d2), comes (a) when all the boy does is accede to Socrates' suggestion that the line that produces the 8 sq. ft. square will have to be longer than the one that produced the 4 sq. ft. square and shorter than the one that produced the 16 sq. ft. square (*M.* 83c6–d1), and (b) when there really is no other answer he might have given. Socrates encourages, if anything, the boy's utter docility.

No matter how subtle and ingenious, all attempts by scholars to justify Socrates' denial that he teaches are doomed to failure. There is, for Socrates, but one criterion by which it is determined whether or not one is teaching, and that is whether or not one has knowl-edge.[44] His claim in the *Apology* that he does not teach (*Ap.* 20b–c)

---

44. The fact that Socrates lacks knowledge means that regardless of whether he uses elenchus or myth or speeches, he still does not teach.

cannot be divorced from his claim that he does not know (*Ap.* 21b).
Indeed, all his protestations in the *Apology* that he is no teacher can
be traced to his adamant insistence that he has no wisdom to impart:
all he knows is that he does not know. There is great irony, therefore,
in Socrates' denial that he is teaching the slave-boy. Since Socrates
has knowledge with respect to doubling the square, what difference
does it make whether he leads the boy by questions or whether he
uses only declarative sentences? He has proof; and no matter how
he conveys that proof, he teaches.

Vlastos (1991a), 119, and others[45] maintain that although there
is teaching in the slave-boy-demonstration, it is restricted to the demonstration's final stage.[46] But Socrates' insistence that he does not
teach is no less adamant as the demonstration enters its final stage
than it is earlier. If anything, it is more adamant: "But be on guard
(*phulatte*)," he admonishes Meno, "in case you should find me somewhere teaching and instructing him rather than asking him his opinions" (*M.* 84d1–2).[47]

The fact is that Socrates teaches the slave-boy at every stage of the
demonstration: at earlier stages, he teaches the boy that his answers
are wrong; at the last stage, he teaches him the right answer. Why,
then, does he deny that he teaches? And why, moreover, does he
deny it (or imply its denial) three times (at *M.* 82a6–7, 82e4–5,
84c11–d2)? He denies it so that the slave-boy-demonstration will
seem to Meno like elenchus.[48] Only if Meno thinks the slave-boy-
demonstration is like elenchus will he proceed with the inquiry into
virtue. As we review the course of the demonstration, we shall be on
alert for the many ways in which Socrates disguises his instruction in

45. See, for example, Klein (1965), 107.

46. Vlastos (1991a), 119, recognizes that, as he puts it, the slave "could have gone
on until doomsday" without getting anywhere if Socrates had not drawn the diagonal.
Vlastos departs here from his earlier view (1965), 157, according to which, given
Socrates' perversely restricted sense of "taught," even in the demonstration's final
stage the slave-boy is not taught.

47. We may compare the rather forceful expression "be on guard," *phulatte*, with
the milder expression "pay attention," *proseche ton noun* (*M.* 82b6), that Socrates uses
earlier when Socrates' teaching is somewhat less overt.

48. For a contrasting view, see Benson (1990a), 136. Benson argues that Socrates'
denials "are necessary because Socrates knows the answer to the question under consideration in the particular example. Plato, however, is concerned to make clear that
the fact that he does is playing no essential role in the slave-boy's progress." As I see
it, Socrates' repeated denials—and particularly the last one at *M.* 84e11–d2, which
warns Meno to "be on guard" lest any teaching slip by him—are Plato's comedic
"winks" to his readers: he lets them in on the joke (Socrates really is teaching!), even
as they watch Meno gullibly fall for it.

geometry, that is, his teaching, his proving, the solution to the geometrical problem at hand, as an elenchus, that is, as a method of
question-and-answer in which the ignorant questioner elicits his interlocutor's opinions and tests them against one another.

Perhaps the first order of business is to state the two important
ways in which the slave-boy-demonstration departs from recollection
as limned in the myth. The first way is that the demonstration, unlike
the myth, makes the questioner indispensable. The myth suggested
that the learner, as solitary inquirer, having lived numerous lives
before the present one and having seen and learned all things,
namely, the things both here and in Hades, is able to recollect what
he knew previously since all things have a natural kinship. How jar-
ring a non sequitur, then, must Socrates' buoyant declaration at the
close of the mythic presentation have seemed to Meno: "Putting trust
in its truth, I am willing to search *with you* for what virtue is" (*M.*
81e2–3). The second way is that whereas the recollection in the
slave-boy-demonstration is said to be sequential (*M.* 82e12–13), progress in recollection in the myth seems somewhat haphazard. In the
myth, because of the alleged kinship of nature, from recollecting a
single thing one recollects all others; in the slave-boy-demonstration,
proof of the rightness of the correct answer follows upon proof of
the wrongness of the incorrect ones.

It is striking that these two ways in which the slave-boy-
demonstration differs from the myth are also distinctive marks of
elenchus: the need for a questioner and the need to have the interlocutor come face-to-face with his own ignorance before meaningful
progress in inquiry can be made. According to the myth, new discoveries can be made on one's own since they are really rediscoveries
of what is old. The myth's version of recollection can better account
for, say, how Pythagoras (presumably) made the discovery of his
eponymous theorem than can the slave-boy-demonstration. What the
slave-boy-demonstration shows is how a person who already knows
teaches another who does not; it does not show at all how someone
who lacks knowledge can attain it on his own.[49] Yet in order to show
how a person who already knows teaches another who does not, the
slave-boy-demonstration need not have taken the form it takes. Socrates could easily have conducted his geometry lesson without asking
the slave-boy any questions at all and without ensuring that the slave-

49. As Flew (1971), 404, notes: "What has to be recognized is that whoever taught
Meno's slave, no one ever taught Pythagoras."

boy propose wrong answers. The only reason that the slave-boy-demonstration proceeds as it does is to mimic elenchus, the method of inquiry that Socrates must ultimately defend if it is to be the one to which he and Meno soon return.[50]

Let us now consider directly the slave-boy-demonstration. Socrates has Meno summon one of his attendants and proceeds to guide the mathematically unsophisticated young slave to the solution of a fairly challenging problem in geometry. By way of preliminaries, Socrates asks only if the boy speaks Greek (M. 82b4–5); he implies thereby that the boy need know nothing else—in particular, that he need know not even the rudiments of arithmetic—for the impending inquiry to succeed. In fact, Socrates knows full well that there are quite a few things that the boy needs to know besides how to speak Greek, some of which he has surely been taught:[51] how to count, how to multiply, what a square is, the relations of double and half, the concepts of larger and smaller. Indeed, as Socrates proceeds, he checks to make sure that the slave does know these things. But, in order to

50. The slave-boy-demonstration has been seen by some as Socrates' ideal method for teaching geometry. See Grube (1935), 234: "this striking passage might well be taken for all time as a pattern of the proper method to teach even the facts of mathematics." See also Crombie (1963), II, 51: "Socrates gives an instance of how to teach by getting an uneducated slave to prove a geometrical theorem simply by asking him the right questions in the right order." Socrates, however, uses this method to show that geometry is *not* taught—not to illustrate how it ought to be taught. Were Socrates prepared to admit that geometry is taught, there is no reason to think that he would recommend the demonstration in the *Meno* as a superior teaching method. In fact, in light of how leading the questions Socrates asks are, it is not clear just how different this method really is from standard methods. Socrates teaches geometry this way in the *Meno* to make it seem as if he is not teaching at all. His method simulates elenchus, which is not a teaching method at all insofar as the "instructor" lacks knowledge.

51. It is likely that Socrates asks only whether the slave-boy is Greek and speaks Greek because Greek is something that one does not need to be taught; it is something that one picks up "spontaneously." (This is not to say that Greek cannot be taught formally—only that, ordinarily, one does not need to be taught one's native tongue formally.) Indeed, Socrates assumes that if the boy is Greek, he speaks Greek, and Meno confirms that he certainly speaks Greek insofar as he was raised in Meno's home, that is, in a place where Greek is spoken. See *Prot.* 319e–320a, where Socrates contrasts virtue, which fathers permit their sons to pick up "spontaneously," with crafts, in which fathers see to it that their sons are taught. From Socrates' perspective, as Protagoras recognizes (*Prot.* 327e–328a), anything that everyone teaches everyone, like Greek (!) (*Prot.* 328a1), is not taught at all; any subject or skill learned in this way is picked up "spontaneously." (The contrast between what one learns by being taught and what one learns spontaneously is featured in Socrates' conversation with Anytus [M. 92e7–93a1], and the contrast between acquiring something spontaneously and acquiring it by one's wisdom and effort is prominent in his description of Anthemion, Anytus's father [M. 90a2–6].)

maintain the pretense that the slave-boy is learning solely by recollection, Socrates suggests that the boy is wholly untutored, knowing nothing more than the language required for understanding Socrates' questions.[52]

Twice during the demonstration the boy stumbles. He answers incorrectly, and Socrates refutes his false answers. As was noted earlier, the boy must answer incorrectly if the slave-boy-demonstration is to resemble elenchus. Nevertheless, since the demonstration is not a real elenchus, the refutation of the slave-boy's false answers in the early stages of the demonstration only seem like, and are not quite like, the corresponding refutation of an interlocutor's views in a virtue elenchus. Elenchus examines an interlocutor's beliefs, exposes the inconsistencies among them, and strives to replace inconsistency with consistency. When, for example, Polus in the *Gorgias* believes that a good thing is something that benefits the one who has it, yet believes also that power is (always) a good thing, he is forced to give up one of those two beliefs for the sake of consistency—for as Socrates argues and as Polus concedes, power in the hands of someone foolish will lead not to his benefit but to his harm (*Gorg.* 466–67).[53] The slave-boy-demonstration, by contrast, begins not with an individual's personal beliefs but with a set of truths upon which it seeks to build without contradiction; the slave-boy has no option concerning which of the two propositions—his incorrect answer or a known mathematical fact—to give up in order to avoid inconsistency: he must abandon those answers of his (the wrong ones) that contradict basic mathematical truths with which he is quite familiar. The slave-boy is not, then, in Polus's position: it is not that, for the sake of consistency, he must give up either his answer, "double," or his view that 4×4 is not 8 (since these two views contradict each other); it is rather that he must forfeit his incorrect answer, "double," because it is inconsistent with the plain facts of arithmetic. In geometry, if x is true and if, furthermore, $y \Rightarrow \sim x$, then it follows that y is simply

---

52. See Grote (1888), II, 252: "If Plato had taken pains to study the early life of the untaught slave, with its stock of facts, judgments, comparisons, and inferences suggested by analogy, etc., he might easily have found enough to explain the competence of the slave to answer the questions appearing in the dialogue. And even if enough could not have been found . . . still we don't know all the things the infant, child, youth assimilates." In my view, Socrates in the slave-boy-demonstration does, in full view of Meno, check on the knowledge that the boy already has; indeed, he rather explicitly builds on knowledge that the slave acquired in this lifetime.

53. Socrates' hope in conducting an elenchus is, of course, that the interlocutor will give up those opinions that Socrates suspects are false.

false; anyone who holds y is mistaken. In virtue elenchus, by contrast, if the interlocutor holds view x and also admits to holding belief y, and if $y \Rightarrow \sim x$, then the interlocutor must choose between x and y; he is not entitled to hold view x as long as he also holds y.[54] Whereas in elenchus one hangs oneself, in geometry the truth is what hangs one. The slave-boy does not bear witness against himself;[55] the facts bear witness against him.[56]

Another instance of Socrates' attempt to make the slave-boy-demonstration resemble an elenchus—when it really is just a lesson in geometry—is the amusingly gratuitous remark he directs to the slave-boy at *M.* 83d2: "Well said, for you should answer what seems right to you," *to gar soi dokoun touto apokrinou.* As we saw earlier, Socrates makes this remark just after the slave-boy simply went along with what Socrates had suggested, and when no other response was even thinkable. Whereas Socrates' remark might have served some useful purpose had it appeared either before the boy gave any answer or even after he gave an incorrect one, it is difficult to see what purpose it could serve coming, as it does, right after the boy endorses an obviously true proposition urged on him by Socrates. Yet Socrates' invoking of the "say-what-you-believe" constraint, as Vlastos (1983), 35–37, calls it, does bring to mind the elenchus. Indeed, this constraint is featured fairly regularly in the elenctic dialogues, where we find Socrates encouraging the interlocutor to say what he believes, so that not only his view but he himself can be examined.[57]

---

54. As at *Gorg.* 480e: "Then either we should abandon those, or else these necessarily follow."

55. *Gorg.* 474a.

56. See Aristotle, *Soph. El.* 170a22–27: "for whenever something can be demonstrated, it is also possible to refute one who accepts the denial of this truth. For instance, if someone accepts that the diagonal is commensurate, someone could refute him with a demonstration that it is incommensurable."

57. Vlastos (1983) cites *Gorg.* 500b, *Rep.* 1.346a, 337c; *Crito* 49c–d; and *Prot.* 331c. Nehamas (1990), 15, n. 19, adds *Gorg.* 495a–b and *Lach.* 193c. We should note, however, that there are times when Socrates relaxes his demand that the interlocutor say what he believes. That is because once the interlocutor has said something, he may be held to its consequences even if he seeks to bail out of the discussion. See Kahn (1992), 256, where Kahn discusses Socrates' deliberate luring of Gorgias into an insincere claim, a claim mocked for its insincerity by Callicles at *Gorg.* 499b–c. As Kahn rightly notes, Socrates allows Protagoras to discuss the views of the many rather than his own views as long as Protagoras will answer (*Prot.* 333b–c); Thrasymachus asks Socrates what difference it makes whether he believes what he is saying or not (*Rep.* 1.349a10), and Socrates says it makes no difference. Kahn concludes: "If there is a rule here, it is that the interlocutor is expected to make, and to stand by, a categorical

Typically, much is at stake for the interlocutor—his reputation, his position, his pride, perhaps even his livelihood—if he is unable to defend the view to which he commits himself.[58] Is anything at stake, however, for the slave-boy such that Socrates would need to emphasize the importance of his answering as he thinks? He is no self-proclaimed expert; he has neither reputation nor standing nor pride nor livelihood on the line.[59] Moreover, the question he must answer is itself of no great consequence—not for his life, not for Socrates', and not for Meno's. Socrates' praise of the slave-boy for answering as seems right to him is, then, but a parody of a caveat that figures importantly in real *elenchoi*.

Perhaps the most significant way in which Socrates assimilates the slave-boy-demonstration to elenchus, however, is in referring to the slave-boy's answers as his "opinions." The term does not appear during the demonstration until the final stage, where it is featured prominently in both introduction and conclusion. As the final stage is about to begin, Socrates says to Meno, "Watch out in case you find me teaching and instructing him rather than just asking him his opinions" (*M.* 84d1–2); and when it has just ended, "What do you think, Meno? Is there any opinion that he answered that is not his own?" (*M.* 85b8–9). As inaccurate as it would have been for anything the slave-boy offered in the earlier stages of the demonstration to be called his "opinion," it is particularly inappropriate for that term to be applied—indeed, restricted—to what he says in the demonstration's final stage, when he is at his most reticent and least forthcoming. There is no little irony in Socrates' reserving the term "opinion" for the "I do not know" and the grunts of assent that constitute the

assertion." Socrates permits his interlocutors to retract assertions or make new ones, but he is less tolerant of other ways in which they seek to dissociate themselves from positions they have taken that are now faring badly in the argument.

58. As a self-proclaimed expert at something, the interlocutor must come across as having expertise if he is to retain his clientele; if he comes off badly, his professional standing is compromised and so, too, as a result, is his economic status.

59. In all the passages cited in n. 57, there is a reason behind Socrates' telling his interlocutor to say what he believes. An especially interesting example cited by neither Vlastos nor Nehamas is *Euthyd.* 275d–e, where Socrates says: "Cheer up, Cleinias, and choose bravely whichever seems to you to be the right answer." In this instance, Cleinias's innocent answer has just been unscrupulously demolished by Euthydemus; surely, under circumstances such as these, it is difficult for one to take heart and answer honestly. Of all the instances in which the say-what-you-believe constraint appears, it is only in the case of the slave-boy-demonstration that the constraint seems both vacuous and intrusive.

greater part of the boy's responses in the demonstration's final
stage.[60]

Why does Socrates insist on speaking, particularly here, where the
term seems so ill-suited, of the slave-boy's "opinions"? Once again,
what Socrates attempts to do is to close the gap between the slave-
boy-demonstration and elenchus: it is, of course, in elenchus that
the interlocutor subjects his opinions to Socrates' critical scrutiny.
Since the slave-boy has, especially at this stage of the demonstration,
no opinions of his own to offer on doubling the square—indeed,
the issue of how to double the square is not, in *any* sense, a matter
of opinion[61]—one can only conclude that Socrates illegitimately and
by design appropriates for the slave-boy-demonstration the term
most clearly associated with elenchus.[62] In this way he impresses

60. One of the boy's "opinions" is, of course, "From this one" (*M.* 85b2), which
he utters as he points to the diagonal that Socrates has drawn. It might be thought
that in this instance even if the right answer is not the slave-boy's own opinion, nevertheless his recognition that the right answer is right *is* both the slave-boy's own
opinion and does occur, in some sense, within his soul. Recollection, however, requires that the right answer be itself within—not simply that one's reaction to that
answer take place within (as all reactions do). One's reaction to learning something,
the "click," the "aha" experience, is certainly one's own and may well occur "in one's
soul," but that hardly means that the thing one learned itself emanated from one's
soul. If recollection is nothing more than the experience of catching on, then recollection is not a way of learning that is opposed to teaching; on the contrary, it is the
mark of successful teaching.

61. Compare the following two sets of questions, only the latter of which asks for
an opinion: (a) "Is this not our figure of 4 sq. ft.? Do you understand? And we could
add this one here, equal to it . . . ?" (*M.* 84d3–5). (b) "Do you add anything to this
acquiring, Meno, namely doing so justly and piously? Or does it not make any difference to you, and even if someone gets them unjustly, you call this virtue just the
same?" (*M.* 72d3–6).

62. It is not until the demonstration's final stage and the summary that follows
that Socrates uses the term "opinion," *doxa*, to characterize what the boy "has within
him" (*M.* 84d2, 85b8, c4, c7, c10), in its noun form. During the rest of the demonstration, even the verb *dokein* appears only twice, both times in the passage in which
Socrates commends the slave-boy for answering as he thinks right: the slave-boy says,
"It seems (*dokei*), so to me, at any rate" (*M.* 83d1); Socrates replies, "Well [said], for
what seems (*dokoun*) to you is what you should answer" (*M.* 83d2). As we have noted,
this remark of Socrates' is otiose in its context and is itself just a way of recalling
elenchus to mind. By contrast, *dokein* appears at least twenty-four times in Socrates'
exchange with Meno: at 71d1, 72d4, d7, e2, e7, 73a4, d4, d5, 74a4, 76d6, e8, 77b2,
c1, c5, c6, d5, d7, 78a5, c2, 79a2, c7, c10, e3, and e4. Interestingly, in the exchange
about shape and color, *dokein* appears only twice: at 76d6, where Meno says he thinks
Socrates has given a superlative answer; and at 76e8, where Socrates says that Meno
would come to think this answer not a good one if only he could stay long enough
to be initiated. In the entire exchange, no proposed definition is presented as an
"opinion."

upon Meno's mind the false notion that the slave-boy-demonstration is just like an elenchus.

By including in his slave-boy-demonstration elements reminiscent of virtue elenchus, Socrates accomplishes half his task: he blurs the distinction between geometry instruction and his own method of moral inquiry. It is not enough, however, for the slave-boy-demonstration to mimic elenchus; it must, in addition, make good on its promise to be an illustration of how *recollection* works. How does Socrates connect elenchus with recollection?

As each of the slave-boy-demonstration's three stages commences, Socrates addresses Meno. He introduces the first stage (*M.* 82b9–e3) with the following instructions: "Then pay attention to how it seems to you: whether he [the slave-boy] is recollecting or whether he is learning from me" (*M.* 82b6–7). Before beginning the second stage (*M.* 82e14–84a3), Socrates, in effect, settles the issue: "Do you see, Meno, that I am not teaching him, but I am asking him everything?" (*M.* 82e4–5). And before the demonstration's final stage (*M.* 84d3–85b7), Socrates again instructs Meno (*M.* 84c11–d2): "Well, investigate what he will discover from out of this perplexity by inquiring with me—with me just asking and not teaching; but be on guard in case you should find me somewhere teaching and instructing him, rather than asking him his opinions."

Let us take note of the two options that Socrates offers Meno for characterizing the demonstration he witnesses: either (1) the slave-boy is recollecting/Socrates is only asking questions or (2) the slave-boy is learning from Socrates/Socrates is teaching and instructing him. These options are presented as both exhaustive and mutually exclusive.

There is nothing innocent in Socrates' offering of just these options. For given these and only these two options, if Meno is unable to deny that Socrates is just asking questions (and there is every reason for Socrates to trust that Meno will be taken in, as Socrates intends, by the question mark that closes each of Socrates' points),[63]

---

63. Meno, it seems, cannot formulate an objection that he has not heard before. He is generally submissive, accepting whatever Socrates suggests to him. On those occasions when he is resistant, it is because what Socrates proposes conflicts with something else that he has heard and has come to accept. Such a case is the one in which Meno doubts that virtue, like health, size, and strength, is the same in all those who possess it: Gorgias has said that it differs for man, woman, child, old man, slave, and so on (*M.* 71e1–73a5).

then he will be constrained eventually to admit that the slave-boy is recollecting. Because of the way in which Socrates structures Meno's choices, the admission that Socrates is just asking questions compels the conclusion that Socrates is not teaching or instructing; the notion that Socrates is not teaching or instructing is equivalent to the notion that the slave-boy is not "learning from me"; but once Meno concedes that the slave-boy is not learning from Socrates, the only alternative left to him is that the slave-boy is recollecting.

But, of course, the slave-boy is not recollecting.[64] He does not recall to mind something that is (or was) already in his mind.[65] If the process in which the slave-boy is engaged is not a process of mental retrieval, then it is not really recollection—even if that is what Socrates elects to call it (*M.* 82e12–13, 84a4–5). The only process in evidence is the slave-boy's reckoning, that is, his doing multiplication and counting. It is by multiplying 4×4 (as well as by counting the four 4 sq. ft. squares in the 16 sq. ft. square) and by multiplying 3×3 that the slave-boy comes to know that his answers 4 ft. and 3 ft. are incorrect. And when the slave-boy does finally recognize the diagonal as the answer sought, the recognition follows the counting of half-squares. We note that not once throughout the demonstration is the slave-boy asked to recollect, to try to recollect, or to try to remember anything. The word "remember" appears only once, when Socrates checks to make sure that the slave-boy remembers what is being sought, namely, a square double the size of the original (*M.* 84e3); it is, in other words, the question—not the answer—that he is asked to remember! By contrast, the earlier elenctic exchanges between Socrates and Meno are replete with references to remembering, recollecting, and being reminded. Meno, then, is the one who recollects. The slave-boy does not recollect; what the slave-boy does is compute.[66]

64. See Ebert (1973), 166, cited in n. 66 below.

65. The continuing presence in the mind of what is recollected is what Moravcsik (1971), 58, calls recollection's "entitative" aspect.

66. See Ebert (1973), 166: "It is, however, in no way evident that Socrates' young pupil is *recollecting* something in this process of finding an elementary geometrical truth. . . . The boy corrects his mistakes and makes his discovery by way of trial and error combined with a method of testing the proposed answers: by counting segments of equal size in the squares to be compared" (emphasis in original). Williams (1972), 9, stresses that mathematical truth comes through proof, and that it is this point that "the Platonic model of *recollection* precisely serves to obscure" (emphasis in original). Williams is surely right. In my view, however, when Socrates calls the computation that constitutes proof "recollection," he does so deliberately to obscure the role of proof in mathematics, for which there is no real analogue in virtue.

Socrates, as noted at the beginning of this chapter, need not deny that the slave-boy learns. Indeed, he says that the slave-boy will inquire into and "learn," *manthanein* (*M.* 84c5), what he previously thought he knew, and Socrates openly anticipates that the investigation will culminate in "discovery," *aneurēsei* (*M.* 84c11). Moreover, since Meno must become convinced that he, too, will learn if he resumes his elenctic investigation with Socrates, the slave-boy in Socrates' slave-boy-demonstration must learn. What Socrates needs to deny, however, is that the slave-boy learns "from me" (*M.* 82b7); for the clear implication of the slave-boy's learning from Socrates is that Socrates teaches him. Although Meno would be glad to learn from Socrates were Socrates to claim to be able to teach him what virtue is (it is not the notion of learning from a teacher that Meno resists but that of learning without one), nevertheless since Socrates denies being able to teach what virtue is but still wants Meno to pursue the investigation with him, he must maintain that just as the slave-boy learns in the slave-boy-demonstration without being taught, so would Meno learn without being taught, were the elenchus to continue. The case for the claim that Meno, just like the slave-boy, will learn without being taught can, however, be made only disingenuously. For the slave-boy *is* taught; he learns *from Socrates.*[67]

iv. The Summaries

The slave-boy-demonstration contains two summaries. The first consists of a brief interlude that takes place at *M.* 82a4–c10. The second is the rather lengthy recapitulation that takes place at the conclusion of the demonstration, at *M.* 85b8–86b5. The first of these provides the key to the interpretation of the second: just as in the first summary the things that Socrates says about the slave-boy are true, not of what the boy himself experienced in his exchange with Socrates, but of what Meno (or anyone like him) experiences in elenchus, so

67. See n. 5. Moravcsik (1971), 62, thinks Socrates equivocates on "learning," which, Moravcsik says, in one place is something that can be achieved by recollecting and in another is a process that is contrasted with and excludes recollecting. He goes on to call the first of these "learning*" and the second "learning**." What Moravcsik fails to notice, however, is that Socrates himself calls the first "learning" and the second "learning from me," *par' emou* (*M.* 82b7); it is only "learning from me" that is opposed to and precludes recollecting. There is, then, no real equivocation here. See *Ap.* 33a5–b8: "I have never been anyone's teacher. . . . If someone says that he has ever learned something from me (*par' emou*) . . . know well that he does not speak the truth."

in the second summary what Socrates says about the slave-boy is to be understood as referring, not to what the slave-boy has and has not yet accomplished, but to what those who engage in elenctic moral inquiry can and cannot accomplish.

Let us consider the first summary. Much of what Socrates says about the slave-boy in the interlude seems plainly untrue of him: whereas it is true that the slave-boy does, indeed, as Socrates says, answer "confidently," *tharraleōs,* at first, "as one who knows," *hōs eidōs* (*M.* 84a7–8),[68] there is little reason to think (a) that the slave-boy thought at first that he had knowledge,[69] (b) that he might now have a new eagerness, resulting from his realization that he does not know, to inquire into the matter, or (c) that he formerly believed himself able to speak well to many people on many occasions about the double square, "saying that it must have a side twice the length" of the side of the original square. Although the slave-boy ventured various answers to Socrates' questions (the answers that Socrates' questions disposed him to think were "clearly," *dēlon* [*M.* 82e2], the right ones), there is little reason to think that he ever thought he had knowledge of the matter: he betrays no sign of surprise or frustration or resistance when Socrates proceeds to discredit his answer; nor is he likely to be any more or any less eager to inquire now that he has been "numbed" than he was at the demonstration's inception; and it most certainly never crossed his mind that he could give speeches before crowds on the matter of doubling the square.

If Socrates' characterization of the slave-boy's beliefs and dispositions seems to strike rather wide of the mark, let us observe that the very same description, were it aimed at Meno's beliefs and dispositions, would be perfectly—even wickedly—on target.[70] For it is not the slave-boy but Meno who believes, in his foolish conceit, that he can speak well before many people on many occasions on a sub-

---

68. There is an unmistakable reference here to the way Gorgias teaches his students to answer, namely, "fearlessly and magnificently," *aphobōs te kai megaloprepōs* (*M.* 70b6–7), "as is appropriate for those who know," *hōsper eikos tous eidotas* (*M.* 70b7–c1).

69. At *M.* 82e7, Meno says that the slave-boy "thinks he knows" what sort of line produces the figure of 8 sq. ft. But the slave-boy never says so. Socrates never asks him. The boy just continues responding to Socrates' questions.

70. See Guthrie (1956), 107: "Socrates has been able to construct a working model of his own method of discussing which will give to Meno, who has up till now regarded it as a form of mental torment, an unmistakable impression of its advantages. With this in mind, he makes explicit references back to their own discussion, to show how it corresponds to the model and what stage in the Socratic process he and Meno have now reached."

ject that he clearly knows nothing about; it is not the slave-boy but Meno who thought he had knowledge; and it is not the slave-boy but Meno who might, Socrates hopes, as a result of being numbed by Socrates, now be eager to inquire. The only point at which Socrates' description applies no less to the slave-boy than to Meno is in his assessment that the boy did not at first and does not now have knowledge; indeed, in their respective areas of inquiry, they manifest remarkably comparable ineptitude: both consistently fail to utilize what they have already learned. The slave-boy, though perhaps not an abysmally dull student, is, like Meno, not an especially able one either: whereas he is quite capable of thinking along with Socrates and grasping what Socrates teaches him, he takes no initiative in applying what he already knows to the questions at hand. The slave-boy, instead of thinking to multiply 4×4 or 3×3 himself—even though he knows that that is how to calculate the area of a square—proposes with great assurance the incorrect answer 4 ft. ("double"), followed by the similarly incorrect 3 ft. In this way, he certainly resembles Meno, who cannot seem to remember, from one vigorously proposed definition to the next, the lesson he should have learned—a lesson to which he himself agreed—namely, that nothing totally devoid of justice and temperance can count as virtue. Yet, whereas the slave-boy and Meno are about evenly incompetent when it comes to answering Socrates' questions, Meno's incivility clearly outstrips the boy's: when the slave-boy's ignorance is exposed, he neither becomes belligerent nor devises unflattering comparisons of Socrates to ugly sea creatures nor raises eristic objections to inquiry. By holding up the slave-boy as a model for Meno, Socrates subtly indicates that the slave-boy is, in at least one respect, better than Meno: though not blessed—or because not blessed—with Meno's worldly advantages of wealth, good looks, and noble birth, the slave-boy *is* better able to admit his ignorance openly. In order to encourage Meno to admit to his own lack of wisdom, Socrates shows him that acknowledgment of ignorance is beneficial to the slave-boy. Indeed, Socrates designates as the point at which the slave-boy is benefited not, as one might expect, the end of the demonstration, where the boy learns the solution to the geometrical problem, but its middle, where after offering two wrong answers, he sees that he does not know.

Socrates' second summary (*M.* 85b8–86b5) begins just as the slave-boy has pointed to the diagonal and said, "From this one" (*M.* 85b2). Socrates immediately confirms with Meno (a) that the boy has not answered with any opinions not his own (*M.* 85b8–9),[71] (b) that he nevertheless did not *know* (*M.* 85c2), and, therefore, (c) that the slave-boy has opinions in him—opinions that are true (indeed, the last of his opinions *are* true)[72]—yet without knowing (*M.* 85c6–7).

How faithfully does Socrates' second summary reflect the slave-boy's condition at the demonstration's close? As we saw in Section iii, it is not quite right to say that the boy has answered with "opinions" of his own. But is it any more accurate to say that the slave-boy has now, concerning the mathematical truth that the double-size square comes from the diagonal, only true *opinions* in him (*M.* 85b8, c4, c7) but still does not know? Having witnessed and participated in a proof that he certainly understands—the proof does not, after all, exceed his mathematical capabilities[73]—may he not rightly be said now to *know*?[74] Why, then, does Socrates withhold from the

71. Socrates makes it appear as if the diagonal was the slave-boy's own suggestion: "Then it is from the diagonal, as you say, Meno's boy, that the double square comes to be?" (*M.* 85b5–6). This passage is reminiscent of an earlier one, *M.* 78c–79a, where Socrates pretends that the view toward which he pushes Meno, namely, that nothing done without justice, temperance, or piety can count as virtue but that anything done with them does, is not his but Meno's: "but you . . . say to me that virtue is being able to acquire good things with justice" (*M.* 79a11–b2).

72. We recall (see Section iii) that Socrates reserves the term "opinions" for the answers the slave-boy offers in the final stage of the demonstration. Not coincidentally, these are the only answers of his that are correct. If the only "opinions" that the boy expresses are true ones (since the wrong answers he gives are not called his "opinions"), Socrates is able to avoid the issue that has troubled many commentators, namely, that the boy—and, by extension, everyone—will have not only true but false opinions in his soul for all time.

73. As Brumbaugh (1954), 32, notes: "This theorem, however, can be proved intuitively by a construction which is clear without any special mathematical training." See also Crombie (1963), II, 51, who grants the slave-boy knowledge now insofar as "the course of questioning showed him that no other answer was possible. Knowledge then is the state of mind in which you are certain because you have seen why the answer was right." Gould (1955), 138, although he grants that "the slave . . . has discovered the right answer by concrete demonstration," and "his certainty, *in this particular instance,* is as sure as that of Socrates, based as it is on personal examination of the sufficient evidence" (emphasis in original), nevertheless withholds knowledge from him, holding that, for Plato, knowledge is only of Forms. (But do not crafts, *technai,* appear as the very paradigms of knowledge in the "Socratic" dialogues?) Similarly, Hansing (1928), although she argues, 238, that knowledge comes after much effort and exertion, concedes, almost grudgingly, 236, "In the realm of mathematical truth, absolute certainty is reached at once."

74. One could, of course, insist that the boy does still fail to know: perhaps he has not fully grasped what he has been shown; perhaps he will be unable to reproduce it. Socrates, however, suggests neither of these possibilities. Indeed, Socrates does not attempt to substantiate in any way his conclusion that the boy does not now know.

boy the full measure of his success, especially when the boy's success is also his? If the slave-boy has come to know something he did not know before as a result only of having been asked questions, will Socrates not have successfully demonstrated that recollection works?

Taking our cue from the first interlude discussed, in which the description Socrates offered of the slave-boy's progress in the demonstration up to that point reflected, not the boy's situation, but Meno's, we may speculate that the description Socrates offers now, at the demonstration's end, of the slave-boy's current and future epistemic states also tells us, not what has happened or will happen to the slave-boy, but what has happened or will happen to Meno (or others like him) in virtue elenchus.

Let us look at the description. Having just said that the boy has true opinions in him, although he does not know (*M.* 85c6–7), Socrates continues. The boy's opinions, he says, are (a) "newly aroused in him as if in a dream," but (b) if someone asks him "these same things many times and in many ways," then in the end, he "will know" (c) "no less accurately than anyone" (*M.* 85c9–d1).

Each of these elements is problematic. With respect to (a), we might ask what there is in the boy's response, "Yes, certainly, Socrates," *panu men oun, ō Sōkrates* (*M.* 85b7), that could be reasonably construed as dreamlike. (b) is troubling because it is not at all clear why asking the boy further questions—in many ways—will extract knowledge from him: if asking questions delivered up only opinions the first time around, why should it deliver up knowledge in the future? As Bostock (1986), 112, astutely remarks: "What difference will mere repetition make?"[75] And concerning (c), we want to know what the significance is of the qualification "no less accurately than anyone" (*M.* 85c11–d1). Why does Socrates not simply say that the boy will know?

All three of these questions are easily answered if we substitute Meno for the slave-boy, and virtue for geometry. (a) It is in elenctic exchanges that the interlocutor becomes perplexed and cannot seem to understand how or why he hears himself saying things he

75. For the boy to become more secure in his understanding of the proof or for him to be able to reproduce it on his own it would certainly be worthwhile for him to review it several times. But Socrates wants the boy to be asked the same questions repeatedly. What is unclear is how repeated questioning could do the job when questions, on Socrates' account, only bring to the surface what is already inside. If the boy already has knowledge inside, the first round of questioning should have elicited it. And if he does not have knowledge inside, then, no matter how many times he is asked questions, the questions will not produce knowledge.

would never have expected himself to be saying. Meno, of course, finds himself agreeing, in opposition to what he formerly recognized as his own views on virtue, that virtue cannot be present unless a part of virtue—justice, temperance, holiness, etc.—is present. And just as he concedes this point to Socrates, Socrates informs him that he is quite mistaken if he thinks that defining virtue in terms of its parts "will make clear," *dēlōsein*, to anyone what virtue as a whole is or, for that matter, will make anything else at all clear (*M.* 79d6–e1). Meno is now thoroughly at a loss. Socrates, he is convinced, has put him under a spell and bewitched him (*M.* 80a–b). Is the slave-boy in any way comparably dazed?

Concerning (b), it is with respect to virtue elenchus that there is always a need to raise the question anew. Three times in his earlier exchange with Meno, and in virtually the same language as that used here, Socrates urges a return to "the same question," *tēs autēs erōteseōs* (*M.* 79c4, c8, e4–5). It is in elenchus generally, and in the elenchus with Meno in particular, that asking the same question over and over again is appropriate,[76] for it is in *elenchoi* that the matter is never quite settled: even when a conclusion is agreed to, it remains tentative and open to challenge.

With regard to (c), it is in elenchus—though clearly not in a geometry lesson in which the solution may be demonstrated—that the participants never come to know (simpliciter); at best, they will come to know, in the end, "no less accurately than anyone." Since, in the Cave, no one has knowledge of what virtue is—indeed, Socrates says at the beginning of the dialogue that neither he (*M.* 71b1–3) nor anyone he has ever met (*M.* 71c3–4) has such knowledge (and he, in particular, knows not "at all," *to parapan,* what virtue is!)—an interlocutor in an elenchus who ends up not having actually attained knowledge might still be said to know "no less accurately than anyone."[77]

---

76. See *Gorg.* 513c8–d1, where, when Callicles says he is not convinced by Socrates' argument, Socrates says: "But if we closely examine these same matters often and in a better way, you will be persuaded." Repeated examining, like repeated questioning, might make a position more convincing; it will hardly lead to knowledge. See also *Phil.* 24d–e, where Protarchus says: "It certainly looks that way, Socrates, though, as you said, these matters are not easy to follow. Still, if things are said again and again, there is some chance that the two parties to a discussion might be brought to an acceptable agreement."

77. It might be thought that the point of Socrates' saying that in the end the slave-boy will know no less accurately than anyone is to counter the (to him) odious idea, an idea that Meno probably endorses, that a slave could not possibly be as wise as others. We recall, in this regard, Socrates' insistence, against Meno and Gorgias, from

What is a most inaccurate account of the slave-boy's achievements, past and future, turns out to be a fairly faithful representation of Meno's past and future accomplishments: Meno has indeed had a true opinion aroused in him, by Socrates, "as if in a dream"; and if Meno is repeatedly asked the same question in many different ways, he might, in the end, know virtue no less accurately than anyone. Perhaps Meno will come to know, like Socrates, that he does not know.

Had the recapitulation really been about the slave-boy, then Socrates, having said that the slave-boy will know, in the end, no less accurately than anyone, might have cut straight to his conclusion. He might have said now to Meno what he does not in fact say until much later, at *M.* 86b2–4: "Therefore, you must confidently try to search for and to recollect what you do not happen to know now—that is, what you do not happen to remember." Since, however, the recapitulation is not really about the slave-boy but about interlocutors in virtue *elenchoi*, Socrates takes another route: he offers up an argument that, by reducing to absurdity the notion that the slave-boy has within him knowledge to recollect, actually undermines the very possibility that the boy will recollect knowledge—*ever*.[78]

the dialogue's very inception, that virtue is the same for all: for men, women, children, old men, *and* slaves. We note Socrates' attempt to quash Meno's elitism by contending against him that all men are the same with respect to their wants. In defining shape, Socrates prefers the simple to the *tragikē*, that which is understood by all to that which only the few understand ("effluences," for example). In the myth, he makes no distinction among souls: they all knew everything. And his use of the slave-boy for his experiment is surely intended to show Meno that the slave is quite as capable as anyone else of learning geometry. Nevertheless, is there not detectable, in Socrates' way of putting the point, the barest hint of skepticism about just how accurately others know these matters? Had Socrates wished only to insist that the slave-boy need not lag behind others, could he not simply have said that the boy will come to know, in the end, just as others do now? (For a very different view of Socrates' relation to the slave-boy, see Gera [1996], 97–101. Gera contends that the slave may well be a man rather than a boy; that the demonstration, therefore, humiliates him; that Socrates treats the slave impersonally, never laughing or having any sort of camaraderie with him as he does with his other interlocutors; that Socrates directs questions about the slave to Meno rather than addressing the slave directly; and that Socrates discusses geometry rather than virtue with him because a slave is not worthy of the kind of elenchus that examines not just one's beliefs but oneself.)

78. That the passage at *M.* 85c9–e6 contains a reductio ad absurdum argument goes unnoticed by scholars. Bluck (1961a), 313, thinks: "It is not at all clear at this point which of the alternatives *elaben poti* [acquired at some time] or *aei eichen* [possesses always] Socrates would wish to accept. . . . But either way both *aei eichen* and *ēn epistēmōn* [was knowing or a knower] must refer at least partly to *latent* knowledge" (emphasis in original). For the most part, it seems to readers of this passage that Socrates goes back and forth between true opinions and knowledge for no apparent good reason (see, for example, Klein [1965], 178, who speaks of the "sudden" switch

Socrates reasons as follows: if recollecting is, indeed, one's recovery of the knowledge "within oneself," *auton en autōi*, then, even if the recovery will take place in the future, the knowledge recovered at that later time would surely have to be within one *now*. Does the slave-boy, though he does not now know, nevertheless have knowledge inside him now?[79] Well, Socrates continues, if he does, he will have come into possession of that knowledge somehow: he will either have acquired it at some time or else have possessed it always (*M.* 85d9–10). Yet neither of these options is viable. He does not possess it always, since to possess knowledge always is to be always knowing (*M.* 85d12), but, as was just said (*M.* 85c2), the slave-boy did not know—he is specifically said to be "one who does not know," *tōi ouk eidoti* (*M.* 85c6). Nor did he acquire it at some time—not in this life, at any rate[80]—because, as Meno attests, no one has taught him ge-

to true opinions). In a dialogue, however, in which the distinction between knowledge and true opinion is critical, it is unlikely that Socrates would carelessly confuse them. What I argue is that Socrates carefully crafts an argument for the boy's having only true opinions—and no knowledge. I will suggest in Chapter 4, Section i, that the method of hypothesis that Socrates seems to introduce for the first time at *M.* 86e–87b is not only not new to the dialogues but is instantiated here in the recapitulation of the slave-boy-demonstration.

79. Scholars are puzzled by Socrates' expression "the knowledge he now has" when Socrates has just said that the slave-boy does not have knowledge. Some (Fine [1992], 223, n. 40, for example) have argued that, by "now," Socrates means the future of which he just spoke. This proposal seems odd, however, in light of how emphatically the present is indicated: in addition to using the present tense, Socrates also uses the term "now," *nun*. Moreover, Socrates' discussion of the knowledge the slave-boy has now, *nun*, comes directly on the heels of his assertion that what the slave-boy has now, *nun*, is dreamlike opinions as opposed to knowledge. The solution, it seems, is to notice that Socrates does not say that the boy has no knowledge now but that he does not now know. He has apparently, as of now, had only his opinions aroused but not yet his knowledge. Further questions, however, will presumably unleash the dormant knowledge he has now, just as the questions he has been asked heretofore have awakened his dormant opinions. Among those who think that the knowledge of which Socrates speaks is latent knowledge are Bluck (1961a), 313; Calvert (1974), 147; Sharples (1985), 155; and Scott (1995), 16.

80. It may seem that Socrates (deliberately) overlooks the possibility that the boy acquired his knowledge at some time prior to this lifetime. (That the overlooking could not be accidental is clear from Socrates' saying, "not in his present lifetime, at any rate" [*M.* 85d13]; Socrates could not have added the qualification "at any rate" unless he saw that the slave-boy's present life is *not* the only time the boy might have acquired knowledge.) As we shall see very soon, however, in connection with Socrates' contention that the boy did not acquire his true opinions in this lifetime but possessed them always, the reason that Socrates does not consider the possibility of acquisition in an earlier lifetime is that for the purposes of the current argument, unlike in the myth, Socrates is assuming that the whole of the slave-boy's existence consists of his current lifetime, during which he is a human being, and the time preceding this lifetime, during which he is not human. Since Socrates has at last acknowledged (see

ometry (*M.* 85e6). The slave-boy, it seems, does not have knowledge now, after all. The argument may be stated as follows:

1. The slave-boy did not know at the demonstration's inception how to double the square (*M.* 85c2).
2. The slave-boy had (latent) true opinions at the demonstration's inception with respect to how to double the square (*M.* 85c6–8).
3. The slave-boy's (latent) true opinions were aroused in the demonstration through questioning, as if in a dream (*M.* 85c9–10).
4. The slave-boy will come to *know* in the future how to double the square by being questioned further but without being taught—in other words, by "recollecting" (*M.* 85c10–d5).
5. In order to recollect in the future the slave-boy must have knowledge now (recollection is the recovery by oneself of knowledge that is in oneself) (implicit in *M.* 85d9).
6. If the slave-boy has knowledge now, he either acquired it at some time or possessed it always (*M.* 85d9–11).
7. If the slave-boy possessed knowledge always, he would always be knowing (*M.* 85d12).
8. The slave-boy does not possess knowledge always (implicit inference, 7, 1).
9. No one taught the slave-boy in this lifetime (*M.* 85d13–e1, e6).
10. The slave-boy did not acquire knowledge in this lifetime (*M.* 85d12–e6) (9).
∴11. The slave-boy has no knowledge now (implicit inference, 6, 8, 10).
∴12. The slave-boy will *not* come to recollect, that is, he will not recover, out of himself, in the future, knowledge of how to double the square (implicit inference, 5, 11).

Socrates makes two rather startling points in the course of this argument. The first is that if the boy has knowledge always, he would have *known* the answer to Socrates' question. The second is that if the boy *acquired* knowledge (that is, did not have it always), he would have been *taught* it. The first point is startling because one would have thought, in light of recollection theory, that it is precisely knowledge that is possessed always that is not actively known at all

steps 9 and 10 of the present argument) that acquisition of knowledge comes by teaching, and since it is unlikely that nonhumans are taught, he would have little reason to think that the slave-boy would have acquired knowledge before this lifetime.

times but lies dormant until it is "recollected." The second point is startling because one would have thought, in light of recollection theory, that knowledge is acquired, not by teaching, but by recollection. There is great irony, then, in Socrates' question "Or has anyone *taught* this boy geometry?" (*M.* 85d13–e1),[81] for it tacitly acknowledges what Socrates was at pains to deny all along, namely, that geometry is teachable and is taught. But not just geometry. For when Socrates goes on to say that the slave-boy "will do the same with respect to every part of geometry and with respect to all other *mathēmata*" (*M.* 85e1–3),[82] the message he conveys is that all forms of knowledge are like geometry: if the one can be taught, all can be taught. And so Socrates continues, "Is there then anyone who has taught this boy everything?" (*M.* 85e3).[83] As far as Socrates is concerned, then, the boy might, in principle, have been taught any of the things that one might know.[84] Furthermore, by adding that insofar as the slave-boy was brought up in Meno's household, Meno ought to know whether or not he was taught these things, Socrates indicates that the teaching of these subjects is a fairly commonplace and easily identified activity. If Socrates really thought that no sub-

81. Brown (1971), 199–200, argues that Socrates initially conceived of the question he asks the slave-boy as arithmetical and only reluctantly settles for a geometrical solution. Socrates' question "Or has anyone taught this boy *geometry*?" however, suggests that from the first, Socrates conceives of his question as a geometrical one. We may note that geometry is quite prominent in the dialogue generally: Socrates offers two definitions of shape, and he is about to use as his model for inquiry a method of hypothesis that he attributes to the geometers (*M.* 86e–87b). In addition, we have already noted that Socrates poses his question geometrically, in *poia* terms—what sort of line?—early on in the investigation (see n. 33). Nor does Socrates seem to be, as Brown urges, dissatisfied with the slave-boy's answer: he seems to have planned the slave-boy's initial stumbles in advance and even seems, as we have seen, to lead him directly to them. Moreover, the slave-boy's success at the end makes Socrates nearly jubilant, as it gives him hope that Meno will, as a result, return with him to the investigation into virtue.

82. Later on in the *Meno*, the term *mathēmata* embraces all matters taught and learned, including flute playing (*M.* 85e2). The term is treated similarly in the *Protagoras*, at *Prot.* 327a4.

83. The notion of being taught everything is probably an ironic reference to Gorgias, who claimed to teach his students to speak well on everything as if they knew everything. See n. 68.

84. Grote (1888), II, 251, thinks that since "Plato does not intend here to distinguish . . . geometry from other sciences, as if geometry were known *à priori*, and other sciences known *à posteriori* or from experience," they must all, for Socrates, "lie equally in the untaught mind." As I see it, Grote is right to recognize that Socrates does not differentiate among the various *mathēmata*, but he is mistaken in thinking that they all equally lie in the mind awaiting awakening; on the contrary, as *mathēmata*, none is in the learner's mind until such time as he is taught.

ject, no *mathēma*, is taught but all are recollected, why would he require Meno's *empirical* verification to establish that the slave-boy was not taught everything? Indeed, we note another ironical twist: since the slave-boy *did* acquire knowledge of this bit of geometry in this lifetime—Socrates just taught it to him!—Meno, as it turns out, is a wholly *un*reliable witness concerning whether or not his slave has been taught: he fails to detect the teaching that is going on before his very eyes.

Why, we may wonder, is Socrates willing to assert (a) that the slave-boy does not possess knowledge always, and (b) that knowledge is acquired by teaching, when each of these points seems flatly to contradict the recollection thesis that he has worked so hard to promote? What is Socrates up to?

If Socrates is to defend elenchus, he cannot leave standing the idea that what is recollected by questioning is knowledge. Elenchus does not recover knowledge. What elenchus recovers is opinions—eventually, it is hoped, the true opinions that are always in the soul. Thus, as soon as Socrates establishes that the slave-boy neither possesses knowledge always (since he was caught not knowing) nor acquired knowledge (since no one has taught him), he immediately asks: "But he does have these *opinions*, or does he not?" (*M.* 85e7).

Socrates proceeds now to look into the provenance of the slave-boy's true opinions, just as he had, a moment ago, considered where the boy's putative knowledge came from. Socrates argues that the slave-boy's true opinions were in his soul always. This is his argument:

1. The slave-boy has true opinions in this lifetime about geometry (*M.* 85e7–8).
2. Either the slave-boy acquired in this lifetime his true opinions about geometry, or else he possessed them and had already learned them at some other time (*M.* 85e9–86a1).
3. If the slave-boy acquired his true opinions in this lifetime, someone would have taught him (implicit).
4. No one taught the slave-boy geometry in this lifetime (*M.* 85e6).
5. It was not in this lifetime that the slave-boy acquired true opinions about geometry (*M.* 85e9) (3, 4).
6. The slave-boy must have possessed his true opinions and had already learned them at some other time (2, 5).
7. The time at which the slave-boy must have possessed his true opinions and had already learned them is the time that he was not a human being (*M.* 86a3–4).

8. The slave-boy has true opinions in him throughout the time that he is a human being and throughout the time that he is not a human being (*M.* 86a6–7)[85] (1, 7).

9. For the whole of time, the slave-boy either is or is not a human being (*M.* 86a9–10).

∴10. For the whole of time, the slave-boy is in a state of having learned (*M.* 86a8–9) (9, 8).

According to this argument, true opinions are like knowledge in that one can acquire them by being taught. They are unlike knowledge, however, in that they can be in one's soul always—even if one is unable to produce them on demand. Moreover, it is the true opinions that are in one's soul always that Socrates elicits through questioning.

Why, we might ask, could the slave-boy not have acquired his true opinions at some time before he was born; why does Socrates suppose that if the boy was not taught these opinions in this lifetime, he must possess them always? The reason is that specifically according to the current argument—and here it departs from the recollection myth—the soul undergoes but one incarnation: a person begins as a nonhuman being and then becomes a human one. Might a nonhuman being acquire true opinions? Not, to be sure, if opinions are acquired by one's being taught. On the assumption, then, that the slave-boy was taught neither in this lifetime nor earlier, it follows that he never *acquired* his opinions. But if he nevertheless has true opinions and, moreover, has them both before and after he is born, he must have them always. (Possession always is the only alternative Socrates recognizes to acquisition at some time.)

To review. The only way for one to *acquire* knowledge is to be taught. Thus, if the slave-boy was taught geometry neither in this lifetime (setting aside that he was—by Socrates!) nor before this lifetime (he was not then human), he never acquired it. And if knowledge that is possessed must always be known, then the slave-boy also does not possess knowledge always (he did not know at first how to double the square). That leaves true opinions. The slave-boy's true opinions, too, were not acquired—for the same rea-

---

85. Most translators translate the *an* in *an ēi chronon kai on an mē ēi anthrōpos* (*M.* 86a6) as something shy of "throughout." An exception is Canto-Sperber (1991): "*durant tout le temps qu'il est un homme et tout le temps qu'il ne l'est pas.*" Aside from the fact that this is the correct translation, it is also the case that unless the boy has held his true opinions throughout both stages of his existence, it certainly would not follow that for "the whole of time his soul was in a state of having learned" (*M.* 86a8–9).

sons that knowledge was not acquired. But unlike knowledge, his true opinions can be, and are, possessed always. For unlike knowledge, true opinions can be present in one even if they are not active. That is why true opinions, but not knowledge, can be "recollected" through Socratic questioning.

At *M.* 86a, Socrates keeps alive the hope, for Meno's sake no doubt, that the slave-boy will eventually attain knowledge—not, however, by further questioning. Since it has by now been established that the only thing the slave-boy has in his soul at present is his always-present true opinions, the only thing questioning can call forth is true opinions. And so, at *M.* 86a, what Socrates says is that questioning will awaken the slave-boy's true opinions and that once awakened these opinions will "become knowledges," *epistēmai gignontai* (*M.* 86a8), that is, become known things or known truths.[86] This rather unusual use of the plural form "knowledges"[87] may be accounted for by the one-to-one correspondence that Socrates posits here between the individual true opinions that are aroused by questioning and the knowledges, that is, the *known* truths, that they will eventually somehow become. The process by which this transformation is to occur, however, is left a mystery.[88]

As we have seen, Socrates concludes from the slave-boy's having true opinions throughout both his nonhuman and his human states that his soul is, for the whole of time, "in a state of having learned," *memathēkuia* (*M.* 86a6–10). Being for the whole of time in a state of having learned is, of course, tantamount to being in a state of never having had to learn.[89] True opinion is, then, on Socrates' account, the natural state of the soul.

The immortality that was a precondition in the myth for recollection (understood as the way to attain knowledge) is now but an afterthought, tacked on to the conclusion that truth is always in our

86. It is clear that it is the opinions—not the knowledges—that are awakened by questioning. The passage reads: "if . . . there are going to be in him true opinions that, having been awakened by questioning, become knowledges. . . ."

87. The plural *epistēmai*, "knowledges," usually refers to branches of knowledge, that is, to the various sciences, rather than to individual truths that are known within a discipline.

88. The expression "become knowledges," *epistēmai gignontai*, is found again at *M.* 98a6, where Socrates speaks of the tethering of true opinions by "working out the reason." Could this be the process left unspecified at *M.* 86a? See the discussion of this passage in Section v of Chapter 4.

89. Davis (1988), 129, notes: "It is not possible for the soul to exist for all time in a state of having learned. What Socrates must mean then is that strictly speaking there is no time at which the soul learns."

soul: "Then, if the truth about the things that are is always in our soul, will not the soul be immortal?" (*M.* 86b1–2).[90] Although Socrates reinstates immortality of the soul—no doubt in order to create the illusion that he has not strayed from the notions with which the discussion of recollection began—it is quite plain that he has moved beyond those notions: he has abandoned the idea that what human souls contain within themselves always is knowledge and has embraced, instead, the idea that what they contain is true beliefs.

What manner of true belief is always in the human soul?[91] Is it the truths of geometry? Or the truths of all *mathēmata*? Surely, the truths that all human beings have always in their souls are moral truths. The truths of the various *mathēmata* are, as Socrates finally admits (*M.* 85d13–e6), taught and learned. Moreover, they are external to us: they are not in our souls and they are not about our souls. By contrast, the truths of virtue, truths that are not successfully taught by anyone, truths that are learned, if they are learned, without one's being taught, are not only recovered *from within* the soul but are, in addition, *of* the soul.[92]

90. It is frequently noted that in the *Meno* immortality begins as the ground for recollection but ends as a consequence of it. See Klein (1965), 180; see also Andic (1971), 267. Despite appearances, however, the soul's immortality is not really a consequence of recollection at the *Meno*'s end. The *Meno*, unlike the *Phaedo*, contains no argument to support the inference from recollection to immortality. The only way immortality could be construed to be a consequence of recollection in the *Meno* is if it were taken as an inference from the proposition that the truth about the things that are is always in our soul: if (a) the truth about the things that are is always in our soul, then (b) the soul "is" (exists) always (= is immortal). Needless to say, such an "inference" would be worthy of only the shabbiest of sophists, men like Euthydemus and Dionysodorus who, in the *Euthydemus*, shamelessly exploit words like "always," a word that, Socrates notes, can easily "trip us up," *hēmas sphēlēi* (*Euthyd.* 296a9). Since immortality is also not needed for the derivation of the recollection demonstration's moral lesson, namely, that Meno ought to inquire confidently into what he does not know now (*M.* 86b2–4)—that lesson follows straightforwardly from the proposition that the truth about the things that are is always in our soul—the most reasonable conclusion to draw is that Socrates simply wants to conceal from Meno just how far the argument has drifted from its beginnings in the mystical Pythagorean idea of immortality with which he was so at home.

91. Let us note the shift from talk about the slave-boy's soul to talk about "our soul" or "the soul" (*M.* 86b1–2) to talk about, finally, Meno himself (*M.* 86b2–4). As I have been arguing, Socrates speaks about the slave-boy and geometry for the sake of advancing the cause of virtue inquiry for "our soul," or for the soul in general. Ultimately, however, the whole argument is designed to persuade Meno to return to the inquiry.

92. If, one day, philosophers do come to have knowledge of virtue through "seeing" the Forms of Justice, Temperance, Courage, and so on, the virtue they will come to know will be, like other Forms and, indeed, like mathematical truths, neither in

People are exposed in their lifetimes to a myriad of false views, views that glamorize power, wealth, honor, good looks, nobility of birth—all the superficial and worthless things that are pursued in the name of happiness and human fulfillment.[93] But these false beliefs are not etched into the human soul; they are but a meretricious overlay, concealing the soul's deeper, more ennobling truths. If Socrates can get his interlocutors to move past the glitter and to see that power, wealth, honor, good looks, and noble birth are ultimately not humanly satisfying, that, indeed, these things present an obstacle to human flourishing, then he will have replaced their false beliefs with true ones that are, in a sense, their own: it is the interlocutors' true beliefs—not their false ones—that accord with their most basic human needs and wishes.[94]

Through his two summaries, Socrates has shown us what elenchus hopes to accomplish—by whom and for whom—as well as why it is able to succeed. In the initial stages of elenchus, the nonknowing questioner seeks to disabuse a pompous interlocutor of his false conceit of wisdom concerning the most important matter, virtue. As the elenchus progresses, the questioner labors to ease the interlocutor past the false opinions he holds on the surface so that the interlocutor can "recollect" the true opinions he holds, if unawares, deep down in his soul.[95] Recollection, in this restricted sense, belongs, not to all learning, but to moral inquiry by way of elenchus.

nor of their souls. Like the truths of geometry, truths of virtue will be external to human beings—out there in a reality that exists apart from us, not inscribed in our souls or in our nature. Virtue will, moreover, be learned differently—no longer by looking in, but by looking out. It will no longer involve self-knowledge but will require instead the knowledge of eternal, unchanging entities: Forms.

93. See Klein (1965), 45: "For most opinions of most men—and not only those of Meno—are derived from, and identical with, opinions of 'somebody else.' "

94. See *Theaet.* 149 ff., where those who associate with Socrates "discover within themselves" "a multitude of beautiful things" that they "bring forth into the light"— with the help of Socratic midwifery. It is only when they take leave of Socrates and consort with "harmful company" that they begin to set value on lies and phantoms. It is necessary, therefore, Theaetetus concludes, for people to try their hardest to bring out the beautiful truths within—rather than, it would seem, to accept the ugly untruths without.

95. The role of the ignorant questioner in the *Meno* is the precursor of that of the midwife in the *Theaetetus* (149a–151d). Burnyeat (1977), 10, argues that the *Meno*'s stingray metaphor is significantly different from that of the midwife. But that is, in part, because he assumes that the *Meno* offers a general theory of knowledge and is meant to show how Socratic inquiry can lead to knowledge. Since I make no such assumptions about the *Meno* (in the recapitulation, as we saw, Socrates substitutes true opinions for knowledge as that which the slave-boy has now in his soul), I see no reason that the stingray metaphor cannot be seen as the forerunner of the midwifery

v. The Disavowal

Having ended the slave-boy-demonstration with the affirmation that the soul must be immortal (*M.* 86b2) insofar as (a) the slave-boy's soul is for the whole of time "in a state of having learned" (*M.* 86a8–9) and (b) the truth about the things that are is always "in our soul" (*M.* 86b1–2), Socrates draws the moral of the preceding exercise: Meno "must confidently try to search for and to recollect" what he does not happen to know now, that is, what he "does not remember" (*M.* 86b2–4).

Now that what was found to be in the soul is not knowledge but true opinions, Socrates seems to be urging Meno to try to "recollect," that is, to search for (taking the *kai* linking "to search for" and "to recollect" epexegetically),[96] the true opinions that are in his soul. Socrates hopes to have persuaded Meno, though without permitting him to see it too clearly, that it pays to search even if the search will not culminate in knowledge, that is, even if it does no more than stir up those moral truths that reside in the soul.

Meno accepts all of what he is told—though with a trace of skepticism: "You seem to me to speak well, Socrates, but I do not know how" (*M.* 86b5). Socrates, however, reacts in a way that is utterly astounding. Although, as he says, it seems to him, too, that he spoke well, he adds:

> As far, at any rate, as the rest is concerned, I would not all out (*panu*) swear to the argument; but that we will be better, both more manly and less lazy, if we think that one must search for those things that one does not know rather than that those things that we do not know we neither can discover nor ought to search for—for this I would fight all out (*panu*) if I could, in both word and deed. (*M.* 86b7–c3)

one. According to both metaphors, Socrates is ignorant (numb/barren); according to both, Socratic questioning is painful to the interlocutor (it induces numbness/labor pains); according to both, progress is made (the interlocutors' true opinions/many beautiful things are brought forth, "himself out of himself," *autos ex hautou* [*M.* 85d4]/"themselves from themselves" *autoi par' hautōn* [*Theaet.* 150d7]). According to neither is there anything properly called "learning from Socrates" (he only asks questions), and according to neither does Socrates' interaction with his interlocutor culminate in knowledge.

96. See Umphrey (1990), 11.

How little of what Socrates has so arduously argued for is he willing now to swear to![97] Apparently, once he has won Meno over to the idea that it is necessary to search and recollect, Socrates feels free to abandon the things he has pretended to prove: that all learning is recollection and that the soul is immortal. Indeed, Socrates commits himself to no more than that we will be better—more manly and less lazy—if we subscribe to the view that we should inquire than if we endorse the notion that we cannot discover what we do not know and need not search for it. It is this maxim alone for which he is willing to fight.[98]

Scholars have noted this peculiar state of affairs. Shorey (1933), 157, for example, says: "the only thing that Socrates after all is prepared to affirm positively is the practical answer to Meno's difficulty. We shall certainly be better men, more valiant and less idle in the pursuit of truth, if we believe that it is somehow possible to learn what we do not know, than if in the belief that it is impossible we supinely abandon the search." Umphrey (1990), 20–21, too, rec-

97. There are three places in the *Phaedo,* the dialogue in which the humanly unknowable matter of the fate of the soul before birth and after death is discussed at length, where Socrates declares that there is something to which he would not "swear," *diischurizomai.* The first is at *Phdo.* 63b–c, where Socrates says that he would not swear to joining, after death, the company of good men but that he would swear to joining that of good gods. The second is at 100d6–7, where Socrates will not swear to his stated conception of the nature of the relationship between the Beautiful Itself and the many beautiful things, but he will swear to the minimal claim that it is by the Beautiful that the beautifuls are beautiful. The third is at 114d1, where Socrates says that it would not be fitting for a man of intelligence to swear that these things (the fates of various souls as described) are as he describes them, but that it is fitting and worthwhile for a man to risk believing—for the risk is a noble one—that either his description or something like it is true about our souls and their dwelling places, "since really the soul is evidently immortal, and a man should repeat such things to himself as if it were an incantation." (The *Phaedo*'s notion of "running the risk" is very much like the *Meno*'s notion of "putting one's trust" in something's truth, *pisteuōn alēthei einai* [M. 81e2].)

98. Socrates' declaration of his determination to fight for the worth of inquiry reminds the reader of his use of military metaphors in similar contexts in the *Apology* and the *Phaedo.* In the *Apology,* Socrates says he will remain at the post at which the god stationed him, risking his life in the pursuit of wisdom, that is, in the examination of himself and others (*Ap.* 28e–29a). In the *Phaedo,* Socrates marshals his forces to combat misology (*Phdo.* 89a). Socrates, however, will only fight "all-out," *panu* (*M.* 86c2), as he says, "if I could," *ei hoios t' eiēn* (*M.* 86c2): he is hampered in his fight by those who, like Meno, quote eristic paradoxes to stop him and by those who, like Anytus, seek to silence him by the far more drastic means of ending his life. See *Rep.* 1.327c, where Polemarchus observes that Socrates and Glaucon can either prevail by force or give in but that they cannot successfully persuade "if we will not listen."

ognizes that all Socrates insists upon is "that we are better if we believe that we must investigate the nature of things than if we believe we need not." And there are many others who make the same or nearly the same point.[99] But what does it mean for Socrates to be willing to affirm no more than the practical benefit of embracing the belief that one ought to inquire, while spurning Meno's paradox? For some scholars, Socrates' severely restricted commitment signals that he does not, after all, hold the views from which he now distances himself or, at the very least, that he has grave doubts about them. Thus, Umphrey comments that whereas "in the end he [Meno] agrees that there is something to the doctrine that learning involves the retrieval of true opinions latent in the soul . . . Socrates himself is no believer in this doctrine."[100] Arieti (1991), 27, agrees: "Socrates himself admits that he doesn't subscribe to the theory (86B)." And Brumbaugh (1990), 300, remarks on the oddity in Socrates' ending the slave-boy-demonstration "by doubting whether any part of the myth other than its practical moral may be true (see 86b6–c2)."[101] For others, however (among them Bluck [1961a], 318; Taylor [1948], 138, n. 2; and Guthrie [1975], 258), Socrates' disclaimer signifies only that he does not take himself to have conclusively *established* the doctrines that he nevertheless subscribes to: recollection, immortality of the soul, and reincarnation. Yet Socrates does not say that he has failed to prove his doctrines; what he says is that he will not swear to them. The simple fact is that he refuses to commit himself to them.[102]

Both Taylor and Guthrie, let us note, do each identify one thesis

99. See Ebert (1973), 164; Brumbaugh (1990), 300; and Woodruff (1990), 82.

100. This, in my view, is precisely the "doctrine" that Socrates does subscribe to—albeit only with respect to virtue. He does not, as Umphrey rightly observes, subscribe to the view that all learning is recollection. This Socratic response to Meno's paradox is, as Umphrey (1990), 21, says, "more pragmatic or dramatic than theoretical. It is an attempt to help Meno forget the Meno-Problem, to give up this excuse for giving up philosophy."

101. See also Ebert (1973), 164, who says of Socrates' remarks at the close of the slave-boy-demonstration that they "look in fact as if they were a sort of revocation of what has just been proved in a somewhat dogmatic way"; and Woodruff (1990), 82, who reluctantly agrees, calling Socrates' attitude toward his recollection thesis "puzzling": "On the one hand, he says he believes it to be true (81e1); on the other, he declines to affirm the theory with any strength (86b7). The most he will fight for is his view that we are better off not submitting to the eristic paradox (86c: cf. 81de)."

102. No matter how loosely one construes Socrates' declared unwillingness to swear to anything but, or to fight for anything but, the practical value of inquiry, there can be no doubt that his commitment to the things he has so strenuously been arguing for—most of all, to the idea that all learning is recollection—is a weak one.

that they think Socrates not only endorses but takes himself actually to have proved. For Taylor (1948), 138, it is that "we can arrive at truth"; this is, for him, the "main point" of the recollection thesis, a point that, according to Taylor, Socrates thinks the theory "proves." For Guthrie (1975), 258, it is the invalidity of the eristic argument; he argues that even if we take, as he agrees we must, Socrates' words "at their face value," in which case Socrates' disclaimer would extend to "the whole 'priestly' doctrine of immortality, reincarnation, and truth learned in a disembodied state," nevertheless "the experiment with the slave has *demonstrated* that our minds *somehow* contain latent knowledge which we can recover without having it put there by someone else, and this is sufficient to invalidate the eristic argument" (emphasis in original). Moravcsik (1971), 62–63, taking greater liberties with the text than do Taylor and Guthrie, contends that "a closer examination of the context shows . . . that Plato expresses reservations only with regard to some of the details of his theory; he has no doubt about the general claim that learning is recollection."

The fact is, however, that Socrates is unwilling to endorse anything but the practical moral that people will be better if they believe they should search than if they embrace Meno's paradox. Indeed, it is this moral lesson that frames the slave-boy-demonstration on both ends—at *M.* 81d5–e3 and at *M.* 86b7–c3. What is important is that men be "better," that is, that they seek vigorously, that they be energetic, manly, and not lazy. Any theory that fosters these qualities in those who put their "trust" in it is to be preferred to one that would make men soft, idle, and reluctant to inquire.[103] From Socrates' perspective, then, if the full-blown recollection thesis, that is, the thesis that all learning is the recollection of knowledge from within the immortal soul, has anything to recommend it, it is the

---

103. We may compare with this passage a similar one in the *Phaedo*. At *Phdo.* 85c–d, Simmias recognizes the limitation of the human capacity to acquire knowledge with respect to the soul's continued existence after the death of the body: "in these matters certain knowledge is either impossible or very hard to come by in this life, but . . . even so, not to test what is said about them in every possible way, without leaving off until one has examined them exhaustively from every aspect, shows a very soft [*malthakou* (*Phdo.* 85c6) = *malakois* (*M.* 81d7)] spirit; on these questions one must achieve one of two things: either learn by instruction [*mathein*] how things are or discover [*eurein*] how they are; or, if that is impossible, then adopt the best and least refutable of human doctrines, embarking on it as a kind of raft, and risking the dangers of the voyage through life, unless one could travel more safely and with less risk, on a securer conveyance afforded by some divine doctrine" (trans. Gallop [1993]).

beneficial effects it is likely to have on the character of its adherents; its worth does not lie in its truth.

Inasmuch as Socrates stands behind none of the conclusions of the myth or slave-boy-demonstration—he swears neither to the soul's immortality nor to "all learning is recollection" nor to the successful outcome of every diligently pursued inquiry—it is most improbable that he has intended, in the myth and in the slave-boy-demonstration, to promote the metaphysical and epistemological doctrines he proposes. His overriding concern, as he makes abundantly clear, is to make Meno a better man by encouraging him to continue to probe with Socrates the question of what virtue is. When Socrates proclaims that although he is not prepared to *swear* "all out" to anything more in the entire argument, he is prepared to *fight* "all out" for moral inquiry, he does no more than describe what he has just done: he has, in fact, just fought, in both word and deed, for moral inquiry. He has fought in word by way of the myth, in which what he does is speak: he tells Meno a story. And he has fought in deed by way of the slave-boy-demonstration, in which what he does is act: he "shows" Meno, *endeixai* (M. 82a6), how recollection works. Socrates is compelled to marshal all his forces—those of word and those of deed—to combat the eristic miasma that threatens to impair permanently the inquiry into virtue.

4

The Road to Larisa

Knowledge, True Opinion, and Eudoxia

One chooses dialectic only when one has no
other means. . . . Nothing is easier to erase
than a dialectical effect.

> Friedrich Nietzsche, *The Twilight of*
> *the Idols* (trans. Kaufmann [1968] 476)

i. Hypothetical Method

Socrates fought hard to get Meno to reopen with him the investigation into the question of what virtue is. But he lost. Meno, despite
having no grounds upon which to refuse to go on with the inquiry
into the nature of virtue, nevertheless revives instead his initial question, namely, how does virtue come to be present in men?[1]

Once more, Socrates rebukes Meno—even as he accedes yet again
to his wishes. On the one hand, Socrates complains that Meno, who
associates freedom, not with self-mastery, but with dominating others, seeks now to rule, not himself, but Socrates.[2] On the other hand,
Socrates capitulates to Meno by giving priority to a *poion* question,
a question concerning what sort of thing something is, what its characteristics are, over a *ti esti* question, a question concerning the

---

1. Meno craftily phrases his question as if its ultimate purpose were to answer
Socrates' question of what virtue is, saying that he would like most to consider and to
hear from Socrates whether the attempt (to search together for what virtue is) should
be made taking virtue as teachable, as natural, or as coming to men in some other
way (*M.* 86c8–d2). We note that Meno's idea of "considering," *skepsaimēn*, is just "to
hear," *akousaimi*, from Socrates. He has an aversion to thinking for himself.

2. Socrates thinks that one who is truly free rules himself. In the *Gorgias*, he
staunchly opposes Callicles' characterization of self-rule as enslavement to oneself. See
Gorg. 491d–e.

thing's nature. Socrates asks only that Meno relax his domination just enough to make one small concession to him: Socrates would like, if he may, to consider Meno's question, the question of whether virtue is teachable, "from a hypothesis," *ex hypotheseōs* (*M.* 86e4).

That Socrates is willing to consider this question at all is utterly astonishing. He has just expended considerable energy on proving in the slave-boy-demonstration that all learning is recollection—not teaching (*M.* 82a1). How can he now even begin to entertain Meno's suggestion that virtue might come to men by teaching (*M.* 86c10)?[3] In light of how Socrates, before the slave-boy-demonstration, jumped on Meno for (innocently) asking him to *teach* him that learning is recollection (*M.* 81e6), it is nothing short of astounding that he objects not at all when Meno asks, after the slave-boy-demonstration, a demonstration whose sole purpose was, ostensibly, to prove that no learning comes through teaching, whether virtue comes by teaching. Moreover, as if Socrates' eerily subdued reaction to Meno's question were not inexplicable enough, Socrates is about to utter his most stupefying and unfathomable remark to date. "Let it make no difference to us," *diaphēretō de mēden hēmin* (*M.* 87b9), he will say, whether we say "teachable" or "recollectable." How is it possible that Socrates is willing to allow it to make no difference which of these terms is used when, for the whole of the slave-boy-demonstration, these terms were not only not interchangeable but were contradictories? In the slave-boy-demonstration, learning was either recollection or teaching; it could not be both and it could not be neither.[4]

---

3. Meno specifies two possible ways in which virtue might come to men: by teaching and by nature. He then trails off with "or in some other way" (*M.* 86c10–d2). He drops the "by practice," *askēton*, of his opening question (*M.* 70a2). And he does not, even now, mention recollection.

4. Some scholars seek to blunt the edge of Socrates' willingness to have it make no difference which term, "teachable" or "recollectable," is used. See, for example, Cornford (1952), 52, 60, n. 1; Bluck (1961a), 21–22; Desjardins (1985), 276; Devereux (1978), 120. Guthrie (1975), 264, maintains that by "teachable" Socrates means, as in the *Theaetetus*, assisting in bringing to birth truths with which another is pregnant. Yet in the *Theaetetus* (149–51), Socrates does not call his midwifery teaching. Moreover, if helping to deliver the views of others were teaching, Socrates would have no reason to deny that he teaches. In the *Meno*, neither in the slave-boy-demonstration nor later does Socrates mean by "teaching" helping someone to bring forth his beliefs. We note that the slave-boy-demonstration refuses the name "teaching" to the practice of helping someone recover his own opinions; in it, teaching is emphatically contrasted with helping one recollect. And, later, it is crafts that are paradigmatic of what is taught. See Irwin (1977), 141, and (1973), 755, who recognizes that the model of learning by way of recollection is incompatible with the learning model associated with what he famously calls the CA (craft analogy). (Interestingly, Irwin thinks that

What clearer indication could there be that Socrates has at long last given up on Meno's returning to the inquiry than that (a) he permits him at this juncture to ask, with impunity, if virtue comes by teaching and (b) he collapses "recollectable" into "teachable"? And why should he not despair? He extended himself for Meno, inventing and then defending at length, for Meno's sake, the elaborate recollection thesis, only to have Meno revert, despite it all, to the question of whether virtue comes to men by *teaching*. That Meno raises this possibility anew shows, not only that he has no compunctions about reneging on an implicit agreement to go on with the inquiry into what virtue is should Socrates successfully counter his paradox (*M.* 81e4–6), but that he is also incorrigibly impervious to what Socrates has gone to such lengths to persuade him of, namely, that all learning comes by recollection—not by teaching. Once Socrates recognizes that it is futile to try to deflect Meno from the question that interests him, or even to hold him to a conclusion to which he has quite explicitly committed himself (*M.* 86b5, c4), he throws up his hands: "Let it make no difference to us which term we use" (*M.* 87b9–c1). Socrates knows full well that the extent to which he can fight for philosophy is determined not solely by his own fortitude but also by the intelligence and openness of his interlocutor. As he says at the close of the slave-boy-demonstration: "For this I would fight all out *if I could*, in both word and deed" (*M.* 86c1–3). Meno's obtuse intransigence limits how long Socrates can fight.[5]

What are Socrates' options at this point? Given that Meno, as it is now clear, will never lead a philosophical life, that this man's soul will not be turned to inquiry no matter what Socrates does, how should Socrates proceed? Socrates can, of course, suddenly remember an appointment he has forgotten—and leave. Or he can reproach Meno not just for his unbecoming desire to control others rather than himself but for the utter intractability of his mind. Or he can try, working within rather constrictive limitations, to help

once Socrates introduces recollection, he abandons the CA; how, we must wonder, does Irwin, then, account for the prominence of crafts in the dialogue's latter part?) Some scholars do acknowledge the strangeness of Socrates' remark. Sharples (1985), 162, for instance, says: "in the present context, and in view of passages like 81e4–82a3, 82e4–5 and 84c11–d2, it seems likely that the statement that the distinction is not to matter is not to be taken at face value." The great irony of Socrates' permitting it to make no difference which term is used is that what was called recollection in the slave-boy-demonstration really *was*, despite Socrates' insistence to the contrary, just teaching.

5. See Chapter 3, n. 98.

Meno. To be sure, the only thing that, from Socrates' perspective, is really of benefit to a man is to be initiated into philosophy: any life but the examined one is, he believes, not worth living for a human being. But since Socrates no longer harbors any hope that Meno will lead a life of that kind, is there not still some other sort of help that he can offer him? In this chapter I intend to show that Socrates does, indeed, attempt to help Meno—no longer in the optimal way but as best he can under the circumstances. He tries to steer him away both from the corruptive influences to which he is most susceptible and from his own self-satisfied arrogance.

Recollection, as the recovery by the soul of the knowledge nestled within it (M. 85d6–7), is, let us note, entirely absent from the final part of the dialogue (from M. 86d to the end)—the momentary revival of the *term* "recollection" at M. 98a4–5 notwithstanding (see Section v). Being no great fan of recollection's to begin with, and having failed to sway Meno anyway by his intensive labors on recollection's behalf, Socrates returns to the themes in whose company he is most at home: all knowledge is teachable; everything teachable is knowledge; and the paradigms for knowledge as well as for teachability are the *technai*—medicine, shoemaking, flute playing, music, athletics, and even wrestling and javelin throwing.[6]

Let us turn to the text before us. As we have seen, Socrates proposes to proceed in the latter part of the dialogue "from a hypothesis." This way of proceeding, referred to by scholars as "hypothetical method,"[7] is widely seen to be yet another momentous "Platonic" encroachment into the *Meno*,[8] along with recollection and the immortality and transmigration of the soul. The "method," however, is neither really new nor really "Platonic."[9] If one looks away from the

6. Socrates never suggests that craftsmen or statesmen help anyone "recollect."

7. However hypothetical method is understood here, it is certainly not the same as the method at *Phdo.* 100 that goes by the same name. Nor is it like the hypothetical method that appears in *Rep.* 7 or *Parm.* 136. See Robinson (1953), 122.

8. According to Robinson (1953), 122, what makes the method of hypothesis "an important methodological breakthrough" is that it attempts to say something positive about virtue. Yet although the method does, in fact, initially say something positive about virtue, namely, that it is knowledge, it ends up saying something negative about it, namely, that it is not knowledge. The complete argument is as follows. If virtue is knowledge, then it is teachable; there is nothing good or beneficial besides knowledge; virtue is good and beneficial; hence, virtue is knowledge. But if virtue is knowledge, then it is teachable; in anything teachable, there are teachers and pupils; there are no teachers or pupils of virtue; virtue is not teachable; hence, virtue is not knowledge.

9. Vlastos (1991a), 123, contends that this new method requires the "scuttling" of the elenchus. Yet elenchus thrives in the latter part of the dialogue (along with the

method's new name and looks instead at the argument presented in its name, one sees just how old and familiar this method is. Indeed, at the end of the *Protagoras*, and on the very same issue, Socrates explicitly commends this procedure: he observes at *Prot.* 361a–b that the best way to prove that virtue is teachable is to prove that every virtue—justice, temperance, courage, and so on—is knowledge and, similarly, that the best way to prove that virtue is not teachable is to prove that these virtues are not knowledge. The *Charmides*, too, employs the hypothetical method. At *Charm.* 169d, Socrates and Critias, in order that the argument be able to proceed, *assume* that a science of science is possible—leaving for a later time the investigation into whether or not this is so—and go on to consider how such a science would enable one to distinguish what one knows from what one does not know. In neither of these cases is there an intimation that elenchus is or will have to be abandoned for a new method; in both instances it is presupposed that the inquiry will proceed, as always, by elenchus.

More significant, however, than the examples of hypothetical method unearthed in other dialogues is the one that has already occurred in the *Meno* itself. In his recapitulation of the slave-boy-demonstration at *M.* 85b–86b (as interpreted in Chapter 3, Section iv), Socrates introduced the following question: what must the slave-boy have at present in his soul for it to be possible for him to recollect (that is, to recover knowledge out of himself just by being asked questions) in the future? His hypothesis was: if the slave-boy already has knowledge in his soul, recollection in the future is possible; if not, not. Socrates then considers the conditions under which the slave-boy might already have knowledge in his soul. He determines that the slave-boy fails to satisfy those conditions. And he concludes that the slave-boy will, therefore, not recollect in the future. The pattern of this argument anticipates the pattern of the argument that runs from *M.* 87b to *M.* 98a, in connection with which it is identified (*M.* 86e3) as "starting from a hypothesis." In this latter argument, Socrates raises the following question: what would have to be the case if virtue is to be teachable? His hypothesis is: if virtue is knowledge, then it is teachable; if not, not.[10] Socrates then consid-

familiar *technē* model for knowledge and teachability, which was also presumably abandoned in favor of recollection [see n. 4]).

10. In my view, the full hypothesis upon which the investigation proceeds is as follows: "If virtue is knowledge, then it is teachable; if virtue is not knowledge, then it is not teachable." In order to do as the geometers do, Socrates proposes that he

ers the conditions under which virtue would be knowledge. He determines that virtue fails to satisfy those conditions. And he concludes that virtue is, therefore, not teachable. Interestingly, not only do both arguments follow the same course, but there is a strong

and Meno test for the teachability of virtue on the assumption that anything that is knowledge is teachable and anything that is not knowledge is not. On that hypothesis, they will investigate whether virtue is knowledge: if it turns out that it is, they can answer the teachability question in the affirmative; if not, not. The hypothesis "if virtue is knowledge, then it is teachable; and if not, not," has its precise counterpart in the geometry case, in which, too, the hypothesis takes the form of a conditional: if p, then q; if $\sim p$, then $\sim q$ (see *M.* 87a1–b1). In my view, by calling something a hypothesis, Socrates intends neither to suggest that it is uncertain nor even to imply that it is something that serves as the argument's starting point; what he intends to convey is that it is something whose truth will not be questioned in the argument: once it is agreed to, it is set. Thus, there is one other proposition called a hypothesis in the argument even though it is neither uncertain nor the starting point of the argument but simply an assertion not open to question once it is accepted by Meno: at *M.* 87d2–3, Socrates calls "virtue is good" a hypothesis. By contrast, the proposition that virtue is knowledge does not, though many scholars maintain that it does, bear the label "hypothesis" in this argument: it does not qualify as a hypothesis (and certainly not as *the* hypothesis) for the very reason that it is the proposition tested; it is not one whose truth is assumed. Therefore, it is not correct to derive from the passage at *M.* 89c3–4, "And it is clear, Socrates, according to our hypothesis, since virtue is knowledge, that it is teachable," that the hypothesis of this section is "virtue is knowledge." For even here, the hypothesis, though unstated, is "if virtue is knowledge, that it is teachable." What Meno means is that given their hypothesis that if virtue is knowledge, then it is teachable, it follows from virtue's having been shown to be knowledge that virtue is teachable. That this is the correct reading is supported by the passage *M.* 89d3–5, where Socrates says that he still does not doubt that virtue is teachable if indeed it is knowledge. He implies here that whereas the hypothesis remains firm for him (that is what hypotheses do) the testable proposition that virtue is knowledge is in doubt. Another passage where the referent of "hypothesis" is unclear occurs at *M.* 87b4. Here, too, I believe, it is the whole "if . . . then" proposition that is intended; if so, the virtue hypothesis perfectly parallels the geometrical hypothesis at *M.* 87a3 (referred to again at 87b1). (Friedländer [1945], 255, contends that the parallel with the geometrical example requires that one take "it," *auto,* at *M.* 87b5 as the object of "hypothesizes" and read "hypothesizing it," where the "it" refers to "virtue is knowledge." On this point alone Bluck [1961a], 325, disagrees with him. Bluck contends, rightly in my view, that the "it" is the object of "let us consider," *skopōmen,* and refers to virtue.) For a fuller discussion of the issue of what Socrates' hypothesis is, see Robinson, who claimed in his first edition of *Plato's Earlier Dialectic* (1941) that the hypothesis is the conditional "if virtue is knowledge, then it is teachable," but then changed his mind in his second edition (1953), 114–22, as a result of criticism he received from Cherniss (1947), 140, and Friedländer (1945), 255. Stokes (1963), 297–98, argues that Robinson should have held to his earlier view, as do Zyskind and Sternfeld (1976), 132. See also Rose (1970), 3–5. Sharples (1985), 167, sides with Cherniss and Friedländer against Robinson's earlier view, but his translation, both as it appears in the text and as it is quoted in his notes, supports the earlier view with which he claims to disagree.

resemblance between their respective results as well: in both cases, Socrates abandons knowledge to settle for true opinion in its stead.

Although the hypothetical method is nothing new and is, therefore, hardly the cataclysmic event that scholars have taken it for, Socrates does, admittedly, introduce it with much fanfare. He associates it with the method of the geometers and illustrates it by way of a geometrical problem that still has scholars scratching their heads as they attempt to reconstruct it.[11] The elaborate pomp with which the method of hypothesis is ushered into the dialogue is, however, surely for Meno's sake. First, as we have had occasion to note, Meno has some measure of mathematical sophistication, of which he is clearly quite proud. Second, the hypothetical method as practiced in geometry promises success: if Meno believes Socrates' method is like that of the geometers, he will trust that his question about virtue will be answered just as surely as the geometers answer their geometrical one. (As in the slave-boy-demonstration, so now, too, however, there is no reason to expect comparable results in virtue and geometry. The hypothesis in virtue will introduce, as in geometry, a proposition to be tested; but the geometrical test will yield results that are certain; the virtue test will not. As long as we do not know what virtue is, we will not know—even if we test "from a hypothesis"—if virtue is teachable.) Third, Meno is, as we know, fond of the *tragikē*, of the dramatic and ostentatious;[12] he is appeased and his resistance is disarmed when he is catered to and flattered by the presentation of an arcane mathematical problem. We recall his saying to Socrates after having been given the effluences definition of color, "But I would stay, Socrates, if you were to give me many answers like this" (*M.* 77a1–2). It is no wonder, then, that Meno scarcely notices—and far less thinks to object to—Socrates' replacement (courtesy of Meno's "small concession") of Meno's question (is virtue taught?) with Socrates' own (is virtue a kind of wisdom or knowledge?). As we shall see, however, Socrates' propo-

11. Lloyd (1992), 181, argues that since Plato's math skills were not poor, the example's obscurity must be viewed as deliberate. Why, he asks, is Plato deliberately obscure? Because "we stand in need of initiation." In Lloyd's view, the initiation is for Plato's readers b: cause "Meno was too impatient for initiation."

12. Vlastos (1991), 123, calls the example "ostentatiously technical" and thinks Plato "is preening himself on his own expertise in geometry." In my view, it is not that Plato is preening himself but rather that Socrates is pandering to Meno's need to preen himself—especially in the wake of the slave-boy's success in the slave-boy-demonstration.

sition that virtue is knowledge is not really, as he pretends, just a means to the end of testing virtue's teachability; he has a stake of his own in it. The concession he asks of Meno, then, is not as small as he would have it appear.[13]

ii. Is Virtue Knowledge?

Socrates provides a rather extended argument for the proposition "virtue is knowledge." The basic structure of the argument is as follows:

1. Virtue is good/beneficial.
2. If nothing else is good/beneficial besides wisdom,[14] then virtue will be (some) wisdom.
3. No goods, whether goods of the soul or goods not of the soul, are either harmful or beneficial in themselves: they are made bad by the addition of folly; they are made good by the addition of wisdom.
4. Nothing but wisdom is [unqualifiedly or always] good/beneficial.
∴5. Virtue is either the whole of, or a part of, wisdom.

Socrates provides an interesting, if somewhat odd, amalgam of goods in connection with (3). Some are old, some new; some are fairly stock goods found in other such lists, others rather unusual— selected, it would seem, just for Meno. The goods not associated with the soul are health, strength, good looks, and wealth. The soul-related goods are temperance, justice, courage, the ability to learn easily (*eumathia*), good memory, and magnificence. Twice before,

---

13. As Canto-Sperber (1991), 281, points out, Socrates' request for Meno's concession is, in context, no pis aller: once Socrates gives up hope of considering with Meno the *ti esti* question, the concession he asks of Meno constitutes his *preference* for how to proceed. This passage resembles *M*. 84a, where Socrates tells the slave-boy to point if he does not wish to calculate. In both cases, Socrates settles for something other than his first choice, but given that he cannot have his first choice, the alternative he proposes is one that he favors over others.

14. Socrates seems to use indiscriminately in this argument *epistēmē* (knowledge), *nous* (intelligence), and *phronēsis* (practical wisdom); later on, *sophia* (wisdom) is used as well. (A similar conflation occurs later between true opinion and right opinion.) I have no good answer for why he does so, although I assume there is one. I do see, however, how the extensive use of *phronēsis* for *epistēmē* helps pave the way for the claim that the practical value of true opinion (or perhaps of true opinion as "right" opinion) is equivalent to that of *epistēmē*.

earlier on in the dialogue, similar lists appeared. At *M.* 74a, when Meno mistakenly identified justice with the whole of virtue and Socrates asked him if there are no others, Meno enumerated courage, temperance, wisdom (*sophia*), and magnificence (*megaloprepeia*) as the other virtues. And at *M.* 78c, where Socrates mentioned the standard goods health and wealth, Meno brushed past health and, for his part, counted as goods such things as acquiring gold and silver, as well as political honor and office (*M.* 78c7–8). We can see, then, that Socrates includes at *M.* 88a nearly, but not all, the virtues and goods mentioned in the earlier passages, and adds some new ones as well.

If we look at the goods *not* of the soul, we see that Socrates has, again, included health among them. Once health is included, strength is a natural addition. Good looks are a standard enough "good," but *Meno*'s good looks, we may note, figure rather prominently in the dialogue: they are alluded to by Socrates as being in part responsible for Meno's overbearing ways. (In this way, good looks serve to illustrate what is to be Socrates' point: the "goods" named are not necessarily good or beneficial; when not directed by wisdom, when not used rightly, they can actually be bad and harmful.) Although Socrates allows wealth a place on the list (it made his earlier list at *M.* 78c as well), he conspicuously omits political honor and office.[15]

As we turn to the goods of the soul, we find the three cardinal virtues of temperance, justice, and courage, plus three more: *eumathia*, good memory, and magnificence. Somewhat surprisingly, Socrates says of all these "goods," including the virtues of temperance, justice, and courage, that unless they somehow are knowledge, they cannot count as genuine goods, since they can all, when separated from knowledge and right use, end up doing harm. Yet were not two of these goods, temperance and justice, found, in the dialogue's early attempts to define virtue, to be "parts" of virtue that were necessary (and, finally, even sufficient) conditions for the presence of virtue itself?[16] What Socrates must be doing, then, in his current list of goods is identifying a conventional way of conceiving of courage

15. It is interesting, though, that in speaking to Meno he ends by stressing wealth: "and wealth, of course," *kai ploutos dē* (*M.* 87e7).

16. Courage, a part of virtue not mentioned earlier, is mentioned now, probably because Socrates' immediate goal here is not, as it was earlier, to challenge Meno's elitism. Piety, by contrast, has been dropped—but probably for a similar reason. Piety, unlike courage, is, after all, one of the humbler virtues. See Chapter 1, n. 56.

and temperance (and ability to learn easily)[17] according to which these goods of the soul do not necessarily involve any sort of wisdom. And so conceived, even the cardinal virtues would not be, for Socrates, really goods, since they would not be, in themselves, always beneficial. If courage and temperance are to qualify as goods, a different conception of them is required—the Socratic conception—according to which each is, in some sense, wisdom. Since on this latter conception of them, the possibility that they could be exercised foolishly is excluded, they would qualify as genuine goods.[18]

The three additions, *eumathia*, good memory, and magnificence, make their appearance here largely to indulge Meno. Magnificence is something that Meno proposed earlier (at *M.* 74a) as one of the virtues. Not a stock Socratic/Platonic virtue (it does not appear in the lists at *Euthyd.* 279a–c, *Gorg.* 451e and 467e, *Prot.* 354b, or *Rep.* 2.357b–c and 367c–d), it is, instead, a virtue that reflects Meno's fascination with the grand.[19] Good memory, though incontestably a fine quality (as in *Theaet.* 144a–b), is also not regularly featured as a standard good in the various lists of conventional goods (it, too, fails to make any of the lists noted above); it appears here, no doubt, because of Meno's purportedly prodigious memory. By including it, Socrates flatters Meno: he assures him that at least one of the goods of the soul is a good that he possesses in abundance. *Eumathia*, usually rendered "quickness of mind" (Guthrie [1956]), "ability to learn easily" (Sharples [1985]), or "quickness in learning" (Day [1994]), also means, however, "docility" (Klein [1965]). Socrates, perhaps, puns on this word—at Meno's expense: Meno is, as we have seen, hardly a quick learner (though he may be a quick memorizer); what he both is and wants to be is passive in learning—one who uncritically imbibes the words of others, one who is, indeed, docile. He raises objections only when either he, personally, or the views he holds—views of others that he has committed to memory and thus

17. *Eumathia* is a peculiar good to lump together with courage and temperance. But Socrates apparently wants what he says to apply both to the standard list of virtues and to the three ad hoc additions.

18. Perhaps Socrates cannot see how justice might be exercised foolishly. If justice is, for that reason, necessarily wisdom, it might automatically count as an unqualified good of the soul.

19. Socrates says of Gorgias at the dialogue's opening (*M.* 70b6–c1) that he has gotten the Thessalians into the habit of answering fearlessly and "magnificently," *megaloprepōs*, any time they are asked a question. But Socrates points out that answering this way is a reasonable thing to do (only) for those who have knowledge.

made his own—are threatened. In Meno's case, then, memory and *eumathia*—as docility—go hand in hand.

Given his docility, Meno is sympathetic to Socrates' argument that virtue is wisdom. Since Meno is only too happy to learn from others, it suits him fine that virtue be a form of wisdom, and hence teachable. Socrates, however, does not let this proposition stand; indeed, he deliberately brings about its dissolution. Let us sketch in brief how the proposition "virtue is knowledge" is made to unravel.

Once Socrates determines that virtue is wisdom, he goes on to draw the immediate inference that virtue does not come by nature (*M.* 89a6–7), assuming, apparently, that wisdom does not come by nature. (Since right from the start [*M.* 70a1–4], Meno distinguished what is *matheton/didakton* from what comes by nature, *phusei*, it is unlikely that he would resist the notion that wisdom or knowledge does not come *phusei*.) Despite the decisiveness of this inference, Socrates, nevertheless, sees fit to supply an additional argument in order to cement the idea that virtue does not come by nature. He points out that if virtue were natural, good children would be discernible early on; there would be people to discern them; and every effort would be expended to shield them from corruption so that they grow up to be useful to their cities (*M* 89b1–7).

Unlike the first argument, an argument so succinct as to require no assumption other than that wisdom does not come by nature, this supplementary argument contains so many undefended assertions that its soundness, even its bare plausibility, defies assessment. Indeed, Meno pays it no mind: he concludes that virtue is teachable simply on the grounds that virtue is knowledge (*M.* 89c2–4), a proposition for which Socrates had argued earlier.

Socrates' efforts in the second argument are not without purpose. Through it Socrates conveys what it would mean for virtue really to come "by nature." For virtue to come by nature is, as is now clear, for it to come solely by nature, without being supplemented by teaching.[20] If virtue were really natural, Socrates says, it would be so noticeable in those who have it that surely some people would notice it. Moreover, those who had it would simply have it; their virtue would require no development, no work or effort. For the gifted

---

20. As we shall see in Section iv, when a young man who has natural ability in a particular skill (Cleophantus, the son of Themistocles, is used as an example) develops his talents in that area by being taught, Socrates regards the discipline in which the young man excels as a teachable—not a natural—one (*M.* 93d1–6).

child to grow up to be virtuous and, as such, useful to his city, all that would be needed is that he be sequestered and protected from corruption. (It is the promise of future usefulness, no doubt, that would provide the inducement for strangers to care for the good-by-birth youth in this way.)[21] Socrates contends that since no such thing as he has described in fact happens, virtue does not come by nature.

Socrates, we note, draws from his finding that virtue is not natural the conclusion that virtue must come by learning, *mathēsei*: "Then, since good men are not good by nature, is it not by learning?" (*M.* 89b9–c1). For Meno, however, as we saw, this conclusion follows from their earlier hypothesis (if virtue is knowledge, it is teachable) and from the conclusion of Socrates' earlier argument (virtue *is* knowledge). Since Meno sees no difference between something's coming by learning and something's coming by teaching, he immediately agrees to Socrates' conclusion that virtue comes by learning: "That [that virtue comes by learning] now seems necessary to me; and it is clear, Socrates, according to our hypothesis, since virtue is knowledge, that virtue is teachable" (*M.* 89c2–4).[22]

Meno, as we have seen,[23] regularly conflates learning with teaching: (a) his opening question at *M.* 70a equates the option that virtue is "taught," *didakton*, with the option that it is "learned," *mathēton;* (b) it is this conflation that, at least in part, motivates his paradox at *M.* 80d; and (c) he takes Socrates' contention that all learning is recollection (that is, that it does not involve teaching) to entail that "we do not learn" (*M.* 81e4–5). That Socrates concludes from virtue's not being "natural," *phusei, not* that it is "teachable," *didakton*, but that it comes to men by "learning," *mathēsei*, signals his commit-

---

21. The parallels to certain aspects of how the *Republic* would have budding philosopher-kings treated have been noted by Thompson (1901), 162–63. In particular, the idea in the *Meno* that these young children are to be guarded like precious gold is reminiscent of the metals metaphor in *Rep.* 3. There are differences, however. For example, whereas the "golden" children of the *Republic* are to be educated rigorously until well into middle age, the children in the *Meno* need only be shielded from corruption. Cf. the *Peri Aretēs*, according to which the young are to be kept from the harm (*phlauron*) that might come from war (*machē*) or any other danger (*kindunos*) but not specifically, as in the *Meno*, from corruption (*M.* 89b6). (The *Peri Aretēs* is a short dialogue of unknown date and authorship. Its basic argument follows the general contours of the *Meno*'s argument. Moreover, the dialogue reproduces almost verbatim entire sections of the dialogue. Its main character is Socrates; different manuscripts, however, pair him with different interlocutors.)

22. Brague (1978), 201, notes the difference between Socrates' question at *M.* 89c1 about whether virtue comes from learning and Meno's answer at *M.* 89c3 that virtue is teachable.

23. See the beginning of Chapter 3.

ment, once again, to the difference between learning and being taught. It is this difference that lies at the heart of elenctic examination: in elenchus, one learns—though without being taught. When, then, Socrates reverses, as he is about to do, his initial conclusion that virtue is knowledge, we need not suppose that he means to concede, at the same time, that virtue is not learned.

Meno, as was noted above, finds the notion that virtue is teachable pleasing. Thus, when Socrates, for no apparent reason, seeks to undermine this conclusion, "Well, perhaps; but maybe we did not do well in agreeing to this" (*M.* 89c5–6), Meno protests: "But it just now seemed that we spoke well" (*M.* 89c7). Why, we must wonder, does Socrates suddenly find it doubtful that virtue is teachable?

Socrates explains his doubts, not by identifying any flaw in the argument he presented for "virtue is knowledge," but by suggesting that there may be neither teachers nor pupils of virtue. If there are neither teachers nor pupils, then, surely, virtue is not teachable. Furthermore, if virtue is not teachable, then, alas, it is not knowledge after all.

If Socrates thinks that virtue's teachability, as well as its status as knowledge, can be toppled by the empirical observation that there are no teachers of it, why, then, did he insist on approaching the question of virtue's teachability by way of the hypothesis that would have virtue's teachability depend solely on whether or not it is knowledge? If he can test directly the proposition "virtue is teachable" by checking to see if there are teachers of it, and if he is going to allow that test, and not the one "from a hypothesis," to decide the matter, why did he need to consider virtue's association with knowledge at all?

It is clear that Socrates must have his own reasons for introducing the proposition that "virtue is knowledge," reasons having nothing to do with his needing to answer Meno's question concerning virtue's teachability. Socrates must want, for his own purposes, to establish links (a) between virtue and benefit, (b) between wisdom and benefit, and (c) between virtue and wisdom. Socrates must want to make the point that in theory, even if not in fact, virtue *is* knowledge, and that in principle, even if not in fact, virtue *is* teachable. Were it possible for human beings to know virtue, those same human beings could teach it. The reason virtue is not actually taught is, quite simply, that it is not known. The absence of teachers shows, not what is theoretically impossible, but what is factually so. Human beings have no access to moral knowledge; that is why there are no teachers of virtue. Moral wisdom is, as Socrates says in the *Apology*, wisdom

greater than human. Until such time as either ordinary human beings somehow gain access to wisdom greater than human or extraordinary human beings do so,[24] what is teachable in principle will, of
necessity, remain unteachable in fact.[25]

We note how emphatically Socrates maintains that if virtue is
knowledge, it *is* teachable: "That it is teachable if it is knowledge,
that I do not retract as not well said" (*M.* 89d3–5). He holds far less
vigorously that since there are no teachers and pupils of knowledge,
virtue is not teachable: "Then, conversely, if there were neither
teachers nor pupils of something, would we not be guessing well in
guessing (*kalōs . . . eikazontes eikazoimen*) that it is not teachable?" (*M.*
89e1–3).[26] The absence in fact of teachers and pupils is insufficient
to sever the connection between knowledge and teachability-in-
principle; what it can do—indeed, all it can do—is render virtue
unteachable in fact.[27]

If Socrates appreciates the tie that binds virtue, knowledge, and
teachability to each other, even if only in principle, why is he so
determined to eliminate teaching as a source for virtue? Why, having
established that virtue is wisdom, does he so quickly retreat from
that position, disqualifying it by way of the actual absence of teach-

24. Socrates raises, at the end of the dialogue, the possibility of the advent of
someone who, like Teiresias among the dead, is able to do what ordinary mortals
cannot, namely, make another like himself—in other words, teach virtue. Someone
among the living who is like Teiresias among the dead is someone who transcends
the Cave.

25. Andic (1971), 306–7, raises the question of just what follows from the absence
of teachers: even if it follows that virtue is not taught, why would it follow that virtue
is not teachable? Of course, the ambiguity in *didakton* only serves to confuse the matter
further. Koyré (1945), 17, contends that there is a deliberate flaw in the argument.
Bluck (1961a), 22–23, counters that the absence of teachers of virtue does constitute
reasonable grounds for assuming it not to be teachable. As I see it, the fact that there
are no teachers of virtue suggests, not that it is in principle unteachable, but that it
is unteachable in fact, that is, given the very real limitations of ordinary human beings.
Virtue would be taught if someone could teach it, but no one can. Meno should,
therefore, not expect to find a teacher of virtue.

26. We may compare this instance of guessing with one that occurs later, where
Socrates says, concerning his characterization of the difference between knowledge
and true opinion, that he speaks, not as one who knows, but as one who is guessing.
He does add, however, that when he says that right opinion is different from knowledge, he does not at all seem to be guessing, since this is one of the few things he
would claim to know (*M.* 98b1–5).

27. Though the *Protagoras* suggests, at *Prot.* 356–57, that virtue is knowledge and
that it is teachable—in the form of a hedonic calculus—the context strongly implies
that this is not a serious suggestion on Socrates' part. See Weiss (1990).

ers? The same impulse that motivates Socrates to eliminate, first, teaching as a way in which virtue comes to be in men motivates him to eliminate, second, as we have already seen and shall see again, "by nature," *phusei*, as well as, as we shall soon see, third, "spontaneously," *apo tou automatou.* That impulse is his concern for Meno. For were Meno to believe that any of these three ways is the way in which virtue comes to be in men, his chances for moral improvement would be seriously compromised. Were Meno to believe that virtue comes by teaching, he might head straight for the sophists, the only professional teachers of *aretē* there are; were he to believe that virtue comes by merely associating with the "right" people, which Socrates calls "spontaneously," Meno might simply seek out the company of such *kaloi kagathoi* (gentlemen) as Anytus; and were he to believe that virtue comes by nature, he might just do nothing, holding fast, with thoroughgoing complacency, to faith in his own innate excellence.

iii. Father and Son

"But do you not think there are teachers of virtue?" an incredulous (and not very perceptive) Meno asks Socrates at *M.* 89e4–5. Socrates says he has searched long and hard along with others for such teachers of virtue but has not found any (*M.* 89e7–9). Felicitously, just at that moment, Anytus sits down beside them.

Socrates proposes that he and Meno make the most of their good fortune and ask Anytus who the teachers of virtue might be. What qualifies Anytus to answer? Apparently, it is certain facts about his father, Anthemion. Anthemion is wealthy and wise and became wealthy neither "spontaneously," *apo tou automatou,*[28] nor by some-

---

28. "Spontaneously," *apo tou automatou,* suggests, in Plato, the absence of voluntary, purposeful action on the part of an agent; it conveys the idea of things happening of their own accord. It thus excludes willful intervention, even when divine. In the *Apology* (*Ap.* 41d2–3), for example, Socrates reassures his "judges" that his present troubles have arisen neither as a result of the gods' having no concern for a good man's troubles nor on their own, *apo tou automatou:* since the gods do have a hand in Socrates' predicament, his troubles cannot then be *apo tou automatou.* What is spontaneous is also by chance, *tuchēi,* though *tuchēi,* "by chance" or "by luck," does not preclude divine agency. At *M.* 99a, things that come out right by chance, *tuchēi,* are contrasted with things that come out right by *human* guidance, but the possibility that they might come out right by divine guidance remains open. For a somewhat different view of the relationship between "spontaneously" and "by chance," see Aristotle, *Physics* 2.6.

one's having given him a gift; he acquired his wealth, instead, by his own wisdom and diligence (*M.* 90a2–6); moreover, he conducts himself as a citizen in a way neither arrogant nor pompous nor offensive and is generally moderate and well behaved (*M.* 90a6–b1). Although Socrates will go on to say a few words about Anytus himself, he directs his attention first and primarily to Anytus's father. How can we explain Socrates' surprising initial interest, not in Anytus's qualities, but in those of Anthemion, when it is not Anthemion but Anytus whom Socrates will consult on the matter of whether or not there are teachers of virtue?

The following two suggestions might go some way toward providing an explanation. First, Socrates uses the father and son pair to illustrate in advance a point he is about to make, namely, that fathers do not transmit their virtue to their sons. For, unlike his father, Anytus *is* arrogant, pompous, offensive, quick to anger, and vindictive; he rushes to judgment without exercising reason and, as the reader is all too aware, is destined to slander and to persecute Socrates and to bring an unjust indictment against him, an indictment that will culminate in Socrates' execution. All Socrates seems to be able to say in Anytus's favor is that "the majority of the Athenians" *think* that Anthemion brought up and educated Anytus well and that they therefore elect him to the highest offices. That Anytus has a favorable reputation,[29] however, hardly means that it is deserved.[30] Anthemion may have tried to make Anytus a good man, but good fathers do not necessarily raise good sons.

Second, and more important, there can be little doubt that Socrates' unlikely interest in the sources of Anthemion's wealth points beyond itself to a more likely interest in the source of something else. What matters to Socrates is not how Anthemion did and did not become wealthy but how men do and do not become virtuous. Just as Socrates spoke, on the surface of the slave-boy-demonstration, about the slave-boy and geometry but, beneath the surface, about Meno and virtue, so, too, here Socrates speaks, on the surface, about

---

Aristotle, who focuses not on the agent but on the one who is affected, regards spontaneity as a broader category than chance; chance, he says, unlike spontaneity, can only affect those who are capable of good or bad fortune and action.

29. We shall see in the final section of this chapter that "good reputation," *eudoxia* (*M.* 99b11), is what the great politicians have that enables them to succeed. But that is not virtue.

30. Cf. *Gorg.* 487b6–7, where Socrates says to Callicles: "You are well enough educated, as many of the Athenians would attest."

Anthemion and wealth but, beneath the surface, about Meno and virtue.

The message hidden behind Socrates' assessment that Anthemion did not become wealthy either spontaneously or by being given a gift is, no doubt, that *virtue* does not come spontaneously or as a gift. "Spontaneously," *apo tou automatou*, is the term that Socrates will use at *M.* 92e7–8 to capture the haphazardness of what Anytus will describe as the way he believes one becomes virtuous, namely, by allowing oneself to be influenced by any Athenian "gentleman," *kalos kagathos*, one happens to meet. And being given a gift finds its counterpart in the "divine allotment," *theia moira*, by which virtue is said, at the dialogue's close, to come to be in those who are "without intelligence," *aneu nou* (*M.* 99e6). As we shall see, neither the chance absorption by the youth of the virtue of their elders nor what comes to men by divine allotment gives rise to genuine virtue: the former is erratic and unreliable, and the latter yields, not virtue, but its impostor, "good repute," *eudoxia*.

If, then, virtue does not come by associating with Athenian gentlemen or as a gift from the gods, how does it come? Again, we look to Anthemion. Anthemion, Socrates tells us, acquired his wealth by "wisdom," *sophia*, and "diligence," *epimeleia*. As we have seen, Socrates does indeed first identify virtue as wisdom: since nothing besides wisdom is always and essentially good and beneficial, and since virtue is always and essentially good and beneficial, virtue must be wisdom. Although he acknowledges one obstacle to virtue's being wisdom, namely, the absence of actual teachers and pupils of it, nevertheless, since teachability is never closed off as a theoretical possibility, that is, as an in-principle possibility, that virtue might be wisdom is also not ever quite ruled out: if ever a teacher of virtue were to arise, virtue would surely, then, be wisdom.

What, however, corresponds to "diligence," to *epimeleia?* The only thing that might correspond to diligence is true opinion, the alternative to knowledge that is paired with it from the time it is introduced at *M.* 96d5 as a practical guide no worse than knowledge, to *M.* 99b11, where Socrates abruptly replaces true opinion with "good repute," *eudoxia*. True opinion is, as we shall see, Socratic shorthand for elenctic investigation, which, when pursued with steady and abiding diligence, culminates in the discovery (or recovery) of true moral opinions.

iv. Are There Teachers of Virtue?

Socrates asks Anytus whether there are teachers and students of virtue. He informs Anytus that Meno wishes to acquire the kind of virtue that enables men to manage a household or city, to look after their parents, and to treat guests properly, whether these be of their own city or not (*M.* 91a). (The virtue to which Meno aspires is, we may note, a bit more "gentlemanly" in Socrates' description of it than it is in Meno's own. Meno himself expresses no interest in caring for parents and guests: he assigns care of the household to women. Meno craves wealth and political prominence and the concomitant ability to secure good for his friends and harm for his enemies and to render himself invulnerable to harm.)[31] Are there, Socrates wants to know, teachers of the gentlemanly virtue that Meno purportedly desires to attain? On analogy with other subjects in which there are professional experts to whom one can go if one wishes to learn—medicine, shoemaking, flute playing, horsemanship, wrestling—Socrates proposes, with respect to virtue, the purported professional virtue experts: the sophists.

Anytus is utterly appalled at the suggestion that sophists might be the appropriate teachers of virtue.[32] He is convinced that the sophists pose a grave danger to those who associate with them, and even cause their ruin. Socrates expresses surprise that sophists might differ so much from others who profess to teach a subject and charge a fee for their services: do these others also not only fail to bring benefit to what is entrusted to them but even destroy it? How, if Protagoras is so harmful, has he managed to earn more money alone than Phidias and ten other sculptors combined?[33] Moreover, how did

---

31. Socrates' and Meno's versions of what Meno wants to learn interestingly parallel Protagoras's and Gorgias's respective descriptions of what they teach. At *Prot.* 318e–319a, Protagoras describes his subject as the proper care of personal affairs, resulting in good management of one's own household, as well as of state affairs, resulting in one's becoming a real power in the city, both as speaker and as man of action. At *Gorg.* 452d, Gorgias describes his subject as something that brings freedom to mankind in general and to each man dominion, (*archein*) over others in his own city.

32. The term *sophistai*, used earlier at *M.* 85b4 for the geometers who call the line that extends from one corner of the square to the other the "diagonal," might just as easily have been called *geometrai*, as are the geometers who use hypothetical method (*M.* 86e4). Socrates' use of *sophistai* for both geometers and sophists calls attention to the gulf that separates "wise men" who are really experts at something from "wise men" who only profess to be.

33. The emphasis on the money Protagoras charges for supposedly teaching virtue

Protagoras get away with his malefactions? Those who repair old shoes and mend clothes would soon starve to death if they gave the clothes and shoes back in worse condition than they were in when received.[34] Surely someone in Greece in the forty-year span in which Protagoras plied his trade would have noticed the ruination of those entrusted to him.[35] How has it happened that Protagoras has not lost his good reputation? Do the sophists knowingly deceive and corrupt young men or are they unaware of what they do? Can it be that those whom some call the wisest of men are crazy enough to do so knowingly?[36]

Of course, virtue is hardly like shoe repair and clothes mending. It is not nearly as evident in the case of virtue as it is in the case of these and other *technai* who improves and who corrupts. That Protagoras retained his good reputation for forty years may well be true, but he was certainly not universally esteemed: Anytus is no fan of his, and as is clear from the *Protagoras* (*Prot.* 316c–d), sophists were regularly subjected to persecution. As we have already seen, Anytus, too, was well thought of by the Athenians. It is unlikely that the same Athenians who revered Anytus also held Protagoras in high regard. Insofar as one's reputation reflects the views of others, and insofar as there is unlikely to be unanimity of opinion in the matter of virtue, it is hardly surprising that one man's "virtue teacher" is another man's "corrupter of the young."

belies his claim to do so. The rewards of having morally upright associates are so great that no payment ought to be demanded. See *Gorg.* 520c–e. Also see *M.* 94c–d, where Socrates says that Thucydides would surely have taught his sons virtue, which requires no expenditure, since he had them taught all the things that do.

34. See *Gorg.* 514–15 and *Lach.* 186b for a similar point.

35. This passage is reminiscent of Socrates' earlier assumption that if children were good by birth someone would surely discern their goodness. It reminds us, too, of the defense Socrates used at his trial: none of those he presumably corrupted, he says, or their families have come forth to accuse him (*Ap.* 33c–34b).

36. It is unclear from the wording of the passage whether the sophists would be crazy to ruin young men deliberately or to do so unawares. But how could they be crazy if what they do they do unawares? To be crazy means deliberately to do something harmful or self-defeating. Thus, what is crazy is for sophists knowingly to corrupt those with whom they associate. See *Ap.* 25a–e, where Socrates asks if he is so much more ignorant than Meletus of the effect bad people have on their neighbors as intentionally to corrupt those with whom he associates. See also *Prot.* 327b, where Protagoras makes the point that since no one wishes to live among bad people, everyone makes it his business to teach virtue all the time. Cf. Bluck (1961a), 361, who thinks the sophists would be crazy in either case; and Klein (1965), 228, who thinks the sophists would be crazy in the case of corrupting others unawares. It is interesting that the word used for "unawares" is *lelēthenai*, "having forgotten." Might this be because, in the *Meno*, virtue is "recollected"?

Anytus's opinion of the sophists is not grounded in any actual experience of them, and he seems to believe that experience of them is unnecessary for assessing their worth; he is willing to rely upon hearsay alone. Socrates remarks that Anytus must be a prophet since he is able to divine the character of people with whom he is unacquainted. As we shall soon see, this is no compliment: prophets know what they know by divine inspiration, but without intelligence. Not only does Anytus's condemnation of the sophists reveal his lack of intelligence, but it shows him to be rash, unjust, and, moreover, unconcerned about his evident injustice. Indeed, what Socrates takes exception to in Anytus's evaluation of the sophists is not the substance of that evaluation—Socrates concedes that "perhaps there is something in what you say" (*M.* 92d8–e1)[37]—but the fact of Anytus's making it without having any hard evidence.[38] This is the man who will one day be Socrates' accuser.

Socrates next asks Anytus to name some Athenian to whom he thinks Meno ought to go—if he ought not to go to the sophists. Anytus refuses to name anyone in particular: any gentleman, any *kalos kagathos*, he claims, that Meno should "happen upon," *entuchei*, bar none, will make him better than the sophists will if he is willing to submit to their influence (*M.* 92e3–6).[39] Socrates wonders how these gentlemen got the virtue that they presumably teach others: did they get it "spontaneously," without having learned it from anyone? Whereas Anytus insists that these gentlemen must in turn have learned virtue from their predecessors, Socrates, it is clear, remains skeptical: there seems to be no teaching of virtue that accounts for the virtue that certain distinguished gentlemen manifest. And al-

37. Contra Kraut (1984), 226–27, who contends that Socrates rejects the idea "that the sophists are a corrupting influence. . . . In fact, Socrates welcomed the visits of Gorgias and Protagoras, for his conversations with them and their disciples allowed him to subject his own moral system to the most rigorous examination." That Socrates is able to benefit from conversing with Gorgias and Protagoras hardly precludes his thinking them corruptive. In the *Protagoras*, for example, does Socrates not worry about the potential harm that might befall the young Hippocrates as a result of his associating with the likes of Protagoras? Socrates uses his conversations with sophists to expose the weakness and dangers in their teaching—indeed, in their very claim to teach.

38. It is remarkable that Anytus claims not only to know what sophists are like but who they are as well: "At any rate, I know who these people are, whether I am without experience of them or not" (*M.* 92c4–5).

39. We may compare Anytus's belief that any Athenian Meno would happen upon would teach him virtue with Socrates' exaggerated comment at the dialogue's beginning (*M.* 71a) that any Athenian Meno might encounter would deny knowing both whether or not virtue is teachable and what virtue is.

though they teach their children every teachable skill, they clearly do not teach their children virtue—no doubt because it cannot be taught. How else can one explain the ordinary and undistinguished progeny of the likes of Themistocles, Pericles, Aristides, and Thucydides?

Two critical tensions arise between Socrates and Anytus in this exchange. (1) Socrates not only wants to know who the particular Athenian gentlemen are who pass their greatness on to others, but he also proceeds to name several distinguished men who failed to do so; Anytus resists singling out any particular man for distinction. (2) Socrates challenges Anytus's model of teaching virtue, according to which all gentlemen learn from and teach all others. The clear implication of Socrates' question regarding how the gentlemen who "teach" achieved their virtue is that they themselves were not taught but in fact came by their virtue "spontaneously." Moreover, insofar as they themselves were not taught, they cannot teach: all virtue manifested by those who associate with them is spontaneous—a matter of chance or luck.

Evident in Anytus's view are his democratic leanings. On the model of teaching virtue that he espouses, the teaching and learning of virtue are not limited to a few but are universal. Any gentleman can teach, he claims; any young man can learn (if he is open to being influenced). One generation as a whole teaches the next. Socrates is at pains to point out, however, that (a) the mass teaching and learning that Anytus depicts is not true to the facts (the distinguished men who have undistinguished sons could not teach them virtue), and (b) mass teaching is not teaching: what Anytus describes is the directionless, haphazard, luck-of-the-draw kind of transmission of virtue that takes place *in the absence of* teaching and learning.

The "spontaneous" acquisition of virtue is the democratic counterpart to the aristocratic "by nature" that Socrates had already discussed with Meno. Indeed, the notion of spontaneous virtue arises only during Socrates' discussions with the democratic Anytus; the notion of natural virtue, considered twice, at *M.* 89a–b and at *M.* 96c–d, arises only during his discussions with the aristocratic Meno. Whereas it serves Meno's aristocratic interest to reserve virtue for those naturally born to it, it serves Anytus's democratic purpose to maintain that virtue passes from the many good men of the past and present to those who regularly associate(d) with them.[40] But, Socrates maintains, virtue comes neither by birth nor by osmosis.

---

40. Anytus's view that all gentlemen are effective teachers of virtue is reminiscent

The possibility of acquiring virtue spontaneously, though new to the *Meno*, appears elsewhere in Plato: in the *Protagoras*. Indeed, the notion of spontaneous virtue arises in the *Protagoras* in precisely the same context as that in which it is considered here, that of good men being unable to teach others—in particular, being unable to teach their own children—virtue. In the *Protagoras* (at 320a), Socrates contends that Pericles, rather than teach his two sons virtue, allows them to "browse around like cattle" on the chance that they will pick up virtue "spontaneously." This way of acquiring virtue surely can be identified neither with nature nor with teaching: not with nature because it is assumed that the boys do not already possess virtue but have yet to acquire it, and not with teaching because there is no specific teacher to whom their education in virtue is entrusted.[41] Indeed, when Protagoras seeks to prove—against Socrates[42]—that virtue is teachable and acquired by "diligence," *epimeleia,* he points to its being commonly regarded as neither natural nor spontaneous. What is teachable is, then, neither natural nor spontaneous.[43]

Anytus bristles at Socrates' suggestion that Athenian gentlemen are not teachers of virtue; he takes it as an indication that Socrates

---

of the view Socrates elicits from Meletus in the *Apology,* namely, that the members of the jury—indeed, the entire Athenian population—are able to educate the young and make them better (*Ap.* 24e4–5). We note that, for Socrates, as a rule it is the many who corrupt and the few who improve. One reason, then, that Socrates tends to cast his gaze in the sophists' direction when seeking possible teachers of virtue is that at least they are the few.

41. Cf. *Euthyd.* 282c2: " 'Yes, Cleinias,' I said, 'if only wisdom can be taught, if only it is not something that comes to men spontaneously.' "

42. Protagoras thinks that despite its wholesale transmission, virtue is still taught: "But as it is, you are spoiled, Socrates, in that all are teachers of virtue to the best of their ability, and so you think that no one is" (*Prot.* 327e).

43. Note here that in the *Protagoras, epimeleia,* along with practice, (*askēsis*) and teaching (*didachē*) (*Prot.* 323d6–7), is contrasted with the pair "spontaneous and natural" (*Prot.* 323c5–6). Thus, the contrast in the *Meno* between wealth that one comes by spontaneously and wealth acquired "through *epimeleia*" has its counterpart in the *Protagoras* in the case of virtue. Protagoras also pairs "natural" with "by chance," *tuchēi* (*Prot.* 323d1). It is quite likely that Protagoras regards "spontaneously" as a species of *tuchēi.* The association of the spontaneous acquisition of virtue with luck or chance is preserved in Socrates' use of *perituchōsin,* "browsing," at *Prot.* 320a3 to indicate that the "browsing" children may "chance" upon virtue "spontaneously." Cf. *M.* 92e7–8, where Socrates immediately links the notion of spontaneity to Anytus's remark (*M.* 92e3–5): "any Athenian gentleman whom he chances upon (*entuchēi*) will make him better than the sophists will." Luck is associated at the end of the *Meno* with divine dispensation and good repute. See n. 28.

doubts that there have been good men in Athens. Once again, Anytus is quick to lay blame without reason—at least without reason so
far as he knows.[44] His earlier assessment of sophists was essentially
correct, but he had no adequate grounds for it; his current suspicion
that Socrates is no admirer of Athenian gentlemen is right, too, but
again, at least at the time he voices it, without warrant. Socrates will,
momentarily, in his reply to Anytus's accusation, say something that
might well have warranted Anytus's suspicion—had it occurred before the fact. Socrates will say that he believes that there both are
and have been men in Athens good *at political affairs*; he conspicuously avoids saying that he believes there both are and have been
good men (simpliciter) in Athens.[45] As we learn from the *Gorgias*
(517b–519d), those who rule successfully gratify the people by build-
ing them docks and walls; but as we know from the *Meno*, until we
determine how these men stand in respect of justice, temperance,
and courage, we do not really know if they are good men.[46]

The sophists, then, are discounted by Anytus as teachers of virtue;
Socrates, in turn, disqualifies Athenian gentlemen. Thus, neither
paying dearly for sophistic instruction nor associating, gratis, with
Athenian gentlemen will reliably result in virtue. In other realms,
that is, in "all the things that depend[ed] on good teachers" (*M.*
93d6), someone like Cleophantus, the son of Themistocles, who is
not deficient in natural ability (*M.* 93d9–10), can be trained and
become accomplished; it is virtue alone that remains elusive. And it
is not from a lack of will on the part of fathers to make their children
good that they do not teach them virtue: if they spare no expense
in having them taught what is teachable, why would they not teach

44. Ryle (1976), 2, sees no reason for Anytus to become angry. But given the way
Anytus understands the teaching of virtue, it is no small thing for Socrates to say that
it is not taught. As Taylor (1948), 142, notes, since Anytus understands the teaching
of virtue to be "simply a matter of imbibing an hereditary tradition," he interprets
Socrates' denial of this teaching as a denial that there have been good men in Athens.

45. Anthemion may be the only (unphilosophical but still) good man in the dialogue; and he is no politician—just a good citizen. It is Anytus, the bad man, who is
a politician, elected to the highest offices. We shall see later that being truly good
and beneficial to one's city is also distinct from being good at political affairs: when
Socrates considers at *M.* 98 how men come to be good and come to bring benefit to
their cities (as opposed to being politically "successful," *katorthōsin* [*M.* 99c9]), he adds
the qualifier, "if such men exist," *eiper eien* (*M.* 98c9).

46. We may note that in the *Gorgias*, Socrates says of these men (Themistocles,
Cimon, and Pericles): "For they have paid no attention to temperance and justice"
(*Gorg.* 519a).

them themselves what can be taught at no expense? Would not a well-connected and powerful man like Themistocles have hired someone to make his sons good—if, that is, virtue could be taught?[47]

Anytus—again without justification—accuses Socrates of speaking ill of people. He reacts this time with a threat: good *or ill*, he says, can be done to people in this city as in others (*M.* 94e6–95a1). Socrates diagnoses Anytus's condition as follows: "Anytus is angry because he thinks I am speaking ill of these men and he thinks he is one of them. If he ever comes to know what kind of thing speaking ill is, he will stop being angry; but at present he does not know" (*M.* 95a2–6). Socrates refers, of course, to the slander that Anytus will, in due time, level against him. When Anytus sees what true slander is—presumably, a vicious lie as opposed to an unpleasant truth—he will perhaps realize that Socrates has slandered no one. That is when his anger will abate.[48]

It is now time to bring the message home to Meno. Do the gentlemen in his part of the world teach young men virtue; do they assert that they are teachers of virtue or that virtue is teachable? Meno confesses that there is disagreement on the subject. Does Meno believe that sophists are teachers of virtue? Well, he is not sure; his view wavers—although he is most impressed with Gorgias, who ridicules those who undertake to teach virtue and limits his undertaking to making people clever at speaking. In order to clinch his case, Socrates cites a poet, Theognis—no doubt to satisfy Meno's craving for a quotable source—who, on Socrates' questionable interpretation, contradicts himself, speaking both as if virtue can, and as if it cannot, be taught: if one associates with noble men, Theognis says, you will learn noble things; but it is not possible to make a bad man good by teaching.

---

47. Socrates mentions—and dismisses—the possibility that Themistocles might have guarded his virtue jealously and not wished to pass it on to others, not even to his own son. Interestingly, in the *Peri Aretēs*, Socrates dismisses the possibility that jealousy might be keeping Themistocles, Thucydides, Aristides, and Pericles from teaching virtue, on the grounds that everyone wants to live among good men. Oddly, however, the argument concludes that only a truly good man would be willing to share his virtue. Is there equivocation here on "virtue"? Perhaps the kind of virtue that a man who is not truly good has and might not wish to share is a kind of political virtue that is not cooperative but competitive.

48. It is interesting to note that Socrates says in the *Apology* that he feels no anger toward the accusers who wrongfully brought about his execution, even though he indeed blames them for their evil intent (*Ap.* 41d–e).

Socrates now draws the long-awaited conclusion: if, on the one hand, those who do claim to be teachers of virtue are not universally recognized as such nor are they thought to know virtue or to be virtuous, and if, on the other, those who are acknowledged to be gentlemen sometimes do and sometimes do not believe virtue to be teachable, how could there be teachers of virtue? If it may, then, be asserted that neither sophists nor gentlemen are teachers of virtue, is there anyone else who might be? Meno can think of no one.

What the reader expects at this juncture is a simple ending along these lines: Well, if there are no teachers of virtue, then must we not agree, Meno, that virtue is not teachable? This is not, however, the ending we get. Instead, Socrates asks: "But if there are no teachers, neither are there learners (*mathētai*)?" (*M.* 96c1). Meno agrees. Socrates resumes: "But we have agreed that a thing of which there are neither teachers nor learners is not teachable?" Meno concurs. "And teachers of virtue appear nowhere?" Again, Meno agrees. But Socrates is not finished. At *M.* 96c8, he repeats, without even the slightest deviation, the question he asked at *M.* 96c1: "But if there are no teachers, neither are there learners?" Only when Meno once again assents, then and only then does Socrates conclude that virtue will not be teachable.

Why does Socrates stop the flow of the argument to ask—twice—whether, if there are no teachers of virtue, there are also no learners? It is not as if Socrates is about to launch an independent investigation to determine whether or not there are learners of virtue comparable to the one he undertook in checking for teachers of it. Yet if Socrates' only proof for the absence of learners *is* the absence of teachers, that is, if he *derives* the absence of learners solely from the absence of teachers, he could surely have drawn his conclusion that virtue is not teachable just from the discovery of the absence of teachers. Why then does Socrates ask twice if there are also no learners?

The only reason for Socrates to be so insistent in asking this question twice, in identical language, is to call attention to the possibility that there might indeed be learners without teachers, learning without teaching. Recollection theory was the first allusion to such a possibility: if there is a kind of learning that comes by recollection, there certainly can be learning without teaching. Socrates opened up the possibility a second time when, after arguing that virtue does not come by nature (for, if it did, someone would surely scout out and seal away the naturally good children), he suggested that it comes by *learning* (*M.* 89c1). The passage currently under discussion, then, is the third time. And we are about to encounter the fourth: in Socrates' identification of true opinion as a source of virtue distinct from knowledge.

v. True Opinion and *Aitias Logismos*

Confronted with Socrates' conclusion that virtue does not come by teaching, Meno is moved to raise as a possibility that there are no good men at all. And if there are good men, how, he wonders, do they come to be good (*M.* 96d1–4).

In answer to Meno's question, Socrates now hits upon true opinion as an alternative source for the goodness of good men. He and Meno, Socrates proclaims, have "absurdly" failed to recognize in true opinion a second way besides knowledge by which men conduct their affairs rightly and well (*M.* 96e1–5). Why does Socrates think that he and Meno are absurd? Their absurdity derives, no doubt, from the fact that although true opinion has been with them since the end of the slave-boy-demonstration, they failed to notice it until now. It was, after all, true opinions—not knowledge—that Socrates finally determined were latent in the slave-boy's soul and awakened by questioning. And it was these true opinions that would somehow, in the future, "become knowledges." Moreover, Socrates charged Meno to attempt to search for and to recollect the truth about the things that are—not the knowledge of them—that resides forever in the human soul. Like the slave-boy who cannot see the diagonal right under his nose, so Socrates and Meno, mired in talk of teachability and knowledge, lose sight of the answer that lies directly before them.

Meno does not see at first how anything but knowledge can guide aright (*M.* 97a8). Indeed, it was his resistance all along to anything less than the certainty and finality of knowledge that engendered his hostility to inquiry, the very hostility that gave rise to his paradox. In the face of Meno's resistance, Socrates must now offer a defense of true opinion as a practical guide not in the least inferior to knowledge.

Before turning to Socrates' defense of true opinion, we should pause for a moment to take the full measure of what Socrates is about to defend. In particular, we should note the remarkable—and anomalous (in Plato)—inflation in the *Meno* of the worth of true opinion.⁴⁹ What Socrates will argue is that for practical purposes, true opinion, for as long as one has it, is just as beneficial as knowledge. Nowhere else in Plato does true opinion enjoy such high praise. We may contrast, for example, with our *Meno* passage the following passage at *Rep.* 6.506c: "Haven't you noticed that all opinions without knowledge are ugly? The best of them are blind. Or do men who opine something without true intelligence seem to you any different from blind men who travel the right road?" (trans. Bloom [1968]). The *Republic* portrays even *true* opinions as ugly things; those who have them are like blind men who happen to take the right road. Insofar as this analogy makes reference to traveling on a road, it is, of course, immediately reminiscent of the *Meno*'s about-to-be-discussed road to Larisa. Yet in the *Meno*, those who have true opinion are presented as being, in their role as guides, not a whit less successful than those with knowledge. To speak of them as blind men, as the *Republic* does, is to disparage them in a way clearly foreign to the *Meno*'s representation of them.⁵⁰

Socrates' defense of true opinion consists largely of his adducing a single example in support of its worth. He contends that of two persons who might successfully guide others to Larisa or anywhere else, the one who "opines correctly," *orthōs doxazōn* (M. 97b1), though he has never been there and does not know the road, is as good a guide as one who does know it.

Several points are worth noting in connection with this example. First, the road to Larisa is presented as something that can be

49. See Gould (1955), 141.
50. True opinion fares far better in the *Symposium.* See *Symp.* 202a–204e, where true opinion stands midway between understanding and ignorance; all it lacks is the ability to render an account. (At *M.* 98a4, it is the closely related "working out the reason," *aitias logismos,* that distinguishes knowledge from true opinion.) Insofar as the philosopher, too, is intermediate between wisdom and ignorance, would not the philosopher, the one who loves wisdom but has not yet attained it, be the man of true opinion? Let us note, however, that nowhere in the *Symposium* is it suggested that true opinion is on a par, in *any* sense, with knowledge. One passage in the *Republic,* however, lists together, seemingly indiscriminately, true opinion, knowledge, and *nous,* of which it is said that they jointly constitute virtue and participate more in pure being, in what is always the same, immortal, and true, than do such things as food and drink (*Rep.* 9. 585b–c). One can only assume that Socrates puts together true opinion, knowledge, and *nous* here insofar as they are things of the mind as opposed to things of the body. It is not until the *Laws,* a dialogue in which the Forms fade from view and philosopher-kings are no longer sovereign, that true opinion gains in stature. As Stalley (1983), 47, notes: "The *Laws,* in keeping with its more practical focus, treats right belief as an acceptable alternative to knowledge (632c, 689a–e, 864a)."

known, as a possible object of human knowledge. Second, the road
to Larisa may be the object of both knowledge and true opinion:
unlike the *Republic,* then, the *Meno* does not pair different types of
cognition with different ontological categories.[51] Third, "having been
there" seems to be at least a necessary condition for knowing the
road as opposed to merely having a true opinion about it: it is said
of the guide who has true opinion that he "has never been there"
and (therefore) does not know it. (If having been there were a sufficient condition, then one who traveled to Larisa as a child, was
asleep at the time, paid no particular attention, has a poor memory,
is blind, or has a poor sense of direction would, nevertheless, have
to be said to know the way.) Fourth, there is a kind of recollection
involved in knowing the road to Larisa—recollection not, of course,
of prenatal knowledge but of former sense experience.

The way one knows the road to Larisa, then, seems most unlike
any of the ways of knowing discussed thus far. It is unlike recollection
as described in the myth insofar as nothing prenatal is recollected.
It is unlike the "recollection" in the slave-boy-demonstration since
the slave-boy did not recollect; he computed. It is unlike acquiring
knowledge by learning from professional experts and teachers who
teach one what they know. Moreover, it is unlike learning and being
taught simply by associating with good men (if this were possible).
Perhaps it most closely resembles knowing Meno, the example Socrates uses early on (*M.* 71b); it is reminiscent as well of the eyewit-
ness knowledge discussed in the *Theaetetus* (201c1). Far from being
paradigmatic of all ways of knowing, then, the way in which the road
to Larisa is known is paradigmatic of one kind of knowing, knowing
attained by one's having had prior direct acquaintance or sense experience of something. It is critical to note, further, that knowing
the road to Larisa is knowing something new that one never knew
before—one comes to know the way to Larisa by going there *in one's
current lifetime.* Moreover, as Socrates depicts it, knowing the road to
Larisa comes without any sort of reasoning or thinking; for that mat-

51. Crombie (1963), II, 50, thinks that in the *Meno,* both true opinion and knowledge can be of particulars. Sharples (1985), 11, contends as well that "the proposi-
tional content of true belief and knowledge may be the same." See also Teloh (1986),
158. Yet Gould (1955), 138, n. 1, contends that because the road to Larisa is a "particular" rather than a form, it is not really an example of knowledge. Gould's view
disregards too flagrantly, I think, Socrates' use of the road to Larisa example for the
express purpose of illustrating how something can be at once an object of knowledge
and of true opinion.

ter, it is a knowing that requires no working out of an *aitia*, that is, of a reason, cause, or explanation.

Socrates has even less to say about the nature of the true opinion that guides aright than he does about the nature of knowing. All we are told of the man who has true opinion, but not knowledge, of how to get to Larisa is that he has never been there.[52] Socrates does not dwell on the nature or source of this man's true opinion: regardless of its nature or source, true opinion, Socrates asserts, serves as an entirely reliable guide for as long as one has it.[53]

On the basis of his example, Socrates stands ready to conclude that "right opinion is no less beneficial than knowledge" (*M.* 97c4–5);[54] it is Meno who prevents him from doing so. Meno contends that a person who has true opinion would not consistently go right; only the person with knowledge would. The person with true opinion, he contends, goes right some of the time—but not all of the time (*M.* 97c6–8). Once Socrates points out to Meno, however, that the person who has true opinion does *always* go right—for as long, at any rate, as he has it—Meno errs in the other direction: he is now unable to see what advantage knowledge might have over true opinion.

In order to impress upon Meno the superiority of knowledge to true opinion, Socrates has recourse to the legendary statues of Daedalus. These statues, which Meno may not have encountered where he lives (as if anyone, anywhere, has!), tend to run away, says Socrates, unless they are tied down. In their untied state, they are worth no more than a runaway slave; when tethered, however, they are worth a great deal. True opinions, Socrates insists, are like such statues: they dislike staying put and want to run away; but if they are not prevented from running away, they are not worth much. To be of value, Socrates concludes, true opinions need to be "tied down" by someone's "working out the reason," *aitias logismōi* (*M.* 98a3–4). Socrates calls this process "recollection," in line, as he claims, with what was agreed "in what we said before" (*M.* 98a5). The effect of tying the true opinions down, Socrates continues, is that they first

52. Many commentators think that true opinion results from one's having been given directions by someone else. See Sharples (1985), 182; Thomas (1980), 201.

53. It is not until later, at *M.* 99a, that Socrates qualifies true opinion as a "human" guide, one that, as such, is not a product of luck or chance, of *tuchē*. See Klein (1965), 246, 252.

54. Socrates reaches this conclusion again at *M.* 98b7–9 and 98c1–3.

"become knowledges," *epistēmai gignontai*, and then become permanent. And that is why knowledge is more valuable than true opinion.

According to Socrates, then, the greater worth of knowledge lies in its staying power: true opinions are as good as knowledge for as long as one has them, but they are flighty—they do not, so to speak, "like" to stay put. Unless they are tied down, therefore, they cannot be relied upon to remain in place.

As we have just seen, Socrates identifies the tying-down process, the process by which true opinions "become knowledges," as one of "working out the reason." And he calls this process "recollection," asserting that he and Meno so agreed in what was said earlier. A scholar's immediate impulse upon encountering a phrase such as "as we have agreed in what we said before" is to scour the earlier text for said agreement.[55] As a result, several passages have emerged as contenders for the distinction of being the text in which "we said before" that *aitias logismos* is virtue. Cornford (1952), 125, points to the myth's "all reality is akin," according to which, as he says, if one starts from one proposition, one will uncover "the whole logical structure of truth." Most commentators see the agreement in the passage (*M.* 86c) in which repeated questioning is said to result in one's finally coming to know;[56] still others think "recollection" now, as earlier, refers to the entire process of coming to know.[57]

It must be acknowledged, however, that there really is no earlier mention of any "tying-down" process accomplished by "working out the reason." And since no such process was mentioned earlier, Socrates and Meno could hardly have agreed, in what was said earlier, that this process is recollection. By now, of course, "recollection" has been almost entirely emptied of meaning. Once Socrates abandons his erstwhile stark distinction between "recollectable" and "teachable," allowing it to make no difference "which term we use" (*M.* 87b9–c1), "recollection" becomes so loose and pliable that it can be made to fit virtually any process of learning or coming to know. Like

---

55. See *Gorg.* 499e, where Socrates reminds Callicles of Socrates' and Polus's former agreement that all action should be done for the sake of good things. This passage sends scholars scurrying to identify the precise passage where this agreement took place. As there is no earlier text to which the later passage unambiguously refers, scholars have not unanimously identified the same text.

56. See Vlastos (1965), 156–57; Gulley (1937), 14–15; Sharples (1985), 155; Bluck (1961a), 31–32. Nehamas (1985), 22, does not believe that we actually witness recollection in the dialogue, because, as he sees it, recollection occurs only when, after being asked further questions, the slave-boy at last reaches understanding.

57. See, for example, Hackforth (1955), 75.

the immortality of the soul that suddenly reappears in the recapitulation of the slave-boy-demonstration, to no real purpose (*M.*
86b2), so, too, "recollection" now reappears, it would seem, to no
real purpose. Socrates, in both places, revives a dead notion, hoping,
no doubt, to create thereby the illusion of constancy in his ever-
shifting argument.

Although "working out the reason," *aitias logismos,* as the process
by which true opinions become knowledges was neither mentioned
earlier nor, a fortiori, called "recollection," it may, nevertheless, have
been hinted at. We recall that in the recapitulation of the slave-boy-
demonstration, the identical odd expression, "become knowledges,"
epistēmai gignontai (*M.* 86a8 and 98a6), appears. As was noted in our
discussion of the recapitulation, the process by which recollected
true opinions will presumably, someday, become knowledges is left
unnamed and unexplicated. Perhaps now we can identify that formerly anonymous and undescribed process as *aitias logismos.* But
even if so, *aitias logismos* is not recollection. All recollection can do
is arouse what lies dormant in the soul; *it* certainly cannot be the
process by which newly awakened true opinions are converted into
knowledges.

Let us assume, then, that true opinions become knowledges by
being tied down through a process of *aitias logismos.* What might it
mean to say that true opinions about virtue guide aright, for as long
as one has them, but that they like to run away and are not of much
worth until they are tied down by working out the reason?

Although true opinions' purported predilection for running away
is most frequently taken to mean that true opinions are easily forgotten, is it not true of knowledge, too, that it can be forgotten?[58]
So if it is true opinions in particular that take flight, perhaps it is
not because we have fallible memories but rather because, without
knowledge, we lack the firm intellectual grip on our opinions that
would enable us to stand up for them when challenged: when our
views are challenged, we are as likely as not to surrender our current
opinions and trade them in for others.[59] The road to Larisa example
helps clarify this point: if someone were recently in Larisa and as a
result of his visit had knowledge of how to get there, would it not
be virtually impossible to convince him to take some radically different route now? Yet someone who did not know but merely had

58. But see Klein (1965), 248, who astutely notes that *phronēsis* is a kind of knowledge that cannot be forgotten.

59. See Sharples (1985), 184.

true opinion could easily be persuaded by another or persuade himself to try another route.[60] Moral true opinions, like the true opinion concerning how to get to Larisa, are easily dislodged: when one fails to apprehend the "goodness" that accounts for the goodness of all things, when one lacks understanding of what it is that makes moral truths true, when one lacks the tether, the *aitia,* that ties opinions down, what is to keep those truths from bolting at the onset of competing views?[61] Socrates, it seems, has a partial solution: elenchus. The importance of elenchus lies, for him, in its ability to tether, *to some extent,* one's true opinions. Although the practice of elenchus does not yield knowledge and does not, therefore, furnish a tether that secures one's true beliefs permanently, nevertheless it does furnish a tether of sorts: the constant examination and reexamination of one's moral beliefs provides a way to persevere in the face of other opinions, opinions that exert a hold on one because they are tightly woven into the fabric of one's tradition, advance one's pursuit of pleasure, or dazzle by their sheer newness. Socratic elenchus can, when confronted with such opinions, ask if they are reasonable, test to see how well they stand up to scrutiny, and check whether they cohere with our most deeply held beliefs or bring discord to our souls. True opinions run the gamut from lucky guesses to well-reasoned and solidly defended beliefs: at the one end they fly about, unrestrained, as is their wont; at the other, they are secured, pretty tightly, by frequently practiced elenchus. But only *aitias logismos* can secure beliefs fully.

Socrates alludes fairly explicitly in the *Gorgias* to the elenctic tethering that falls short of *aitias logismos.* While insisting, as always, that he lacks knowledge ("I do not know how these things stand" [*Gorg.* 509a5]; cf. *Gorg.* 506a3–4: "For the things I say, I do not say, at any rate, as knowing"), he says of his conclusions, arrived at earlier in the discussion, that they are "clamped and tethered," *katechetai kai dedetai,* "by arguments of iron and adamant."[62] (The term *dedetai,*

60. See Guthrie (1975), 240, who says, with respect to the man who has been told the right way to Larisa, that he "may meet someone else who tells him differently, find him more persuasive, and go astray."

61. Socrates never makes, with regard to true opinion, as strong a claim as the one he makes about knowledge in the *Protagoras* (to which Protagoras concurs), namely, that it cannot be dragged about by pleasure, pain, hope, love, and fear, like a slave (*Prot.* 352b–d). Perhaps, then, true opinions might take flight in the face not only of other opinions but of these passions as well.

62. In the *Gorgias,* Socrates asserts of his view, which is philosophy's view, that it always says the same things (*Gorg.* 482a7–b1). And the *Crito* repeatedly emphasizes

"tethered," recalls the *Meno's dēsēi* and *dethōsin,* at *M.* 98a4 and a6, respectively, which are its cognates.) We may observe, however, that no matter how strong Socrates' tether is—indeed, even if it is made of iron and adamant—it is not sufficiently strong to eliminate permanently the "if" that attaches to his conclusions: "So, again," Socrates says, "I set down how these things are. . . . And *if* they are so . . ." (*Gorg.* 509a7–b1). In the final analysis, then, not all tethers are equal: elenchus cannot take the place of *aitias logismos,* for elenchus does not yield knowledge.

True opinions, even though they are not knowledge, need not be ugly things. When fastened and bound, they can guide just as well as knowledge does. Unlike lucky guesses, which cannot guide a private life or the life of a city (except haphazardly and unpredictably), examined true opinions can abide for a lifetime and can serve one and even one's city surprisingly well. Until such time as there is moral knowledge to be had, then, true opinions are a worthy substitute.[63] Since they will only stay put, however, if the tether that keeps them down is powerful enough to combat their tendency to take flight, no life but the examined one will be a life lived well.

Socrates worries about the accuracy of the distinction he has drawn between knowledge and true opinion. "I speak," he says, "not as one who knows but as one who guesses" (*M.* 98b1).[64] It is, however, for him, no mere guess that knowledge and true opinion are distinct from one another: if there is anything Socrates would claim to know—"and there are few things of which I would say this"—that knowledge is different from true opinion is surely one of them (*M.* 98b2–5).[65]

Socrates' abiding beliefs: even at the end of his life, as he faces death, he has, because of a lifelong practice of elenchus, views that are strong enough to stand up to death (without, however, counting for him as knowledge).

63. Perhaps one reason for the *Republic's* harsh take on true opinion is that it has already envisioned, and at least to some degree seriously entertained, the possibility of ascent out of the Cave and, with it, the human attainment of moral knowledge. Viewed against the possibility that human beings might actually come to possess moral knowledge, true opinion pales. See Appendix II.

64. Klein (1965), 249, brilliantly translates *eikazōn* as "by making images": Socrates has, after all, sought to convey the difference between knowledge and true opinion by appeal to the statues of Daedelus. I do not believe that this can be the primary sense of *eikazōn,* however, since *eikazōn* appears earlier meaning "guess." At *M.* 89e1–3, Socrates says that we would be "guessing well" were we to guess that if there were neither teachers nor pupils of something, it would not be teachable. Perhaps the term at *M.* 98b1 is intended as a pun.

65. Thompson (1901), notes that this passage (*M.* 98b3–4) has a counterpart at *Ap.* 29b, where Socrates says: "If I should claim to be wiser in anything, it is in that I

It makes good sense that Socrates can do no more than guess at the nature of the difference between true opinion and knowledge, at least with respect to that of which he has no knowledge—virtue.[66] Not actually having moral knowledge, he is compelled to speak about moral knowledge on analogy with other kinds of knowledge. But it is fairly easy to know both that one lacks knowledge (recognizing that one lacks decisive proof should suffice for that) and that knowledge differs from true opinion. In fact, that there is a difference between knowledge and true opinion may be regarded as a corollary of one of the very few other things that Socrates claims to know, namely, that he lacks knowledge of the most important things, *ta megista*, moral matters: If Socrates knows that he stands in some epistemic state with relation to moral matters that is not knowledge, and he calls that epistemic state opinion, then he knows that there is a difference between knowledge and opinion. And if, in addition, at least some of his opinions might be true, he knows, too, that there is a difference between knowledge and *true* opinion.

One might go so far as to say that it is on the distinction between true opinion and knowledge that the validity of elenctic activity depends. Since elenchus cannot hope to achieve knowledge, it would be difficult to defend elenchus if, in the space that separates knowledge from mere opinion, there were nothing worthwhile—that is, if there were no true opinions—toward which elenchus could strive. Without the distinction between knowledge and true opinion, Socrates could not recognize as a possibility the recovery of true opinions—as distinct from the recovery of knowledge—from within the depths of the human soul.

Socrates is now satisfied that he has shown true opinion to be the equal of knowledge in directing action to their good end. As long as a man has true opinion, Socrates concludes, he, no less than the man who has knowledge, will do well and guide aright.[67]

---

know that I do not know." Sharples (1985), 185, and Bluck (1961a), 414, note the similarity between this passage and the one at *M.* 86c, in which Socrates says he will not swear to any of the things just proposed but will fight for but one of them: that men will be better for believing in recollection rather than in Meno's paradox (*M.* 86b–c). As Sharples observes, Socrates, by emphasizing (in both passages) his reluctance to make one set of claims, draws attention to his singular determination to make another.

66. Socrates has knowledge of other things, as he admits in the *Euthydemus*. His knowledge, however, is "of small things," *smikra* (*Euthyd.* 293b7–8).

67. Vlastos (1991a), 125, believes that if it is the case that true belief is as good as knowledge with respect to action, then "the whole row of Socratic dominos will have to fall, including the fundamental conviction that . . . the unexamined life is not

vi. *Eudoxia* and Divine Dispensation

Having established a kind of practical parity between true opinion and knowledge, having concluded at *M.* 98b7–9 that "when true opinion guides, it is no worse than knowledge at carrying out each act to completion," Socrates is ready to turn his attention to the man himself who possesses the knowledge or true opinion by which acts are well executed. The shift from the effect of knowledge and true opinion on the quality of a man's actions to their effect on the quality of the man himself takes place at *M.* 98c3: "nor is the man who has right opinion [less beneficial] than the man who has knowledge." And at *M.* 98c5–6, once Socrates has identified the good man as the beneficial man ("And we have agreed that the good man, at any rate, is beneficial"), he is at last in a position to address head on Meno's question of *M.* 96d1–4 of how those men who do become good, if indeed there are any such men, do so.

The good men who bring benefit to their cities, *if there are such men,*[68] says Socrates, do so in one of two ways: by knowledge *or* by true opinion. And neither of these comes by nature:[69] insofar as both are things that must be acquired anew—they are *epiktēta*[70]—they are

worth living for a man." What I hope to have shown is that it is because true opinion is so valuable that the examined life, the life of moral inquiry, is worth living. For true opinion is the goal of the examined life.

68. Cf. *Crito* 47d1–2, where Socrates inserts a similar skeptical phrase, "if there is such an expert," *ei tis estin epaiōn,* thereby registering his doubts about the existence of experts on what is just and unjust, shameful and noble, good and bad. The source of Socrates' skepticism concerning the existence of good men is not likely to be the same as Meno's. In Meno's case, it is the discovery that virtue is not teachable that makes him wonder if there are any good men at all. In Socrates' case, it is the discovery that reputedly "good" men are not good that gives him pause. See the exchange between Anytus and Socrates at *M.* 93a, where in response to Anytus's suspicion that Socrates might doubt that there have been good men (*agathoi andres*) in Athens, Socrates says that he thinks that indeed there have been good—politicians (*agathoi ta politika*).

69. Socrates had already proposed that virtue does not come by nature because it is wisdom (*M.* 89a3–7). Meno accepted the idea without protest: after all, as we saw in Section ii, Meno assumes from the start, as is implicit in his opening question at *M.* 70a, that *didakton/mathēton* and *phusei* denote distinct ways in which virtue might come to men; natural things are things like good looks, noble birth, and wealth, for the possession of which, unlike for the possession of teachable/learnable things, he need do nothing. But true opinion is something new. That is why Socrates must now raise with respect to true opinion the question of whether it, too, like knowledge, does not come by nature: "neither of these (*toutoin de oudeteron*) belongs to men by nature" (*M.* 98c10–d1); and "Or do you think that either of these (*hopoteronoun autoin*) is by nature?" (*M.* 98d2–3).

70. The phrase *out' epiktēta* (*M.* 98d1) has caused scholars much consternation. In

not achieved effortlessly, as things that come by nature are.[71] Moreover, if neither of these things comes by nature, then men are not good by nature. Yet since, as was argued, virtue is not teachable and, hence, not wisdom, how else might virtue come? On the assumption that (a) virtue guides aright (and, in guiding aright, is both good and beneficial), and (b) there are only two human guides that guide

context, it seems to suggest that "(newly) acquired things," *epiktēta*, constitute a class to which neither knowledge nor true opinion belongs. In order to avoid this result, several emendations have been proposed; for a review and discussion of these, see Bluck (1961a), 417. Bluck's own view is that *ont' epiktēta* was originally a gloss that was corrupted to *out' epiktēta* and found its way into the text. Bluck therefore brackets *out' epiktēta*, as does Sharples. My proposal is to leave the text unemended and to render the text at *M.* 98c10–d2 as follows: "Since, then, it is not only through knowledge that men become good and beneficial to their cities, if there are such men, but through right opinion, and [since] neither of these comes to people by nature— neither knowledge nor true opinion nor newly acquired things [generally]—or do you think that either of these comes by nature?" That is, Socrates makes the point that just as nature cannot be the source for knowledge, so it cannot be the source for true opinion, since both of these and, indeed, all other newly acquired things, *epiktēta*, do not come by nature. Through his *out' epiktēta*, then, Socrates provides some reason for Meno to agree that not only knowledge but true opinion as well do not come *phusei*: nothing that is newly acquired comes *phusei*.

In Plato, there are many examples of *oute . . . oute . . . oute*, where the third *oute* designates the class to which the first two alternatives belong: for example, *Charm.* 160c6, 173b1–2; *Crito* 52e5–6; *Ion* 530c9–d2; *Lach.* 196a5; *Prot.* 345a8–b1; *Gorg.* 475e4. In all these cases, however, some form of *allos* appears immediately following the third *oute*. There are at least two cases, however, in which the third *oute* designates—without *allos*—either the general class to which the first two alternatives belong or the other members of that class, and which thus strongly support my reading of *out' epiktēta*. The better case is *Lys.* 210d3–4: "If not, you will have no friend in anyone, neither in your father nor in your mother nor in your family members (*hoi oikeioi*) [generally] [or, alternatively, 'nor in your other family members']." See also *Rep.* 5.464b9–c1: "These helpers must possess neither houses of their own nor land nor any property (*ti ktēma*) [generally] [or, alternatively, 'nor any other property']."

71. As we have seen, when something comes "by nature," it comes without effort. (That is why Socrates maintained, at *M.* 89b, that if, hypothetically, there were children who were virtuous by nature, nothing more would have to be done to ensure their continued virtuous state than to sequester them and preserve them from corruption.) Thus, even if we are born already having moral knowledge or true opinions in our souls, as long as effort is needed for their recovery, they cannot be rightly regarded as coming simply "by nature." Indeed, Socrates' declared purpose in developing the recollection thesis, with its insistence that we have truths always in our souls, was to encourage us not to be complacent and lazy but to become, instead, energetic seekers after those very truths. We note that in the discussion of Anthemion the two ways in which he might have *become* wealthy, *egeneto plousios* (*M.* 90a3), are the effortless ways of "spontaneously" and by being given a gift. By contrast, the two ways in which he actually *acquired*, *ktēsamenos*, his wealth (*M.* 90a5) are "by wisdom" and "by diligence," *epimeleiāi*. Since, for Socrates, acquisition requires diligence, it stands to reason that insofar as both knowledge and true opinion have to be newly acquired (they are *epiktēta*), neither would, as Socrates says, come "by nature."

aright, knowledge and true opinion, it follows that if (c) virtue does not come by knowledge, then (d) it can only come by true opinion.

Or so one would think. Most oddly, however, as was noted earlier, this is not the conclusion that Socrates draws. Although Socrates quite deliberately sets the stage for true opinion to emerge as the answer to Meno's question about how men become good (true opinion is, after all, the only source for virtue entertained thus far that has not been defeated), he conspicuously prevents true opinion from stepping into what is surely the role for which it was groomed.[72]

Let us take note of just how carefully Socrates lays the groundwork for true opinion to turn out to be virtue's source. At *M*. 99a1–5, having decisively eliminated nature as a contender, Socrates makes it clear that there are two and only two human guides that guide aright: knowledge and true opinion. He then makes sure to disqualify chance, insofar as chance is not a human guide. Socrates then takes knowledge out of the running on the grounds that virtue is not teachable (*M*. 99a7–8). (Knowledge is a human guide generally, in that it guides aright in all teachable matters; it is not a guide with respect to virtue, however, because virtue is not teachable.) He reiterates that, of the two finalists, one—namely, knowl-

---

72. This unexpected turn of events is but the last in a series of such surprise turns in the *Meno*. The dialogue fails to deliver what the reader expects on at least the following occasions: (a) After the final definition of virtue at *M*. 79b, the reader expects Socrates to be pleased that Meno has come around to his way of thinking, but instead Socrates turns on Meno. (b) After Meno states his paradox, the reader expects Socrates to paraphrase both the paradox of inquiry and what I have called the paradox of knowing, but Socrates paraphrases only the paradox of inquiry (*M*. 80d–e). (c) At the conclusion of the slave-boy-demonstration at *M*. 85d, the reader expects Socrates to conclude that the slave-boy, who did not know, has now, solely by having been asked questions, come to know, but instead Socrates confines the slave-boy's achievement to true opinion. (d) In the recapitulation of the slave-boy-demonstration at *M*. 86b–c, the reader expects Socrates to conclude that he will swear at least to that "all learning is recollection," but instead Socrates will swear only to the superior character of those who embrace the recollection thesis. (e) As a result of the slave-boy-demonstration, the reader expects Socrates to rebuke Meno for daring to suggest the possibility that virtue is teachable, and to refuse to entertain it (on the grounds that he has just established that all learning comes by recollection, not by teaching), but instead Socrates not only considers the teachability of virtue but decides to have it make no difference if one says "teachable" or "recollectable" (*M*. 87b–c). (f) After Anytus suspects Socrates of not thinking that there have been many good men in the city (*M*. 93a3–4), the reader expects Socrates to say that he either does or does not think there have been such men, but Socrates says instead that there are and have been men good *at politics* (*M*. 93a5–6). Finally, (g) after Socrates has argued that virtue is wisdom at *M*. 89a, the reader expects Socrates simply to conclude that virtue is, therefore, teachable, but instead Socrates worries that since there are neither teachers nor pupils of it, it may not be.

edge—has now been disqualified (*M.* 99b1–2). That, it would seem, leaves only the other: true opinion. Where else can Socrates now go?

He goes somewhere else: to *eudoxia*, "good repute." Why, we must wonder, does Socrates substitute *eudoxia*, a term that, despite its etymological sense of "good opinion," in fact always means "good repute,"[73] for the expected "true (or right) opinion"? Why does he steer the argument so manifestly off course?

The answer lies in what intervenes between (a) Socrates' recognition at *M.* 99b1–2 that, of the two candidates for the source of virtue—knowledge and true opinion—knowledge is no longer viable, and (b) his heralding of *eudoxia* as virtue's source at *M.* 99b11. In the space of just nine lines, Socrates replaces the question of where the virtue of truly good men who benefit their cities (if there are such men) comes from with the question of how men good at

73. Although Bluck (1961a), 421, translates *eudoxia* simply as "true opinion" (as does Sharples[1985]; Day [1994] has "good opinion"; Canto-Sperber [1991] has "*la bonne opinion*"), he recognizes the possibility that Plato intended it to be a pun, "as though these statesmen owed their *aretē* to 'good reputation.' " Canto-Sperber (1991), 314, also detects here a *jeu de mots*. Cf. Sharples (1985), 187: "Plato may be playing on words here; to say that the excellence of politicians consists in reputation is to say that it is no excellence at all." Thompson (1901), 225, regards the shift to the unexpected *eudoxia* as just another in a series of substitutions in the *Meno* of "the concrete word for the substantive infinitive": *tōi porōi* substitutes for *tōi porizesthai* or *tōi porismōi* at *M.* 78d, e; *aporia* for *to mē porizesthai* at *M.* 78e; *desmōi* for *tōi dedesthai* at *M.* 98a; now *eudoxia* for *to eu doxazein* at *M.* 99b11. *Eudoxia*, however, does not substitute for the infinitive *eu doxazein* but for other concrete words, specifically, "true opinion" or "right opinion," *doxa alēthes* or *orthē doxa*. That *eudoxia* replaces these, when *eudoxia* has a very different sense from these, makes this shift not just another in a series of substitutions. See Klein (1965), 253, who takes *eudoxia* to be significantly different from *doxa alēthes* and *orthē doxa*, and in the very way I do: "Does Socrates mean that statesmen are guided by sound and good opinions in their counsels and actions? Or does he mean that statesmen are reputed to be thus guided in the opinion of their fellow citizens? The term *eudoxia* is chosen with care." Andic (1971), 308, though he translates *eudoxia* as "well-aimed conjecture" or "good opinion," relates these expressions to "public opinion" and sees that politicians who have *eudoxia* do not have true opinion but guide others purely by chance or divine dispensation. "Well-aimed conjecture," a translation suggested by Andic and used by Guthrie (1956) as well, seems a rather odd rendering of *eudoxia*. Its source is most likely Apelt's emendation of *eudoxia* to *eustochia*, the latter of which *is* properly translated "well-aimed conjecture." Apelt emends the term because, as he notes, *eudoxia* never means anything in Plato but "good repute." It is worth noting that of the seventy-odd times that Plato uses the term *eudoxia* or one of its cognates, there is not one in which it signifies anything but good repute, that is, the favorable opinion—deserved or not—that others have of one; it never indicates that one's own opinions are good, right, or true. It is, however, often used sarcastically to imply that one lacks true merit. The substitution of *eudoxia* for "true (or right) opinion" is reminiscent of the pun on *eumathia* discussed earlier, in Section ii.

political affairs, such as Themistocles and the others that Anytus mentioned a moment ago,[74] guide their cities. The switch begins at *M.* 99b2, where Socrates suddenly qualifies "good and beneficial" with the phrase "in political action," *en politikēi praxei*. And it continues at *M.* 99b6, where Themistocles et al. are named. As the text proceeds, it speaks specifically of politicians, *hoi politikoi andres* (*M.* 99c1) rather than of good men or good citizens. And in place of "beneficial to their cities," *ōphelimoi tais polesin* (*M.* 98c9), we now encounter "are successful," *katorthousin* (*M.* 99c9 and d4). The shift from true or right opinion to good reputation, then, corresponds to the shift from good and beneficial men to good and successful politicians.

It is clearly no accident, no slip of the stylus, no mistake, that Socrates substitutes *eudoxia* for the true or right opinion used exclusively up until *M.* 99b11. We note that once *eudoxia* is introduced, it stays: for the duration of the dialogue, there is no mention of true or right opinion. Found consistently in their place are expressions for divine inspiration, possession, and allotment. How are we to understand *eudoxia* in relation to the political realm in which it is now said to function?

Eudoxia, Socrates says, is what politicians use to guide cities aright. What they certainly do not use, he insists, is knowledge: like prophets and oracular priests, who when inspired speak many truths but know nothing of what they speak (*M.* 99b–c),[75] politicians who, without thought, succeed in accomplishing many great things in both action and speech[76] are "divine," that is, inspired and possessed by the god (*M.* 99c-d).[77]

---

74. The irony here, of course, is that Anytus *refused* to name any good men; Socrates named them. This Socratic "report," then, is an instance of Socratic revisionism. It is not the first such instance in the *Meno.* We have already noted Socrates' made-up reference to a presumed earlier agreement reached by him and Meno that the process of tying down true opinions by *aitias logismos* was recollection (*M.* 98a). A second example occurs at *M.* 93b, where Socrates tells Anytus, falsely, that he and Meno "have for a long time been inquiring into" the matter of whether the good men of the present and past know how to pass on to others the virtue that makes them good. No such inquiry took place.

75. See *Ion* 534b–d and *Lach.* 195e–196a: poets have no knowledge; *Laws* 4.719c: poets are "without intelligence," *ouk emphrōn.*

76. It may seem as if the text imputes to politicians, by its use of "too," *kai,* the utterance of truths. Having just spoken about politicians, the text continues: "For these, too [soothsayers and prophets], say many true things when divinely possessed, but they know nothing concerning any of the things they say" (*M.* 99c3–5). Yet, surely, what politicians have in common with soothsayers/prophets is not that they speak truths but that they lack knowledge. Whereas politicians may speak successfully, *kator-*

Since successful politicians like Themistocles exploit *eudoxia* to guide their cities and, at the same time, act by divine possession rather than by human intelligence, *eudoxia* is surely connected in some way to divine allotment (*theia moira, M.* 99e6) and to divine inspiration and possession. The link that joins them is chance or luck, *tuchē.* Insofar as one's reputation is a reflection not of one's own true worth but of other people's opinions—whether good or bad, deserved or undeserved—it is a matter of luck.[78] Indeed, if the *Apology* is to be believed, those with the greatest reputations are most deficient (*Ap.* 22a3). (We may note that in the *Meno* itself, Anytus is *reputed* among the people to have been brought up and educated well; Protagoras, too, is a "man of renown," *eudokimōn* [*M.* 91e9].) On the other side, those who do merit good reputations are persecuted and executed—witness, Socrates.[79] The good reputation, then, that some enjoy and that catapults them into positions of power turns on nothing more than a twist of fate. And the god-given knack for doing and saying the right thing that is the mark of politicians-without-understanding both preserves and promotes the good reputation with which they were already blessed. The esteem in which they are held, therefore, like their political effectiveness, must be credited not to them but to the gods. Both divine inspiration and good reputation create the illusion of human greatness, while they mask human deficit.

As divine, *eudoxia* turns out to be critically different from true or right opinion, to which it bears only an etymological resemblance,

---

thōsi legontes (*M.* 99d4), they do not speak truthfully. Cf. *Ap.* 22, where it sounds as if Socrates is saying that poets have in common with the craftsmen not only that they mistakenly think they know what they do not know but also that they genuinely practice a craft. But, Socrates had just said that the poets have no craft (*Ap.* 22c).

77. See *Gorg.* 456a, where Socrates, in expressing surprise regarding rhetoric's alleged power to advise on a very wide range of matters, says, tongue in cheek, that when considered in this way, rhetoric seems to him to be "something supernatural," *daimonia tis* (*Gorg.* 456a5), in scope. At *Ap.* 33c4–7, Socrates acknowledges his own *theia moira,* as evidenced by oracles and dreams. Yet *his* inspiration, rather than enabling him to say wise things, obliges him to live the life of philosophy, examining those who mistakenly think themselves wise and showing them that they are not.

78. See Aristotle, *Eth. Nic.* 1.5.1095b23 ff., where he argues that the life of honor, (*timē*), the political life, cannot qualify as the highest life because it is not self-sufficient: whether one is honored depends upon others, not upon oneself.

79. The craftsmen, too, are a case in point. Although craftsmen are experts at their crafts, they are, nevertheless, popularly regarded as inferior, *dokountes phauloteroi* (*Ap.* 22a5–6). See *Gorg.* 512c, where Socrates remonstrates with Callicles for being unwilling either to give his daughter to the son of an "engineer" or to take an "engineer's" daughter for himself.

for as Socrates has already emphasized, true opinion is a human guide (*M.* 99a4–5). In addition, *eudoxia* is disqualified from being identified with knowledge on the grounds that it is inspired and involves no thought. The only kind of "guide" that *eudoxia* can then be is *tuchē*,[80] the third, and nonhuman, source of things' turning out well, introduced at *M.* 99a. *Eudoxia* is that lucky—often undeserved—favor one finds in the eyes of others, through which, in turn, one is able to rule them.

In what way, we may well wonder, is *eudoxia* as divine gift, as luck or chance, distinguishable from nature as a source of virtue?[81] Both are wholly adventitious; both neither require effort nor reward merit; and both can be lost (the latter, by corruption; the former, by divine whim).[82] Yet, that they are meant to be distinguished is clear from Socrates' summary at *M.* 99e5–100a1: "virtue will be neither natural nor teachable but something that comes by divine allotment, without intelligence." Wherein lies the difference between them, and how important is that difference?

It seems that the only difference between nature and divine allotment is that whereas natural virtue is present in a man at birth, virtue by divine allotment comes, if it comes at all, later. The significance of this difference can only be appreciated in light of Socrates' project of helping Meno. For if Meno were to believe that virtue comes by nature, he would also surely believe that he already has it—in respect of his noble birth. If he accepts, instead, that virtue comes by divine allotment, then, on the one hand, he cannot be sure that he either has or will ever have it and, on the other, he loses the incentive to pursue potentially detrimental associations with sophists and with "gentlemen" like Anytus.

---

80. Klein (1965), 254, and Andic (1971), 307, make a similar point. *Tuchē* is interestingly linked—though not identified—with divine inspiration at *Rep.* 6.499b–c, where it is proclaimed that no polis can be well ordered until some chance compels the uncorrupted philosophers to take charge of it, or until divine inspiration awakens a passion for philosophy in its rulers or their sons.

81. Nature and divine gift are linked at *Ap.* 22c; cf. *Laws* 642c. See Aristotle, *Eth. Nic.* 10.9.1179b22–23, where Aristotle contends that the virtue that comes to a man by nature may be traced to a divine cause, *dia tinas theias aitias . . . huparchei;* indeed, those who are virtuous by nature are the lucky ones, *hoi eutuchesin.*

82. See *Gorg.* 515e11, where Socrates says of Pericles that he was—at least at one time—held in high esteem, *ēudokimei Periklēs*. Pericles later fell in the people's estimation. As far as Socrates is concerned, the reason Pericles fell from favor is that he failed to "improve" the citizens in his charge. But that he fell from favor also attests to the transitory, fickle nature of *eudoxia.*

Meno, of course, wishes to attain the eminence of a Pericles or a Themistocles; he longs to join their ranks. Socrates makes it clear to the reader, however, by attributing the success of Themistocles and others like him to *eudoxia* rather than to either knowledge or true/right opinion, that *he* means to disparage both their "virtue" and its source. Such men may achieve prominence, they may have fine reputations, they may be favored by the gods, but they certainly are not good men and do not really benefit their cities. They give no thought to what is truly best for the people entrusted to their care, pandering instead to the citizens' appetites, filling cities with harbors, dockyards, and walls, and, moreover, going about their business paying no heed to justice and temperance (*Gorg.* 519a).[83] Socrates, though far less eminent, is nevertheless their superior; he is, as he says in the *Gorgias* (at 521d), the only man who genuinely pursues the political *technē*. For although Socrates too lacks knowledge of the most important matters, that is, knowledge of what constitutes the best life for a human being, he devotes his life to striving to find it. He alone "works at," *epicheirein,* the true political *technē,* practicing and actively engaging in things political, aiming at "what is best," *to beltiston,* for his fellow citizens (as a physician aims at what is best for his patients) rather than at what they find "most pleasant," *to hēdiston* (*Gorg.* 521d9–e1).

Once *eudoxia* is pried apart from true/right opinion, it becomes possible to appreciate the full import of the rather startling fact that true/right opinion has never been shown unfit to be a source of virtue; it has simply vanished from the scene. Of all the options considered, only true/right opinion escapes the argument unscathed; it alone remains an open possibility.[84] Moreover, as we have seen, true opinion disappears from view just as good and beneficial men are replaced by successful politicians who lack intelligence. It is, of course, the "virtue" of prominent political leaders that Socrates attributes to divine dispensation. It is their divinely induced success in doing and speaking that is both traceable to and responsible for their good reputation. But what of the good and beneficial men

83. As we know from the beginning of the *Meno,* nothing can count as virtue if it is done unjustly and intemperately.

84. Klein (1965), 254, sees that since whatever it is that politicians are said to have in common with prophets and soothsayers involves chance, it cannot be any form of *human* guidance. He does not seem to recognize that one of the two identified forms of human guidance, true opinion, need not involve chance and may, therefore, remain a viable option. See also Andic (1971), 306–7.

whose "virtue" does not come from the gods? Might not their virtue come from the true opinion that disappeared from view at the same time that they did?[85]

At the end of the dialogue, Socrates hints at the possibility that a politician might arise who could make someone else a politician. Insofar as a politician who is able to make someone else a politician is necessarily someone who has knowledge, such a man would be among the living what, according to Homer, Teiresias was among the dead: "he alone had wisdom (*hoios pepnutai*) but the rest flit about like shadows" (*M.* 100a5–6). On earth, Socrates says, such a man would be, with respect to virtue, "reality contrasted with shadows." The unmistakable implication of Socrates' reference to Teiresias among the shades, to a prophet whose blind eyes can see clearly in the darkness what sighted eyes cannot, is that we on earth, dwelling in the darkness of the Cave, are truly the blind ones; and no one who is blind in the way we are can hope to relieve our blindness. It is, of course, with respect to virtue that we are blind, lacking the moral wisdom that would make it possible to transmit, to teach, virtue to another. For virtue to be knowledge, for it to be teachable, someone most extraordinary, someone who can see even in the dark, would have to appear. No such man has yet appeared; perhaps someday he will.[86]

Until such time as we on earth are privileged to be guided by a Teiresias among the dead, what will virtue, true virtue, be for us? It will not be knowledge: with no Teiresias, there is no one who knows and no one who can teach. But is there not still true opinion? Is there not always the possibility of elenchus, through which we might hope to gain access to, to "recollect," the moral truths that are, so to speak, always in our souls, that are, in other words, true to our nature? Assiduous and painstaking lifelong inquiry into moral mat-

85. Many commentators contend that Themistocles' virtue cannot be, for Socrates, genuine virtue, for, in Socrates' view, true virtue comes from knowledge. If, however, true opinion is distinguished from *eudoxia*, then it becomes possible to entertain the possibility that true opinion might be the source—or one source—of genuine virtue. See Thompson (1901), 113; Sharples (1985), 14.

86. For an instructive commentary on the role of Teiresias, see Scott (1995), 49–50. Scott draws several interesting connections between Teiresias and Plato's philosopher-kings: (a) Teiresias wanders among the shadows in Hades; Plato compares the Cave to the Underworld. (b) Teiresias cannot see in the world of the living; the philosopher-king has a vision of true reality but is blinded when he returns to the Cave. (c) Teiresias, like the philosopher, sees things differently from how ordinary people see them and, like the philosopher, tends to make himself unpopular with politicians. (d) Both Teiresias and the philosopher see things correctly.

ters holds the promise of true opinion, the sole source for genuine virtue that is still viable at the *Meno*'s end. The great innovation and contribution of the *Meno* is the revelation that it is true opinion, and the quest for it, that make life worth living—when all human beings are *mere* human beings. Virtue comes not, as Meno imagines, by teaching, practice, or nature but rather "in some other way": by the hard work, the *epimeleia,* of moral inquiry, that is, of elenchus aimed at true opinion.

Conclusion

The Examined Life

> It is much better to have reasonable opin-
> ions about useful matters than precise
> knowledge about matters of no use.
>
> Isocrates, Helen 5

What is the end of the examined life? Is it the recognition of one's
ignorance or, perhaps, the attainment of positive, substantive knowledge? It has been argued in this book that for Socrates in the *Meno,*
the end of the life of inquiry is neither of these: the former is insufficient; the latter, out of reach. The goal of a life of moral reflection and critical investigation is, in the *Meno,* true opinion.

Scholars have contended that since the elenchus is able to do no
more than demonstrate that an interlocutor's belief-set contains inconsistency, Socrates' goal in employing it can be no more ambitious
than to cause his interlocutors to recognize their inconsistency and,
thus, their ignorance.[1] To hold this view, however, is to forget that
the Socrates of Plato's elenctic dialogues is concerned, not only that
people come to see that they do not in fact know what they think
they know, but that they come to believe what is right and true. Is
it enough that Euthyphro recognize his lack of expertise in piety; is
he not also urged to relinquish his unenlightened, indeed impious,
view of divine service? Need Polus do no more than take note of the

---

1. If Socratic elenchus regularly employs deliberately unsound arguments and
other forms of verbal trickery, one might wonder if it can accomplish even the limited
aim of exposing the ignorance of Socrates' interlocutors. It can, in one sense. As long
as Socrates' interlocutors become confused and cannot answer cogently Socrates'
questions about matters in which they think they have wisdom, their confidence in
their expertise is shaken and they are revealed to themselves as being certainly not as
wise as they thought they were—even if they do not openly admit it.

inconsistency in his views; is he not encouraged to give up his envy of tyrants and rhetoricians? Is Socrates content to cause Thrasymachus to blush (*Rep.* 1. 350d); or does he seek to persuade Thrasymachus that justice is to be valued more highly than injustice? Socrates says in the *Apology* that he is sent by the god to awaken people from their moral slumber, to weaken their attachment to things of no worth (reputation, honor, and wealth), to impress upon people the need to care for the soul more than for the body. Regardless, then, of how little elenchus can accomplish in the strictest sense, it remains, for Socrates, a powerful instrument wielded in service to the god, that is, in the furtherance of virtue and of those moral principles that are rationally defensible.

Does Socrates hope that his elenchus might eventually yield knowledge? Elenchus, as was argued in this book's Introduction, is a method grounded in opinion and confined to opinion, a method that can do no more than, at most, substitute true (hence, better) opinions for false (hence, worse) ones.[2] Moreover, even these substitutions are never certain; they must be reexamined and retested without end. Were it possible for elenchus to yield knowledge, Socrates would applaud, not a life of endless investigation and examination, but rather one that culminates in knowledge, in moral expertise, in certitude about "the most important things," *ta megista.* The fact is, however, that the life he advocates is the life of moral inquiry, which, he contends, is the only life of value for human beings. Such a life could never satisfy those for whom knowledge is within reach. Such a life could never be prescribed, say, for the gods. Surely one who knows does not—need not—inquire.[3]

It is often thought that Socrates makes many claims to moral knowledge, that there are many moral propositions that he takes himself to know. Yet the fact is that Socrates claims to know only (a) that he lacks moral expertise ("For I am conscious to myself of being not at all wise, neither much nor little" [*Ap.* 21b4–5; see also *Ap.* 21d2–6, 22c9–d1; *Gorg.* 506a3–5, 509a4–6; *M.* 71b3; *Euthyph.* 16d]); (b) that he ought to obey his "better," *beltiōn,* that is, the one who is an expert, whether god or man (*Ap.* 29b); and (c) that knowledge

---

2. See *Rep.* 7.533c3–5: "When the beginning is what one does not know, and the end and what comes in between are woven out of what is not known, what contrivance is there for ever turning such an agreement into knowledge?" (trans. Bloom [1968], very slightly modified).

3. This is Socrates' point in his restatement of Meno's paradox: one would not inquire into what one already knows, for one already knows it (*M.* 80e).

or expertise differs from true belief (*M.* 98b). The first of these claims is Socrates' notorious profession of ignorance; yet, for him, let us remember, the recognition of ignorance constitutes a kind of wisdom, "human wisdom," the highest wisdom regarding *ta megista* that an ordinary human being can achieve. The second claim may seem like a substantive moral belief, but it is really just a corollary of the first: only one who recognizes his own ignorance would admit the importance of obeying the one who does know; it is those who lack awareness of their own ignorance who recoil from seeking the guidance of experts. Socrates appreciates the expertise of craftsmen in those areas of life where they indeed exist, as well as the importance of obeying them; and he laments the absence of experts— himself included—in the moral domain, where, it would appear, he can obey only the god. The third of these claims is, too, but a corollary of the first, for it is Socrates' recognition that he lacks knowledge that enables him to know that knowledge is distinct from true opinion: he knows that he has moral beliefs, but since he also knows that he lacks moral knowledge, it follows for him that if even *some* of his beliefs are true, true opinion is distinct from knowledge.

Socrates cannot—any more than others can—pass with respect to virtue the tests for expertise that he devises (particularly in the *Laches* at 185 and in the *Gorgias* at 465a, 500b–501a, 514a–c):[4] he can point neither to teachers from whom he has acquired expertise at virtue nor to students to whom he has transmitted his expertise;[5] he has produced no "works" that attest to his skill (who, after all, are the people whose souls he has improved?) nor can he give a satisfactory account of the virtues. As he says in the *Crito*, he is a man who always obeys what "*seems best* to me upon reasoning" (*Crito* 46b): a man who knows would surely not have to rely upon what merely seems best. Moreover, Socrates refrains from declaring that he knows even the most basic moral truths.[6] What Socrates knows is that he must prac-

---

4. See also *Euthyph.* 16a; *M.* 90b; *Prot.* 319e ff., 448e ff.

5. Although the *Charmides* seems to suggest that anyone who is not himself an expert is unable to detect expertise in another, there is much evidence in Plato that experts are known and recognized: they are the teachers to whom people send their children for various sorts of instruction; they are the people who build their houses and ships and make their shoes; they are the people who cure their bodily ills.

6. At *Ap.* 29b Socrates seems to be claiming that he knows that it is bad and shameful to commit injustice. As I understand this passage, however, Socrates is actually claiming to know—with respect to a particular injustice or crime, namely (*kai*), that of disobeying one's superior (*apeithein tōi beltioni*)—that it is bad to commit (*adikein*) it. Given the way *adikein* and *apeithein toi beltioni* are linked as the apparently single thing Socrates knows to be bad and shameful, with *adikein* and *apeithein* sharing

tice philosophy, remaining at the "post" at which his divine better, his only moral superior, has stationed him,[7] forever examining himself and others.

Are there, then, no substantive moral truths that Socrates professes to know? As surprising as it may seem, for Socrates, all moral propositions, even so fundamental a proposition as that it is worse to suffer than to commit injustice, are open to debate, and argument is always in order. Moreover, even "proof" is not final.[8] When Socrates remarks to Polus in the *Gorgias* at 479e, "Has it not been proved that what was said is true?"[9] namely, that whoever avoids paying what is due is more wretched than he who pays it, he means no more than that he has constructed proofs upon premises to which Polus has agreed, proofs that will stand as long as the premises do. Indeed, he follows his remark immediately with the caveat "if these things are true" (*Gorg.* 480a). Moreover, in response to Polus's objection, "I think these statements are absurd, Socrates, though no doubt you think they agree with those expressed earlier," Socrates says, "Then either we should abandon those, or else these necessarily follow" (480e).[10] In elenchus, if the interlocutor withdraws the premisses to which he has agreed, the conclusion is no longer secured; often, a new proof is required.[11]

one article, *to*, and with the singular verb *estin* applying to both as one, it seems unlikely that *to adikein* is meant to stand on its own, apart from *apeithein tōi beltioni*, as a second thing that Socrates knows to be bad and shameful. Another passage in the *Apology*, 19b4–5, uses *adikein* just as *Ap.* 29b does. Moreover, it is constructed identically to *Ap.* 29b, containing, like it, an epexegetical *kai: Sōkratēs adikei kai periergazetai*, "Socrates does an injustice/commits a crime: he is meddlesome." *Adikein*, in the *Apology*, is a semi-technical legal term. The official charge against Socrates states that he "commits a crime (*adikein*): he corrupts the young" (Ap. 24c4).

7. Although Socrates in the *Apology* (at 28d–29a) makes a point of saying that he stayed where his commanders, *archontes*, stationed him, he notes that what would be truly terrible is if he, out of fear of death, were to abandon the post at which the god stationed him, that post being the practice of philosophy and the examination of himself and others.

8. In the disagreement between Kraut (1984), 208, n. 37, and Irwin (1977), 71, regarding whether or not it is compatible with expertise to be willing to reopen any moral question, I side with Irwin, who asserts that "this is no expert's procedure.... The expert in a particular craft offers authoritative guidance, supported by a rational account." See *Rep.* 1.340e: "The expert never errs," *oudeis tōn dēmiourgōn hamartanei*.

9. This is the star instance in the case Vlastos (1985), 21, makes for "elenctic" knowledge.

10. See also *Euthyph.* 15c: "Therefore, either we were not agreeing nobly before, or if we did agree nobly then, we are not setting it down correctly now."

11. There are many examples of Socrates' willingness to reopen an argument: *Euthyph.* 4e; *Charm.* 169d; *Prot.* 354e–355a; *Gorg.* 486e; *M.* 86d; *Rep.* 1.337e.

There are, to be sure, things that Socrates says he or others know. But not every utterance of the word "know" marks the presence of a knowledge-claim. When Socrates says, for example, with respect to the craftsmen, "I knew that I would discover that they, at least, had knowledge of many noble things" (Ap. 22d1–2), is he making a knowledge-claim? If he is, why does he proceed to investigate what he presumably "knew." Moreover, all he says he knew is that he "would discover," *eurēsoimi*, that the craftsmen had knowledge of many things. What more could "knew" mean here than something like "strongly suspected"?

Then there are the many occasions on which Socrates uses, with respect to himself or others, the phrase "know well." "Know well" is not the same as "know," nor is it an intensified version of it. Rather, it is an expression that suggests a kind of street-smart confidence, born of experience, about the workings of the world. Typically, experts do not "know well"; they simply know. When Socrates says, for example, "For I know well that, wherever I go, the young will listen to me when I speak, just as they do here" (Ap. 37d6–7), he makes a claim, not to expertise, but only to a certain degree of worldly awareness. He uses the expression "know well" also with respect to the badness of the penalties he rejects (Ap. 36b), appealing to shared common judgments about the undesirability of being a slave to the Eleven or an old man driven from place to place.[12] Similarly, Socrates' assertion at Gorg. 521c9–d3, "But I know this well: that if I do come into court involved in one of those dangers that you mention, the man who brings me in will be a wicked man, for no good man would bring in a man who is not a wrongdoer," is not a knowledge-claim but a defiant repudiation of the naïveté and misplaced complacency with which Callicles just charged him.[13]

In the Socratic dialogues, there are also many instances in which Socrates says simply "I know," yet clearly does not mean to claim any sort of wisdom or expertise. For example, Socrates says of Charmides: "I know him" (Charm. 154b3). Socrates also "knows" what others think, believe, feel, will say, or will do: Crito 49d2; Gorg. 487c6, 512d1; Lys. 204b7; M. 80c3.[14] He "knows" facts that are common

---

12. If the judgment that exile is bad were a "philosophical" one rather than a conventional one, it is unlikely that Socrates' advanced age would have counted for him as a relevant factor.

13. See also Gorg. 486e5–6: "I know well that if you agree with what my soul believes, then that is the very truth." The "know well" here clearly means "I have every confidence."

14. Socrates often uses "know well" both about what others think and value (see

knowledge about famous people: *Gorg.* 515e10; *M.* 91d2. Socrates "knows" things about his interlocutors that flatter them into submitting to elenchus: *Gorg.* 487c1; *Euthyd.* 271c6. He also "knows" the ways of the world: *Gorg.* 511b1, 522b3. He "knows" what is needed in order to reach a firm answer: *Prot.* 360e8. He "knows" that some cities are ruled tyrannically, some democratically, and some aristocratically: *Rep.* 1.338d9. He also "knows" that people have five fingers on one hand: *Ion* 537e4. None of these known things has moral import. Knowing any or all of these things, however, makes neither Socrates nor anyone else a wise man.

Socrates also speaks from time to time of things everyone knows. Since he, too, is someone, must he not be claiming to have knowledge of these things? Yet knowing something that everyone knows is hardly expertise. For Socrates, expertise is always a rare commodity from which the many are excluded;[15] knowing the things everyone knows, the small things (*Euthyd.* 293b7–8), does not confer wisdom on their knowers.

Socrates sometimes claims that someone else knows something, the primary example of this being the sea captain who presumably knows that "for a wicked man it is better not to live, for he necessarily lives poorly" (*Gorg.* 512b1–2). Yet Socrates cannot possibly believe that the sea captain actually has such knowledge. If there is one thing Socrates makes clear in the *Apology*, it is that people who are masters of nonmoral *technai* have no moral expertise to speak of.

Vlastos (1985), 10, includes among the things Socrates must surely know those things Socrates attributes to the moral expert (see, for example, *Crito* 47d1–2, 48a5–7), but, let us note, Socrates reg-

---

Euthyd. 297d8, 303d2, d4) as well as in describing himself (see *Gorg.* 522d8 and *HMi.* 372d2). In all these cases he uses "know" colloquially to express his strong conviction.

15. The point that Socrates makes in his first cross-examination of Meletus in the *Apology* (24d–26b) is that it is never the case, in any field of expertise, that the many are skilled and the few are bunglers. A possible exception might be thought to occur at *Rep.* 1.351a5–6, where Socrates says to Thrasymachus: "injustice is ignorance—no one could still be ignorant of that." Yet not only is Socrates' remark ironic, its purpose being to needle the obstinate Thrasymachus, who withholds assent from a conclusion that follows from premises he accepts, but as Benson (1990b), 27, points out, Thrasymachus does not even now believe—let alone know—that injustice is ignorance. A similar case might be *Prot.* 357d7–e1: "You yourselves, surely, know that wrong action done without knowledge is done because of ignorance (*amathiāi*)." In this case, although Socrates seems to impute knowledge to his interlocutors, he in fact uses the imputation of knowledge to them as a way of disarming their resistance to his argument. Moreover, what they are said to know is, not some moral truth, but a presumably tautologous one: that acting without knowledge is acting in ignorance.

ularly raises doubts (at *Crito* 47d1–2 and *M.* 98c, for example) about the existence of such a man and, through his frequent professions of ignorance, misses no opportunity to disclaim being that man.[16]

Finally, there are many things that Socrates asserts with confidence and conviction but does not say he knows. Some expressions used to convey this confidence or conviction are the following: "It is evident (*dēlon*) (*Ap.* 41d3); "it has been made clear" (*Rep.* 1.335e5, 336a9); "Then I was right in saying" (*Gorg.* 468e3); "We are right, therefore" (*M.* 99c11); "These things having become evident" (*Gorg.* 508e6–7); "they have been clamped down and tethered by arguments of iron and adamant" (*Gorg.* 508e7–509a2); "Has it not been proved (*apodedeiktai*)?" (*Gorg.* 479e8). Far from indicating that Socrates believes he has some sort of knowledge, these utterances represent Socrates' studied refusal to profess knowledge of any kind; in other words, it is precisely in order to avoid claiming to have knowledge that he skirts the term "know." His assertion, for example, that his statements "have been clamped down and tethered by arguments of iron and adamant" is followed immediately by "at least so it would appear" and, but three lines later, by "I do not know how these things stand" (*Gorg.* 509a4).[17] Socrates' views stand only until such time as someone refutes them (*Gorg.* 509a2–3). And although Socrates no doubt thinks it unlikely that his views will be refuted (especially considering that, as he says, up until now no one has been able to hold an opposing view without appearing ridiculous [*Gorg.* 509a5–7]), nevertheless, if it did happen, he would record the refuter as his greatest "benefactor," *euergetēs* (*Gorg.* 506c2–3).

The upshot of this pruning of Socrates' putatively vast stock of knowledge-claims is that Socrates claims no moral expertise, whether for himself or for others. No one—and certainly not someone who engages daily in conversation with others—can go through life confining his use of the word "know" to those occasions upon which he means to make a knowledge-claim. When, however, Socrates does wish either to profess knowledge or to disavow it, he fairly heralds his pronouncement: "Nobody knows *x;* but I, who also fail to know *x,* do know *y*"; or "There are few things I claim to know, but *x* is one of them."

---

16. Does Vlastos really want to say that this moral expert, *epaïon* (*Crito.* 47d2), whose existence is in doubt, has only elenctic knowledge?

17. See *Gorg.* 506a3–4: "For I do not say what I say to you as one who knows."

None of the preceding is intended to imply that Socrates employs systematically two senses of "know." It means to suggest, instead, that Socrates, like all speakers of natural language in natural situations, even in simulated natural situations, cannot but use "know" non-technically rather frequently. Radical proposals, such as Vlastos's (1985) attribution to Socrates of two distinct kinds of knowledge, certain knowledge (knowledge$_C$), which, according to Vlastos, Socrates disavows, and elenctic knowledge (knowledge$_E$), which Vlastos insists Socrates both possesses and claims to possess, are themselves too technical to succeed, for they turn a wooden ear to the necessities of spoken language.[18] Moreover, Vlastos's specific proposal is vulnerable to other objections. First, if, as Vlastos maintains, Socrates recognizes uncertain knowledge as bona fide knowledge, then (a) why is Socrates so adamant in his disavowal of knowledge; and (b) why is he so proud of the very few things he does know? Second, how are we to construe those passages in which Socrates contrasts things he knows with things he does not know? Does he know$_E$ that it is bad and shameful to disobey one's better but fail to know$_C$ whether death is good or bad (*Ap.* 29b)? And, third, is it at all reasonable to think that the things Socrates says he knows, he knows$_E$, that is, as a *result* of practicing his elenchus?

Despite his lack of moral expertise, however, Socrates hardly lacks conviction or commitment with respect to his moral beliefs.[19] As a consequence of his investigation of the views of others, Socrates' own opinions are tested, probed, and repeatedly subjected to critical scrutiny. And they, unlike the alternatives to them that are embraced by Socrates' interlocutors, never strike him as absurd (*Gorg.* 509a).[20] It

18. Woodruff (1990), 65–67, suggests a somewhat more viable distinction, a distinction between expert knowledge and nonexpert knowledge. But he assigns substantive moral propositions to the category of nonexpert knowledge. As we have seen, however, Socrates disavows knowledge of even the most rudimentary substantive moral propositions. All moral knowledge is expert knowledge, knowledge that Socrates claims to lack. Nonexpert knowledge certainly exists for Socrates: it is what everyone knows. But as Woodruff notes, 67, Socrates has no interest in such knowledge—either in asserting or in denying that he has it or in challenging others' claims to have it.

19. See, for example, *Rep.* 1.337e: "How could a man answer who, in the first place, does not know and does not profess to know, and who, in the second place, even if he does have some suppositions about these things, is forbidden to say what he believes . . . ?" (trans. Bloom [1968]).

20. Even Socrates' assertions that his opinions wander (*Euthyph.* 11b) or that he "cannot agree with myself" and is "always changing my opinion" (*HMi.* 37b–c) or that he is "absurd" (*Prot.* 361a) are not, contra Kraut (1984), 287, n. 64, truly admissions of perplexity: they are, instead, a description of what happens to Socrates' opinions in *elenchoi* that proceed from premises that his interlocutors—but not he—endorse.

is even likely that Socrates thinks his beliefs true: at *Gorg.* 472b, he chides Polus for trying to "banish me from my property, the truth." Nevertheless, to hold opinions, even true opinions, confidently is not to have knowledge. And that there is a difference between belief, even when true, and knowledge is one of the very few things Socrates would claim to know (*M.* 98b3–5).

If moral knowledge is ultimately unattainable by ordinary human beings, why, then, does Socrates repeatedly stress the urgency of attaining it; why does he say such things as: "I suppose that all of us ought to be contentiously eager to know what is true and what is false about the things we are talking about" (*Gorg.* 505e4–5) or "the matters in dispute between us are . . . pretty nearly those it is most admirable to have knowledge about and most shameful not to. For the heart of the matter is that of recognizing or failing to recognize who is happy and who is not" (*Gorg.* 472c6–d1)?[21] For Socrates, nothing is as important as knowing the answer to how people ought to live. Indeed, it is the yearning for moral wisdom that fuels the examined life—even when one recognizes that the wisdom yearned for is beyond reach. The way of the skeptic is not Socrates' way: for Socrates, if even truths that cannot be *known* by man might still be discovered, how can the quest for them fail to be worthwhile?

I have argued in this book that the *Meno* affirms (i) the unattainability of knowledge by ordinary human beings, (ii) the value of true opinion, and (iii) the possibility of achieving virtue even without knowledge. To confirm that these convictions are authentically Socratic, that is, that they are true to the Platonic representation of Socrates in the Socratic dialogues, I turn at last to the *Apology.*

Socrates makes it clear in the *Crito* at 49a–d and in the *Gorgias* at 482a–b that his own beliefs do not shift. Indeed, given Socrates' declaration in the *Gorgias* that his views are always the same, one cannot but take ironically with respect to Socrates himself Socrates' conclusion that "it is disgraceful that men in such a condition as we now appear to be in should swagger as though we were something when we are never of the same mind about the same questions—and those the greatest of all. So uneducated are we" (*Gorg.* 527d5–c1).

21. One need not have hope of attaining knowledge in order to hunger for it; one need only harbor the conviction that what is unknown is knowable—if not by human beings, then by gods; if not by ordinary human beings, then by extraordinary ones, the counterparts among the living to Teiresias among the dead.

i. The Unattainability of Knowledge by Ordinary Human Beings

As a result of his attempt to refute the oracle (*Ap.* 20e–22e), Socrates comes to realize that others who seem wise are not so, that, indeed, they are less wise than Socrates because they think, mistakenly, that they know the important things of which they are, in fact, sorely ignorant. That is not all Socrates learns: besides learning that he is wisest, he learns, too, that he is the paradigm for all people who, like him, recognize that they lack wisdom (*Ap.* 23a–b). Yet if it is not Socrates per se but anyone who recognizes his own ignorance who is wisest, then it is no mere accident of history that no one with substantive wisdom, that is, with wisdom that goes beyond the recognition of ignorance concerning *ta megista,* has as yet appeared. Instead, it is a condition of being an ordinary—as opposed to a superhuman—human being that one's wisdom cannot reach any higher than the recognition of one's ignorance of *ta megista,* that is, than the recognition that "in truth [one] is worth nothing with respect to wisdom" (*Ap.* 23b3–4). The god alone is wise with wisdom greater than human; human wisdom is worth little or nothing (*Ap.* 23a). No human being, for as long as he fails to transcend the limits of his humanity, will ever attain in this life the wisdom that is the god's.

Nor will he fare any better in death. In death, at least as Socrates envisions it in the *Apology,* human limitation is not transcended: Socrates will do in Hades precisely what he does here—he will examine and sort through those he meets to determine who is a wise man and who supposes he is wise but is not. If in Hades Socrates does what he does here, then, insofar as he will there encounter men who, though perhaps a cut above his current clientele, are in the final analysis no more than men, he will find, once more, none who is wise with a wisdom greater than human, none who has achieved substantive knowledge with respect to *ta megista.* More important, Socrates imagines his own lack of moral expertise unchanged.

ii. The Value of True Opinion

Among the things Socrates urges those he encounters to care for, more than for money, reputation, and honor, are *phronēsis,* truth, and the condition of one's soul (*Ap.* 29e). These are strictly human ambitions: although *phronēsis* is at times in Plato's corpus used interchangeably with *epistēmē* and *sophia*, here it denotes the moral virtue of practical wisdom, of prudence.[22] The *Apology* conspicuously neglects to encourage the pursuit of moral wisdom; indeed, full-blown moral wisdom (as opposed to mere "human wisdom," which consists of recognition of ignorance) is, it would seem, explicitly closed off to mere mortals. Yet truth remains a valued goal, on a par with *phronēsis*, with the well-being of the soul, with virtue itself. In place of expertise, knowledge, or wisdom, there is to be endless philosophizing in the pursuit of truth.

iii. The Possibility of Achieving Virtue without Wisdom

In the *Apology*, Socrates' purported overintellectualization of virtue is not in evidence. He links, not the possession or attainment of virtue, but its teaching to the greater-than-human wisdom that he imputes, tongue in cheek, to the sophists.[23] Socrates appears to tie possession of virtue to such humanly attainable aims as caring about the right things and avoiding intentional injustice.[24]

Socrates, it is clear, regards himself as a good man, a man who possesses virtue—of the sort, of course, that men can possess.[25] He is, in his view, not only a "better" man than his accusers (*Ap.* 30d1) but a good one: "This has convicted many other good men, too,"

22. Were *phronēsis* in the *Apology* a matter of *epistēmē* or *sophia*, Socrates could hardly have concluded that those "with more paltry reputations seemed to be men more fit in regard to being prudent," *phronimos echein* (*Ap.* 22a5–6). Surely, none of these men had any measure of moral expertise.

23. "And I regarded Evenus as blessed if he should truly have this art and teaches at such a modest rate" (*Ap.* 20b9–c1). "But those of whom I just spoke might perhaps be wise in some wisdom greater than human, or else I cannot say what it is" (*Ap.* 20d9–e2). "Though this, too, seems to me to be noble [viz., to educate human beings and make money from it], if one should, like Gorgias of Leontini and Prodicus of Ceos and Hippias of Elis, be able to educate human beings" (*Ap.* 19d9–e4).

24. See also *Gorg.* 527d, where Socrates states that a man who is good and honorable practices or "pursues," *askōn*, virtue.

25. If Socrates calls himself an *agathos*, he must believe he has virtue, *aretē*: there is in Greek no other adjective but *agathos* to denote one who is virtuous; and *agathos* is related etymologically to *aretē*, through the superlative form, *aristos*. See *Gorg.* 506d2–4: "But surely we are good, both we and everything else that is good, when some virtue has come to be present in us?" See also *M.* 87e1: "And it is by virtue that we are good?"

Socrates says at *Ap.* 28a, implying that he is himself a good man (as are others).[26] A good man is a man who is just, who acts on principle, not relinquishing principle even in the face of death (*Ap.* 28b–c). He is one who cares for the right things, the things that matter (*phronēsis*, truth, and the best condition of the soul), not for the wrong ones, the things of no importance (money, reputation, and honor) (*Ap.* 29e). Indeed, in the *Apology*, a sign that one lacks or has failed to acquire virtue seems to be one's *caring* about the wrong things: "And if one of you . . . asserts that he does care. . . . And if he does not seem to me to possess (or, 'to have acquired,' *kektēsthai*) virtue but only says he does, I will reproach him, saying that he regards the things worth the most as least important and the paltrier things as more important" (*Ap.* 29e3–30a2).[27] Later, at 31b, Socrates says that what he seeks to persuade the Athenians to do is to *care* for virtue, and that his own "whole care," *pan melei*, "is to commit no unjust or impious deed" (*Ap.* 32d2–3). Moreover, he does not do anything unjust. At 36b, Socrates says that he attempts to persuade the Athenians to care first and foremost about how they themselves will be best and as prudent as possible and, at 37a, that he does not do injustice to any human being voluntarily. For all these reasons, Socrates believes himself to be a good man: in comforting his judges, he assures them that there is nothing bad in store for a good man, that is, for him, whether living or dead (*Ap.* 41c–d). In none of what Socrates says in the *Apology* does the possession of virtue await the acquisition of knowledge: it is sufficient never to do injustice voluntarily, no matter what the cost to oneself; to care about the things truly worth caring about; and to live philosophically, examining oneself and others. The "greatest good," *megiston agathon*, for a human being, Socrates says at *Ap.* 38a, is to make speeches about virtue and the other things about which he converses and examines himself and others. Even in death, even in Hades, "the greatest thing," *to megiston* (41b5), is to examine those there "just as I do those here" (41b6); indeed, he continues, "to converse and to associate with and

---

26. It is perhaps noteworthy that the "judges in truth" and the men who were just in their own lives whom Socrates hopes, as he says, to find in Hades all turn out to be demigods (*Ap.* 41a). Is he the only just man (though other men may have been, like him, unjustly accused) to be found there?

27. Somewhat unaccountably, Irwin (1977), 90, cites this passage as proof that Socrates holds that knowledge (or the ability to give an account) determines whether or not one has virtue.

to examine" the likes of Agamemnon, Odysseus, or Sisyphus would be "inconceivable happiness," *amēchanon eudaimonias* (41c3–4). Yet Socrates neither achieves nor hopes to achieve—whether in life or in death—the wisdom greater than human that constitutes expertise in *ta megista*, in virtue. Moral inquiry may be the best life for man; nevertheless, moral expertise, if only it were attainable, would surely be better.[28] As things stand, the best is not within reach; that is why second-best becomes the "greatest good" and "inconceivable happiness."

Yet, it will be objected, Socrates does, if not in the *Apology*, then certainly frequently and regularly throughout the Socratic dialogues, link virtue to knowledge, implying, or so it is thought, that knowledge is, if not identical to virtue, then surely a necessary and sufficient condition for it. A careful consideration of the many passages that connect virtue to wisdom shows, however, that they emphasize, not the necessity, but the sufficiency of knowledge for virtue: *Charm.* 174b–176a;[29] *Prot.* 349e–360e; *Lach.* 199b9–c7;[30] *Euthyd.* 279–282.[31]

---

28. See Aristotle, *Eth. Nic.* 10.7.1177a27–28: "and it is reasonable that the course of life for those who know will be more pleasant than for those who inquire."

29. Socrates asks whether, by acting according to knowledge, we shall act well and be happy; he asks, that is, if knowledge is sufficient for virtue and happiness. But Critias answers that without knowledge, happiness will not be found, that is, that knowledge is *necessary* for happiness (*Charm.* 173d). And when Socrates later says, "none of these things will be beneficially done if knowledge of the good be wanting" (*Charm.* 174d), he is merely echoing Critias's earlier confusion. For Socrates, knowledge guarantees success; only its contrary—not its contradictory—guarantees failure.

30. In the *Laches'* formulation: "Everyone is good in that in which he is wise" (*Lach.* 194d1–2). In other words, knowledge is sufficient for virtue. Nicias goes on to derive, illegitimately, the converse of this proposition, namely, that "if the brave man is good, it is evident that he is also wise" (*Lach.* 194d4–5). Only with respect to the former of these propositions does Socrates say, "You certainly speak the truth, by God, Nicias" (194d3). After the latter proposition, Socrates only asks Laches if he hears (194d6): there is no endorsement. As the discussion progresses, Nicias emerges as just another Euthyphro: the prudence, the wisdom, he recommends as courage is knowing how to deal with gods and human beings so as to guard oneself against terrible things and provide oneself with good things (*Lach.* 199d–e).

31. In the *Euthydemus*, the phrase "without *phronēsis* and wisdom (*sophia*)" means "when he has no sense," *noun mē echōn* (281b), that is, when he is in a state of complete ignorance (*amathia*) (281e). Thus, although the *Euthydemus* rules out the possibility of one's achieving "good use" when one is guided by ignorance, it does not, ipso facto, rule out this possibility for one who falls short of knowledge but is nevertheless not guided by ignorance. (In the context of Socrates' recommending to Clinias the pursuit of wisdom, it is hardly surprising that he is fairly uninterested in finding and specifying some alternative means to happiness.) See also *M.* 88 ff., where the kind of lack of wisdom that is the source of faring ill is folly—not a mere lack of expertise.

Of course, the deeply ignorant cannot be virtuous; but one who possesses true opinion is far from being ignorant. The man who goes right—in belief, in action, in objects of care—is the focus of the second half of the *Meno;* it is in the *Meno* that we come to see how it is that Socrates, or anyone who lives philosophically but lacks moral wisdom, can be a good man, can have virtue, if in a secondary degree: such a man can have, and act upon, true moral beliefs.

In the final analysis, Socrates is a man of good sense. He recognizes that *logoi* that begin with opinions must end with opinions: such *logoi* cannot transcend opinion to reach knowledge. Yet we who read Plato deny to Socrates the very common sense that we arrogate to ourselves. For who among us does not recognize that the study of ethics will not yield anything as definitive as knowledge? Who among us thinks that moral wisdom is like geometry? Moreover, for those of us who toil in the field of moral philosophy, does the awareness that ethical investigation will not yield knowledge render it an enterprise wholly without value? Why, then, do we assume that Socrates cannot embrace a life of moral inquiry that will not, as *he* is well aware, culminate in knowledge?[32] Socrates does, in full awareness of the limitations of his discipline, just what we do—indeed, what we have learned from him to do: he posits as axioms what seem to be the most fundamental and "self-evident" moral or psychological principles, regarding even these, however, as subject to rethinking or revision, and seeks to hold other people, as he holds himself, to the logical consequences of the acceptance of these fundamental principles. In doing as Socrates does, in striving for the moral knowledge that we know full well cannot be ours, we, like Socrates in the *Meno,* hope to attain true belief.

And in the *Meno,* of course, a middle ground, true or right belief, is posited between knowledge and ignorance. In every case, Socrates' point is that knowledge is the guarantor of virtue or happiness. What is lost when knowledge is lost is not the very possibility of benefit but its necessity.

32. See Vlastos (1985), 6: "If after decades of searching Socrates remained convinced that he still knew *nothing*, would not further searching have become a charade ...?" (emphasis in original). Why, we might ask, would searching be a charade if it either confirmed and reconfirmed the likely truth of the searcher's propositions or strongly suggested their likely untruth?

Appendix I

Recollection in the Phaedo

One reason for taking seriously the recollection thesis in the *Meno* is that the *Meno* is not the only place in the Platonic corpus where Socrates advances this thesis. It emerges in full force in the *Phaedo* (primarily at 72e–77a, though it is mentioned again later on in the dialogue); and it turns up again in the *Phaedrus* (at 250) as well. Although some scholars have imagined it present or "implied" elsewhere (*Tim.* 42b;[1] *Rep.* 7.518b6–c2;[2] *Symposium*,[3] and even *Statesman*[4]), it is, in fact, rather conspicuously absent from these dialogues.[5] Indeed, it seems that what lies behind the sightings of recollection in dialogues besides the *Phaedo* and *Phaedrus* is little more than that it strikes scholars that recollection would fit nicely there. That recollection is missing just where it would fit nicely, however, makes its absence even more profoundly felt.

Recollection is, we may note, glaringly absent as well from other

An earlier version of this appendix, entitled "The *Phaedo*'s Rejection of the *Meno*'s Theory of Recollection," appeared in *Scripta Classica Israelica* 19 (2000): 51–70. I gratefully acknowledge permission to reprint.

1. Vlastos (1991b), 54.

2. See, for example, Hackforth (1955), 77; Gulley (1954), 195; Adam (1969), II, 98.

3. Bluck (1961a), 50.

4. Skemp (1952), 76, sees in the *Statesman*'s "sensible likenesses" (*aisthētai homoiotētes*) at 285e "the later form of the earlier doctrine of Recollection."

5. Although there is talk of reincarnation in the *Timaeus*, recollection does not appear there. As for the *Republic* passage, see Klein (1965), 158, who rightly insists that although Socrates does indeed maintain in this passage that there is within each of us the power to know, so that education is not the pouring of knowledge into ignorant souls, "still, there is no mention of 'recollection' in this passage."

Platonic dialogues where one would quite reasonably expect to find it, dialogues in which questions of what knowledge is and how it is acquired are prominent: the *Symposium* and, especially, the *Theaetetus*.[6] Moreover, of the two places besides the *Meno* where recollection is found explicitly,[7] the *Phaedrus* passage is so heavily mythic that perhaps one need not see in it anything literally intended. That leaves, in all of Plato, but one dialogue besides the *Meno* where recollection might qualify as a Socratic or Platonic "doctrine": the *Phaedo*. If the *Phaedo* is, in fact, the only place outside the *Meno* where the recollection thesis is developed with some sustained effort and is proposed more than just mythically, then the strength of the case for taking seriously the *Meno*'s recollection thesis is much diminished. Nevertheless, it is worthwhile to look at the recollection thesis in the *Phaedo* to see whether it sufficiently resembles the theory found in the *Meno* to serve as support and confirmation of it.

I will argue here that the *Phaedo*'s discussion of recollection consciously draws itself away from the *Meno*'s, making reference to the *Meno* for the express and sole purpose of severing all connection to it.[8] I will contend that the *Phaedo* is interested in recollection only insofar as recollection and Forms provide mutual support for one another and, together, help make the case for the immortality of the soul.[9] Yet recollection is not indispensable even in the *Phaedo* to

6. See Klein (1965), 157–72. Hackforth (1955), 77, approvingly quotes Cornford (1934), 28, who explains recollection's absence from the *Theaetetus* by saying that the *Theaetetus* "presupposes that we know the answer to the question here to be raised afresh: what is the nature of knowledge and of its objects."

7. One might say that recollection is implicitly parodied in the *Euthydemus* at 293–96, where Euthydemus and Dionysodorus seek to demonstrate to Socrates that he knows everything, maintaining that he knew "even when you were a child and when you were being conceived. And before you yourself came into being and before the foundation of heaven and earth, you knew absolutely everything, if it is true that you always know" (trans. Sprague [1965]).

8. It is the contention of this appendix, not only that the two versions of recollection are different, but that the *Phaedo*'s deliberately pulls away from the *Meno*'s. Many commentators recognize that the two versions differ, but they are reluctant to assert that Plato rejects in the *Phaedo* the version he proffers in the *Meno*. See, for example, Anderson (1993), 125; Bostock (1986), 63; Ackrill (1974), 177; and Hackforth (1955), 74. Bostock is typical. He says, on the one hand: "As Socrates indicates at 73b3–4, the version now to be presented is not meant to be the same as the *Meno*'s version." But he insists, on the other, that what the *Meno* contains is "an earlier version of this argument."

9. Scott (1995), 56–73, argues forcefully against what I, too, regard as an ill-conceived view of recollection in the *Phaedo*, namely, the view that it is a theory of concept formation.

the case for the soul's immortality: the dialogue offers other arguments for the nonbodily existence of the soul—both in its preexistence and in its postexistence—that are independent of recollection.
Nor is recollection regarded in the *Phaedo* as proved: its truth rests
on the imperfectly established existence of Forms.[10] Indeed, when
Socrates notes that recollection is "out of tune" with the attunement
theory of the soul, he does not presume that it is a foregone conclusion that the theory to be adopted is recollection theory—instead,
he allows Simmias to choose the theory he prefers (*Phdo.* 92c). Moreover, even when Simmias chooses recollection because, as he says, it
is grounded in a "hypothesis," the Theory of Forms, that he is convinced he holds rightly (*Phdo.* 92d–e), Socrates, not content to let
matters be, shores up the first argument he offered against attunement theory with two additional ones.[11]

It is probably fair to say, then, that Socrates is less than wedded
to recollection even in the *Phaedo*. One imagines that, were it to turn
out that people have no preexistent souls that might once have
known but since forgotten the Forms, Socrates would simply seek
some way other than recollection to account for how human beings
come to posit realities that transcend the sensibles that share their
names. Indeed, such an alternative explanation is suggested later on
in the *Phaedo*, where Socrates, in describing his second-best quest for
"causes," arrives at Forms to provide a "safe" solution to logical puz-
zles that are generated by experience (*Phdo.* 100–102).[12]

10. Although the *Phaedo* has its own "method of hypothesis," it instantiates the
Meno's hypothetical method in the way it proceeds, at *Phdo.* 72e–77a, to prove the
soul's immortality by way of recollection. It asks what would have to be true if the soul
is to be immortal. It answers: learning would have to be recollection. And what would
have to be true if learning is to be recollection? Answer: there would have to be Forms.
And do we know that there are Forms? Answer: not quite. So we do not really know
that the soul is immortal. (Although Socrates seems at first to recognize that only the
argument for immortality founders if there are no Forms—"this argument will have
been in vain" [*Phdo.* 76e4–5]—he goes on to speak as if immortality itself is on the
line: "and if not the former [that is, if the Forms do not exist], then not the latter
[that is, our souls do not exist before birth] either" [*Phdo.* 76e]).

11. The first is the rather peculiar argument that since an instrument can be more
or less in tune, it would follow from the assumption that the soul is an attunement
that a soul could be more or less a soul; but since a soul cannot be more or less a
soul, then, if it were an attunement, all souls would have to be, contrary to fact, equally
good (*Phdo.* 93a–94b). The second is the argument that whereas an attunement, qua
compound, follows and indeed cannot oppose its components, the soul often opposes
what, on attunement theory, would be its components, namely, the body (*Phdo.* 94b–
95a).

12. See also *Rep.* 7.524c: "the intellect was compelled to see big and little, too, not
mixed up together but distinguished, doing the opposite of what sight did. . . . Isn't

Socrates in the *Phaedo*, then, avoids dogmatism both about the Forms and about recollection. And this is so despite his meeting no resistance in Simmias and Cebes to either thesis: the same Simmias and Cebes who stubbornly resist virtually everything else Socrates proposes become surprisingly deferential when he speaks either of Forms or of recollection.[13] Indeed, against the backdrop of Simmias's and Cebes' ready endorsement of these Socratic offerings, Socrates' own restraint and circumspection are all the more striking.

Regardless of the degree to which Socrates is committed to the version of recollection he promotes in the *Phaedo*, he leaves no doubt that this version of recollection is incompatible with the version in the *Meno*—and that he means to have nothing to do with recollection as it is presented there. He signals in the *Phaedo* his break with the *Meno* in several ways: (a) dramatically, by challenging rather than defending the kind of recollection he espoused in the *Meno* (and leaving its defense to Cebes); (b) philosophically, by correcting the *Meno*'s version of recollection; and (c) by making parts of the *Phaedo*'s argument incomprehensible unless read as countering the *Meno*'s account. Let us turn now to the *Phaedo*'s discussion of recollection.

After Socrates does his best to establish that the souls of the dead exist (for if they died, eventually everything would be dead) (*Phdo.* 72a–e), Cebes chimes in with a supplementary argument: "And besides, Socrates, [the existence of the souls of the dead may be proved] . . . according to that thesis (*logos*) that you are always accustomed to spouting,[14] that for us learning turns out to be nothing

---

it from here that it first occurs to us to ask what the big and the little are? . . . and so, it was on this ground that we called the one intelligible and the other visible" (trans. Bloom [1968]).

13. Burger (1984), 70, notes how readily Cebes and Simmias accept recollection: "the recollection argument will turn out to be the only one in the entire conversation that both Cebes and Simmias wholeheartedly endorse. It is, therefore, the one too that Socrates shamelessly exploits: he need only appeal to the recollection thesis, and his interlocutors will immediately give up any opinions they believe conflict with it. Socrates takes advantage of their acceptance, despite the fact that it is based upon unexamined, and even preposterous, assumptions about the psyche, knowledge, and the objects of knowledge."

14. What is the best way to understand Cebes' characterization of the recollection thesis as something that Socrates is "always accustomed to spouting" (*Phdo.* 72e4–5)? Are we to think that Socrates regularly put forward the thesis that learning is recollection? Burnet (1911), 51, for one, thinks that "it is very difficult to regard this definite statement as a fiction." But Burnet also believes that the Theory of Forms must be attributed to the historical Socrates, inasmuch as Plato would not, in his

but recollection" (*Phdo.* 72e3–6). In Cebes' understanding of what he calls "Socrates'" thesis, what one is now reminded of one must have learned at some former time, and such "being reminded" would be impossible unless the soul existed somewhere before being born in human form. Unless our souls were immortal, Cebes concludes, we could not learn.

This first stage of Cebes' presentation of recollection theory corresponds roughly to the myth presented in the *Meno* at *M.* 81a–e. Indeed, two of the difficulties that plague the *Meno*'s recollection myth recur in Cebes' account of Socrates' recollection thesis. First, it is not clear in Cebes' account how the "learning" done in the "somewhere" where we presumably existed before we were born is accomplished: if it, too, is recollection, does that not create a regress that cannot be stopped–and, consequently, a chain of learning that cannot get started? It is true that in the *Meno* myth the soul is said to have "seen" (*heōrakuia*) all things; yet insofar as the myth also proclaims that all learning is recollection, it is not clear that there can be a first seeing that unproblematically constitutes the first learning. Second, the nature of the "somewhere" where our souls presumably existed before being born in human form is not clear, although Cebes, like the *Meno* myth, gives us no reason to think it is a place radically different from those places familiar from life and legend. We may observe, however, that whereas the *Meno* myth begins with the assumption that the soul is immortal, Cebes uses recollection to *prove* the immortality of the soul.[15]

depiction of Socrates' dying day, attribute to Socrates views that are not really Socrates' but are "novel doctrines" of Plato himself (xi–xii). I admit that I do not find as repugnant as Burnet does the notion that Plato uses Socrates as a mouthpiece for his own views: if Plato believes that his views are in some way a natural extension of Socrates', then it might well seem to Plato an act of devotion to ascribe his own views to Socrates (as, say, Pythagoreans ascribe their views to Pythagoras). Nevertheless, it *is* rather puzzling that Cebes speaks of recollection as a familiar Socratic thesis. It is true that Socrates, referring to the Forms, says the following in the *Phaedo*: "Well . . . this is what I mean: it is nothing new, but is what I have spoken of incessantly both at other times and in our earlier conversation" (*Phdo.* 100b1–3). The two cases are hardly the same, however. For in the case of Forms we might at least be able to say that the *character* Socrates talks incessantly about them, whereas not even the *character* Socrates is always talking about recollection. Perhaps it is best to suppose that Cebes, in his youthful exuberance, simply exaggerates: it is not, after all, Socrates but Cebes who says of Socrates that he is accustomed to speaking always of learning as recollection.

15. As was argued in Chapter 3, although it may appear that the slave-boy-demonstration ends by deriving the soul's immortality from recollection by way of the idea that the truth about the things that are is in our soul always (*M.* 86b1–2), the

When Simmias cannot "recall" the "proofs," *apodeixeis*, for the thesis that learning is recollection, Cebes rehearses for him the proof in the *Meno*'s slave-boy-demonstration. There is one excellent argument, Cebes says, namely, that when people are questioned, they are able, if someone asks the questions well, to say by themselves all that is; yet they surely would be unable to do so unless knowledge and a "right account," *orthos logos*, happened to be present within them. Thus, he continues, if one leads people to diagrams or anything else of that sort, there is proof positive that this is so (*Phdo.* 73a7–b2).[16]

The reference to the *Meno* is unmistakable.[17] The proof Cebes offers is but a summary of what takes place in the *Meno*'s slave-boy-demonstration. Socrates, there, leads the boy to a diagram and asks his questions well—too well.[18] The boy, in turn, comes up with the

---

fact is that immortality is simply revived and reaffirmed without argument and without any real connection to recollection. See Chap. 3, n. 90.

16. Burnet (1911), 52, following Bury (1906), 13, argues that the matter of leading one to diagrams "is opposed to, rather than included in," the process of asking questions well. This reading, however, is a forced one. It requires bypassing the most straightforward reading of the preposition that introduces the matter of leading one to diagrams: rather than as "thus," Burnet renders *epeita* as "secondly"—and this despite the absence of a prior *prōton men*, "firstly." In the absence of a *prōton men*, Burnet's reading requires that *heni logōi*, "by one argument," be read "firstly," even though he notes that this phrase has a very different sense ("in a word") at *Phdo.* 65d13. None of this is necessary. In the *Meno*, the process of putting questions well to the slave-boy, that is, of asking him leading questions, is not separate from the use of diagrams: the questioning does not occur apart from the diagrams. Moreover, Cebes himself regards the argument he presents as "*one* excellent argument" (*Phdo.* 73a7)—and this despite Simmias's request for "proof*s*," in the plural. We note, too, that Socrates subsequently refers to Cebes' proof in the singular, *tautēi*.

17. Somewhat remarkably, commentators have been hesitant to make the connection definitively. Gallop (1993), 88–89, says that this passage contains what is "possibly an allusion to *Meno* 81e–86b." Burnet (1911), says: "This seems a fairly certain reference to *Meno* 82b9 sqq. . . . No doubt, if we hold this doctrine and its proof to be genuinely Socratic, the reference to the *Meno* is less certain." I am not sure exactly why Burnet thinks that the reference to the *Meno* becomes suspect if one takes the view and proof as genuinely Socratic, unless he takes the *Meno* to be clearly un-Socratic. But whatever he may mean, it is hard to see how there could be anything here but a direct allusion to the *Meno*. See also Hackforth (1955), 74, n. 1, who thinks that with respect to the leading of people to diagrams, there is a clear reference in this passage to the *Meno*, but that with respect to the "proper questioning," there may be only "a quite general reference to that Socratic 'midwifery' which is abundantly illustrated in the early dialogues." I think, however, that, considering how many times Socrates in the *Meno* emphasizes that he is only asking questions and not teaching the slave-boy, it is highly unlikely that there is anything here but a reference to the *Meno*.

18. Cornford (1952), 51, recognizes that the phrase "if one asks well" at *Phdo.* 73a

correct answer, presumably *on his own*. As we saw in Chapter 3, the slave-boy does not really produce the correct answer on his own. Nevertheless, Meno in the *Meno* concurs with Socrates' assessment that he does; and Cebes in the *Phaedo* appears to reach the same conclusion. Furthermore, although Socrates, in his recapitulation of the slave-boy-demonstration, determines that what the slave-boy has in his soul is not knowledge and a correct *logos* but only true opinions,[19] Cebes assumes, just as the *Meno*'s discussion predisposes Meno to assume, that what those questioned must have inside them is knowledge.[20]

Perhaps the most striking feature of the introduction of the *Meno*'s recollection thesis into the *Phaedo* is that the character who both introduces and defends it is not Socrates but Cebes. Not only is Socrates not the one to advance what Cebes presents as a customary Socratic view, but he will propose, momentarily, in his own name, a very different theory, for which he will adduce a very different proof. Moreover, Socrates immediately disparages Cebes' proofs: "But if you are not persuaded by that, Simmias . . . then see whether you might agree by looking at it this way" (*Phdo.* 73b3–4). Socrates even plants doubt in a Simmias who, apparently, has none: Socrates says, "For, you are indeed distrustful as to how what is called learning is recollection?" (*Phd.* 73b4–5),[21] to which Simmias says, "I am not

might point to "some uneasiness" in Plato's mind with respect to the slave-boy-demonstration in the *Meno*, where Socrates' questions are leading ones.

19. We may compare Socrates' expression in the *Meno*, *enesontai autōi alētheis doxai*, "there are going to be present within him true opinions" (*M.* 86a7), with Cebes' *kaitoi ei mē etungchanein autois epistēmē enousa kai orthos logos*, "yet unless knowledge and right account were present within them" (*Phdo.* 73a9–10). Although Socrates speaks at one point in the *Meno* of the knowledge the slave-boy has now (*M.* 85d9), he proceeds, as was argued in Chapter 3, Section iv, to reduce to absurdity the possibility that the slave-boy has knowledge now, concluding that all he has now are true opinions.

20. Whereas Cebes is surely right to connect having knowledge with possessing a correct account, he is wrong to conclude that when those questioned are able to produce the right answer, that in itself demonstrates that they have knowledge and a correct account within. In the *Meno*, although Socrates contends that the slave-boy's arriving at the right answer indicates that he has true opinions within, does he really have, with respect to the diagonal, either knowledge or true opinions within? Surely, what the slave-boy has within is the ability to follow the compelling proof for, and hence to learn, the new bit of geometry that Socrates teaches him.

21. See Hackforth (1955), 74, who says, rightly, that "the description of the *Meno* argument as 'excellent' (*kallistos*) is partly offset by Socrates' doubt whether Simmias finds it convincing." Hackforth resists, however, drawing the conclusion for which I argue, namely, that Socrates is "repudiating the earlier argument for recollection and immortality." The most Hackforth will concede is that Socrates regards the argument he will currently expound as "far superior" (see n. 8). See also Gulley (1954), 197:

distrustful," *apistō ou* (*Phdo.* 73b6). Simmias in fact declares himself "nearly convinced," *schedon peithomai*, by Cebes' way of putting the matter; he is nearly able to "recall," *schedon memnēmai*, that learning is recollection (*Phdo.* 73b6–9). It is clear even to Simmias, however, that Socrates wants him to resist Cebes' account (which is, of course, the *Meno*'s account) of recollection and to hear Socrates' new account instead. He is willing to oblige: he would be pleased, he says, to hear how Socrates would put it (*Phdo.* 73b9–10).

What follows is Socrates' statement of the theory that learning is recollection, accompanied by a new proof. Neither the content nor the demonstration that Socrates presents resembles Cebes' account at all.

Socrates begins his account by distinguishing it from that of Cebes. "I, for my part (*egōge*)," he says, "put it this way" (*Phdo.* 73c1).[22] The way Socrates puts it is, in other words, *not* Cebes' way. In what follows, Socrates departs both from Cebes' opening account of recollection, that is, from Cebes' paraphrase of the *Meno*'s myth, and from the proofs Cebes subsequently provides for it, that is, from his distillation of the slave-boy-demonstration.

In the *Meno*, as we saw in Chapter 3, the slave-boy-demonstration is hardly the defense or proof that it purports to be of recollection as it appears in the recollection myth. On the contrary, the picture of the process of recollection that emerges from the myth is very different from the one that derives from the slave-boy-demonstration. The learner, according to the myth, is a solitary inquirer; no mention is made of his having need of another. Having lived numerous lives before the present one and having seen and learned all things, namely, the things both here and in Hades, he is able to recollect what he knew previously. Moreover, once he recollects a single thing, the recollection of all the others requires but courage and perseverance since all things have a natural kinship to one another. The process of recollection as depicted in the slave-

"In 73c Plato introduces a new aspect of the theory, hinting at its novelty in his suggestion that if Simmias is not convinced by it in its presentation so far, then perhaps he will agree if it is presented in another way (73b)." Let us observe, however, that it is not Socrates but Cebes who calls the *Meno*'s argument *kallistos* (at *Phdo.* 73a7); all Socrates does is immediately offer to replace it.

22. See Burger (1984), 71: "Dissatisfied, apparently, with Cebes' enactment of recollection, Socrates takes over." We shall see at the end of this appendix that Socrates wishes to substitute in the *Phaedo* for the version of recollection in the *Meno* a version suitable to Simmias and Cebes: just as the *Meno*'s version is fashioned for Meno's sake, so is the *Phaedo*'s designed for Simmias and Cebes.

boy-demonstration, by contrast, resembles nothing so much as elenchus, a procedure that requires the participation of both a questioner and an answerer, a procedure that relies on questioning to
arouse opinions held by the answerer but hidden from his view.[23]
The *Phaedo*'s recollection thesis needs to defeat both the *Meno*'s
myth-related brand of recollection and the sort of recollection found
in the slave-boy-demonstration. To that end, it replaces both (a) the
myth's notion that the sole way in which each of us learns is by
recapturing by ourselves, by trying hard, things we saw in a previous lifetime, since "all nature is akin," and (b) the slave-boy-
demonstration's notion that all learning takes place only by "recollecting," that is, by being asked questions and being shown diagrams,
with (c) the distinct notion that *sometimes* when we learn we do so
by recollecting Forms with which we were acquainted before birth.

Two divergences from Cebes' statement of the recollection thesis
thus appear immediately: first, whereas according to Cebes, whatever
was learned previously must have been learned before one was in
human form, according to Socrates in the *Phaedo*, what was previously known could have been learned at any previous time; second,
whereas according to Cebes, the proof of the soul's immortality lies
in that one can only be reminded of what one has learned before
this lifetime, according to Socrates in the *Phaedo*, the soul's immortality is not derivable solely from the phenomenon of "being reminded," since one can be reminded, as Socrates says, as long as one
knew the thing one is reminded of "before," *proteron* (*Phdo.* 73c2)—
that is, at any previous time.

Socrates is not, of course, correcting only Cebes. What he is correcting is recollection in the *Meno*. In affirming that one's being
reminded requires only that one have known "before," he challenges
both the implication of the *Meno*'s myth that all kinds of knowledge
are "seen" prenatally and its assumption that the soul is therefore
immortal. In the *Phaedo*, the immortality of the soul will stand or fall
with the recollection specifically of Forms—entities which, as the
Phaedo argues, cannot be "seen" by embodied souls, but only by disembodied ones.

As Socrates continues, he makes his position even clearer. It is
not that all learning is recollection (as in the *Meno*); it is only when

---

23. The slave-boy-demonstration is not a genuine elenchus, of course, because
Socrates in the demonstration is a knower who, in fact, teaches the slave-boy something the slave-boy never knew before.

knowledge comes to one by one's being reminded that there is recollection (*Phdo.* 73c4–5).[24] Any other way of learning, then, is not
recollection. And how is one reminded? Is it, as the *Meno* would have
us believe, by being asked a question or by being shown the answer
in a diagram? Is it true, in other words, that the slave-boy was "being
reminded" of something?[25] Not according to Socrates in the *Phaedo*.
In the *Phaedo*, being reminded occurs when someone sees, hears, or
in some other way senses something and, upon doing so, recognizes
not only the thing perceived but also, as a result of that perception,
something else (*Phdo.* 73c6–8). Moreover, the knowledge by which
a thing of which one is reminded is known must be, Socrates insists,
not the same as, but different from, the knowledge by which the
original thing is recognized (*Phdo.* 73c8).

Many subtle and ingenious suggestions have been made with respect to what Socrates intends by this last qualification, that is, by
the stipulation that the knowledge by which the reminding thing is
known must differ from the knowledge by which the thing of which
one is reminded is known.[26] Hackforth (1955), 67, n. 4, for example,
thinks that the qualification seeks to rule out as bona fide recollection one's being reminded, when one perceives x, of the characteristics of x that one does not perceive at the moment—since the
knowledge by which one knows x's characteristics would be the same
knowledge as that by which one knows x. For Burnet (1911), 54, it
is knowledge of opposites that does not count for Socrates as genuine recollection—since the knowledge of one of the opposites is
not distinct from the knowledge of the other. For Ackrill (1974),
184, what Socrates wishes to exclude as a true case of being reminded is the case in which "thinking of y is already involved in

24. The term *epistēmē* in this passage refers not to the agent's cognitive state but
to the thing known: it is the just-mentioned necessarily previously known "thing," *ti*
(*Phdo.* 73c1), that "comes," *paragignētai*, to one (*Phdo.* 73c4–5). See *Phdo.* 75e4, where
the "knowledges" (pl.), *tas epistēmas*, are clearly not the agent's many knowings but
the many (previously) known things. The terms "knowledge" and "know" are used
loosely in this passage, sometimes meaning no more than "coming to think of" and
sometimes "having full understanding." It has the former sense in many of the examples Socrates uses of reminding and being put in mind of, as well as at *Phdo.* 74b2–
4 and 74c9.

25. As was noted in Chapter 3, Section iii, Socrates virtually never asks the slave-
boy if he remembers or is reminded of anything; the one time that he does so (*M.*
84e), he asks him if he remembers what the question is!

26. See Bostock (1986), 64, who notes Plato's "obscure condition that the knowledge of the reminding thing, and of the thing it reminds us of, should not be 'the
same knowledge.'"

perceiving and recognizing *x*. One would not want to say that something brings so-and-so to mind if so-and-so is necessarily in mind when that something is." According to Ackrill, if one, on seeing a picture of Simmias, thinks of Simmias, then one has *not* been reminded—for in recognizing that this is a picture of Simmias, one has already, by the same knowledge, as it were, thought of Simmias.[27]

Since the case of one's being reminded of Simmias by seeing his picture serves as Socrates' prime example of what being reminded *is*, it certainly seems that Ackrill must be misunderstanding Socrates' point. And neither Burnet nor Hackforth explains *why* it is so important to Socrates that the knowledge with which the reminding thing is known differ from the knowledge with which the thing of which the reminding thing reminds one is known. Yet if one reads this passage of the *Phaedo* as a correction of the *Meno*'s recollection thesis, it becomes immediately evident what is at stake for Socrates in this otherwise obscure point. In the slave-boy-demonstration, the diagonal that is drawn reminds the slave-boy of no other diagonal. First, if, as was argued in Chapter 3, Section ii, the diagonal was in place in the diagram from the start, the boy's seeing it certainly reminded him of nothing. Second, even if the diagonal was not drawn until the demonstration's end, nevertheless the boy's answer consisted of nothing more than his pointing to the drawn diagonal: there is no other diagonal that this diagonal reminds him of.[28] Moreover, the slave-boy is surely not reminded by the sight of one thing of another thing that is the object of a different knowledge. Only if the slave-boy were reminded, by seeing the drawn diagonal, of, say, the geometer's perfect and purely conceptual diagonal,[29] which surely *is* the object of a separate and distinct knowledge, then and only then would his learning qualify as "recollection."

27. See also Burger (1984), 73, who says: "Of course, one would 'know' the image only if one knows Simmias, and just for that reason, it is unclear how it could satisfy the condition that knowledge of what is recollected be other than knowledge of what causes the recollection."

28. Even if the slave-boy can generalize from this diagonal to all diagonals, he is not "reminded" of anything: generalizing is not the same as being reminded. One can—indeed, one must—generalize whenever one learns; otherwise, one would have to relearn everything each time anew. This rule holds for anything, from math to tying shoelaces.

29. Cf. *Rep.* 6.511d, where Socrates notes that although geometers use visible figures and make claims about them, their thought is directed not to the figures but to the thing they resemble: the Square Itself, the Diagonal Itself, "not the diagonal they draw."

Through this caveat, Socrates sets the stage for what is for him the most important kind of reminding and being reminded, namely, when a thing of "lower" ontological status serves as a reminder of a similar thing of "higher" ontological status. In a case of this kind, the one who knows surely knows the things in question with two different knowledges. When one is reminded of Simmias by seeing a "drawn" Simmias, one is reminded by an ontologically inferior Simmias of an ontologically superior one.[30] Although it is true that one knows Simmias and Cebes by different knowledges, and that one knows Cebes' lyre and Cebes by different knowledges, the more interesting and significant instance of knowing by different knowledges, the instance toward which the discussion progresses and in whose discovery it culminates, is that of knowing the real Simmias from knowing the drawn one. It is by way of the Simmias example that Socrates is able to make the transition to what most concerns him: how one is reminded by sensibles of their corresponding Forms.

Having reviewed several kinds of reminding in which things that are different from one another serve, respectively, as the reminding and reminded things—seeing lyres and cloaks reminds one of their owners; seeing Simmias reminds one of Cebes; seeing a drawn horse or lyre reminds one of a person; seeing a drawn Simmias reminds one of Cebes—Socrates goes on to conclude that recollection occurs especially when the thing recollected has been forgotten, either through lapse of time or through inattention (*Phdo.* 73e).[31] He then proceeds to discuss the last of the cases reviewed, the case in which one is reminded of something by a similar thing—for example, when a drawn Simmias reminds one of the real Simmias. It is only in this

30. It has been asked why Socrates speaks of a "drawn" or "pictured" Simmias rather than of a picture of Simmias. The answer, I think, is that Socrates wishes to contrast Simmiases of different ontological orders. By speaking of a drawn Simmias and of a real one, Socrates speaks of different kinds of Simmiases; it is not as clear that a picture of Simmias is a kind of Simmias. In addition, a "drawn," *gegrammenon*, Simmias, horse, and so on calls to mind the drawn diagonal, the *grammē* that reaches from one corner of the square to the other.

31. "Reminded" and "forgotten" are obviously being used rather broadly here to mean, respectively, "being put in mind of" and "not having in mind at the moment"; otherwise, seeing Cebes could not remind one of Simmias without Simmias's being quite forgotten. Thus, when Gosling (1965), 154, says: "Normally, when I see my wife's handbag it does not remind me of my wife, even if it makes me think of her: I am not that forgetful," he is pressing "remind" and "forget" too hard or reading them too narrowly.

case, says Socrates, that the question arises of whether the reminding thing is deficient with respect to that of which it reminds.[32]

Having broached the issue of deficiency, Socrates is able to take his first step in the direction of what will shortly be his proof for immortality. Socrates speaks of the relationship between equal logs or stones, on the one hand, and the Equal Itself, on the other.[33] Although it is the sensible equals that "remind" one of the Equal Itself, they do so by way of their deficiency:[34] unlike the Equal Itself, they can appear unequal and can change from being equal to being unequal.[35] How, Socrates wonders, could one recognize the deficiency of equal logs and stones unless one were formerly acquainted with the perfection of which these fall short?[36] It is only when things are similar, let us note, that from seeing the one that is deficient, a person comes to think of the other that is perfect.[37]

32. Gosling (1965), 160, is surely right to note that when we ask whether or not a pictured Simmias is deficient with respect to Simmias, we are not asking whether it is a good likeness but whether it is actually Simmias or just a representation of him. If the pictured Simmias lacks not a single feature of Simmias, then it does not remind one of Simmias; one thinks it is Simmias. To speak in terms of being reminded is to recognize an ontological falling short.

33. We should note that the *Phaedo* does not limit the Forms to those of mathematics and virtue. It puts all Forms on an equal footing, mentioning, in particular, largeness, health, and strength (at *Phdo.* 65d). Interestingly, it is just these three that Socrates uses in the *Meno* (*M.* 72d-e) to illustrate his point that in defining a term one looks, not to the variable individual instances of the term, but to what they have in common. Yet in the *Meno*, there are no Forms that correspond to these qualities.

34. Scott (1995), 63, n. 12, asks why the senses are necessary as a catalyst for recollection: "Another possibility, one that Plato ignores, is that we grasp the forms by rational intuition without any need for the senses." What Scott's question fails to take into account is that grasping the Forms "by rational intuition without any need for the senses" is not recollection. For Socrates, it is only learning by recollection that requires a sensible reminder. There are, however, for him, other ways of learning— perhaps even, as suggested at the beginning of this appendix and in n. 12, other ways of grasping the Forms.

35. Here, too, I agree with Gosling (1965), 160, that the sensible equals are not deficient in being less equal than the Equal Itself. To be deficient equals is to fail to be "eternally and immutably equal."

36. The assumption here is that unless one already had the notion of perfection, one could not recognize things as deficient, yet one could (obviously) have the notion of perfection without having perceived deficiency. Perhaps it is because the prisoners in the Cave in *Rep.* 7 do not recognize the deficiency of their perceptions that they never "recollect" the real things of which their perceptions are mere images.

37. The sensible equals are other (*heteroi*) than the Equal Itself. But they are similar (*homoioi*) rather than dissimilar (*anhomoioi*) to one another. When Cebes is asked whether it is in being similar or dissimilar to the many equals that the Equal Itself comes to be known from them, Cebes answers, as if in a comedy routine, "Certainly."

The perfect realities, the Forms, that are known by way of the perception of their similar sensibles, Socrates now contends, must have been known by us before such time as we perceived the sensibles that are similar to them and recognized their deficiency. Since we begin sensing at birth, Socrates reasons, we must have had knowledge of the Forms before birth.[38] We apparently do not hold on to our knowledge of the Forms when we are born and during our lives, because, as Socrates points out to a confused Simmias (at *Phdo.* 76b), we cannot give an account of them.[39] That means we must forget them when we are born. And if we forget them at the moment of birth, we surely could not also get them at the moment of birth. Therefore, we must get them before we are born. By perceiving sensibles, we are reminded of the perfect realities that we once knew— before birth. Therefore, our souls must have existed before birth.[40]

The right answer is "from being similar." Socrates lets the point go. (Later, however, Socrates is careful not to make the same mistake. When he wants Simmias to say whether we are born knowing or are later reminded of the things of which we acquired knowledge before, he says: "Then which do you choose, Simmias?" [*Phdo.* 76a9].)

38. This Socratic argument has caused scholars considerable consternation. See, for example, Cornford (1952), 51. It seems at first that Socrates must be confusing (a) the idea that we start sensing at birth with (b) the idea that at birth we make the determination that our sensibles fall short of the corresponding Forms. It is hard to see how, without this confusion, Socrates could derive from (c) the notion that our knowledge of the Forms must precede our judgment that sensibles fall short of them (d) the conclusion that we must know the Forms before birth, that is, before *the moment at which our sensing begins.* Surely, however, there is a better way of understanding Socrates' point: he is, after all, hardly so foolish as to think that as soon as we begin perceiving we begin making the determination that sensibles fall short of their corresponding Forms. Let us consider, then, the following alternative construal of Socrates' argument. Since, on the one hand, it is from sensibles that we are put in mind of the Forms, insofar as we judge sensibles deficient, and since, on the other hand, *we are unable to get original knowledge of the Forms once we begin using our senses,* it follows that we had to have gotten our original knowledge of the Forms before we were born—since we begin using our senses at the moment of birth. On this construal of the argument, Socrates relies, not on the notion that knowledge of the Forms necessarily precedes the judgment that sensibles are deficient with respect to them, but on a point made earlier, namely, that sentient beings are precluded from knowing the Forms insofar as the senses hinder reason's ability to know them (see *Phdo.* 65b–66a). Indeed, that Socrates' argument depends on this earlier point is confirmed by Simmias's remark: "That must follow *from what has been said before,* Socrates" (*Phdo.* 75b9).

39. Socrates here confirms a point made earlier in Cebes' statement of the Theory of Recollection, that there is a link between having knowledge and being able to give an account. A similar notion is found as well in the *Meno*'s discussion of knowledge as what results from "working out the reason," *aitias logismos* (*M.* 98a).

40. The *Phaedo* highlights, then, specifically that form of recollection that the *Meno* conspicuously avoids in its review of the slave-boy-demonstration (see Chap. 3, Sec.

The recollection in the *Phaedo*, then, that proves the soul's immortality is radically different from the recollection in the *Meno*'s slave-boy-demonstration. The recollection in the *Phaedo* is not "recollection" by way of questions or diagrams; it is recollection of pure Forms by way of deficient sensibles. The recollection in the *Meno*'s slave-boy-demonstration does not even require being reminded; and the drawn diagonal in the *Meno* is never recognized to be in any way deficient. Moreover, being reminded in the *Phaedo* is clearly not the whole of reacquiring knowledge formerly possessed; rather, being reminded is but the first step: it makes the recollector aware of what he does not know by reminding him *that* he once knew it. According to the *Phaedo*, one recollects, that is, is put in mind of, via sense perception, things that one formerly knew; but insofar as one is not able, simply by virtue of having been reminded, to give an account of the things one is put in mind of, it seems that the recollection by which one is put in mind of something previously known does not suffice for coming to know again what one knew before. (On this point, see *Phdo.* 76b5.)

Recollection in the *Phaedo* departs significantly, too, from recollection as it is depicted in the *Meno*'s myth. What the soul in the *Phaedo* remembers is what it cannot know when it is embodied; in the *Meno*, however, it remembers what it learned in previous lives—both here and in Hades. In the *Meno* myth, one is able to recollect what one knew in previous lives because "all nature is akin," *sungenous* (*M.* 81d1);[41] in the *Phaedo*, one is able to recollect what one knew because one's soul is "akin," *sungenēs*, to the Forms (*Phdo.* 79d3, 84b2). In the *Meno*, one has knowledge of the very things of which one has opinions; in the *Phaedo*, one's soul, by following reason, beholds what is true and divine "and *not* the object of opinion," *adoxaston* (*Phdo.* 84a8). In the *Meno*, one's soul recollects what it has seen both here and in Hades; in the *Phaedo*, one's soul recollects what it has seen in " 'Hades' in the true sense," *Haidou hōs alēthōs* (*Phdo.* 80d6–7), that is, in the realm of the nonvisible (*aides*) intelligibles, the Forms.[42] In the *Meno*, no release from the cycle of rebirth

iv), namely, acquiring knowledge at some point before birth and recovering it later, in this lifetime. The only two possibilities the *Meno* considers are possession always and acquiring knowledge in the present lifetime.

41. As was noted in Chapter 2, Section iv, since in the *Meno* all nature is akin, there are no ontological levels that might clear a space for the kind of recollection we find in the *Phaedo*.

42. Plato's fondness for plays on words is in evidence also at *Phdo.* 92d, where Simmias prefers recollection theory to attunement theory because although recollec-

is envisioned: the soul goes from here to Hades and back, over and over again; in the *Phaedo,* the soul of a man who has lived philosophically is returned to its natural home to dwell in the rarefied atmosphere of the pure, the unseen, the intelligible: the Forms.

I have argued that (a) the *Phaedo* is the only dialogue within the Platonic corpus besides the *Meno* where recollection is set forth as a Socratic or Platonic account of human learning, yet (b) the *Phaedo*'s account departs radically from the *Meno*'s, and (c) the *Phaedo*'s account repudiates the *Meno*'s. In light of these conclusions, it seems that if, for reasons internal to the *Meno,* one is inclined to believe that Socrates does not seriously endorse its version of recollection, one need not, for reasons external to it, suppress that inclination.

In closing, it is perhaps worth noting that Socrates is an unqualified fan of recollection in neither the *Meno* nor the *Phaedo.* Just as he limits his endorsement of recollection in the *Meno,* so he does, as we have seen, in the *Phaedo* as well: he raises the possibility that there might be no Forms, in which case there would be nothing for the immortal soul to be remembering when it notes the deficiency of sensibles (*Phdo.* 76d–e). If Socrates is unhappy with the recollection thesis in the *Meno* and, therefore, provides a different recollection thesis in the *Phaedo,* why, we may wonder, does Socrates raise doubts about recollection in the *Phaedo* as well?

Socrates' introduction of recollection in both the *Meno* and the *Phaedo*—in their respective versions—reflects the great care he takes for his interlocutors. Meno is a misologist of the very type described in the *Phaedo* at 90c–e.[43] When arguments conflict or disappoint, he is quick to bail out. For the sake of securing Meno's continued participation in what he, Socrates, regards as all-important virtue inquiry, Socrates tailors a recollection thesis to suit Meno—one that recalls Pythagorean ideas familiar to Meno, plays on Meno's pride in his ability to remember, and capitalizes on Meno's love of the esoteric and ostentatious, the *tragikē.* Unlike Meno, however, Simmias and Cebes are avid arguers. In that sense, they are already

---

tion theory, too, has not been "proved," *apodeixasthai,* it, unlike attunement theory, is worthy of "acceptance," *apodexasthai.*

. 43. This passage of the *Phaedo* is very much in the spirit of *M.* 81d-e and *M.* 86b-c, where Socrates diagnoses as lazy, soft, and cowardly those who refuse to inquire, taking refuge in eristic argument. Socrates warns in the *Phaedo* that when arguments go awry, it is not the arguments but those who present them who are to be blamed. "But we must be courageous and be eager to be sound" (*Phdo.* 90e3). Let us note that Socrates, even in the *Phaedo,* does not promise that there will be knowledge at the end of rigorous argument.

deeply philosophical.[44] We note in this regard Simmias's speech at *Phdo.* 85c, a speech worthy of Socrates in the *Meno:* "I think, Socrates, as perhaps you do too, that in these matters certain knowledge is either impossible or very hard to come by in this life; but that even so, not to test what is said about them in every possible way, without leaving off till one has examined them exhaustively from every aspect, shows a very feeble spirit" (trans. Gallop [1993]). The recollection thesis, then, that Socrates proposes in the *Phaedo* has the goal of turning Simmias and Cebes, not to philosophy construed as the life of argument, but to a different kind of philosophical life, the peculiarly otherworldly life of communing with transcendent Forms. Indeed, it is this latter type of philosophy, the sort that separates one from one's body and frees one's intellect to consort with truth, that is repeatedly called in the *Phaedo* not simply "philosophy" but philosophy "in the proper manner," *orthōs* (64a4–8, 67b4, d8, 69d2). It is also called "real philosophy," *tōi onti,* (68b2–3). When Socrates, then, prevents Simmias from being satisfied with Cebes' presentation of recollection, he intimates, in effect, not simply that that version is defective in certain ways but that it is not suitable for Simmias. For the recollection thesis that Socrates fashions for the sake of Simmias and Cebes is not one that urges the ordinary soul, as the *Meno*'s version of recollection does, to seek to remember all that it has learned here and in Hades but one that inspires the philosophical soul to yearn to recover Forms. Yet Socrates succeeds no better with Simmias and Cebes than he does with Meno. Meno does not turn to the life of argument; Simmias and Cebes do not turn away from it.[45] Despite his failures, however, the valiance of Socrates' efforts and the lengths to which he is willing to go for the sake of his interlocutors attest to the boundlessness of the benefaction he seeks to bestow on all those he encounters—old or young, Athenian or stranger.

44. When the others present show signs of frustration and require a pep talk by Socrates, Simmias and Cebes are the only ones who are not in danger of lapsing into misology. The only thing that might keep them from pursuing an argument is their concern for Socrates—not any unwillingness to continue arguing. See *Phdo.* 88c–91c. See also *Phdo.* 63a1–3: "There goes Cebes again, always hunting down arguments and not at all willing to accept at once what anyone may say." Simmias, too, even near the dialogue's end (107a–b), still admits to having misgivings about the argument; he remains prepared to argue further.

45. Cebes and Simmias endorse a philosophical life they neither live nor understand. Neither Simmias nor Cebes can give an "account" of the Forms—indeed, Simmias believes that once Socrates dies, there will be no one who can. Furthermore, it is not at all clear to them that death is not fearful. And before Socrates suggests otherwise, Simmias counts even Evenus as a philosopher.

Appendix II

The Abandonment of Moral Inquiry in the Republic

It has been the contention of this book that the *Meno*, as other "Socratic" dialogues, portrays philosophy as it is in the Cave, that is, in the world of opinion, from which there is, at least for ordinary mortals, no egress. In the Cave, it has been argued, where there are no true moral experts but only pretenders to expertise, no wise men but only sophists, no one who knows the truths of morality but only those who think they know, the endless search for truth is the best stand-in for the actual attainment of wisdom. The endlessness of the search derives, not from the inability of the search to discover truths, but from its inability to guarantee the truth of the truths it discovers: the search, in other words, fails to culminate in knowledge. And how could it? In the progress to a set of conclusions from a host of unsecured premises, there is no source out of which knowledge could arise.[1]

If, when there are no moral experts, philosophy is ongoing inquiry whose end is truth, what is philosophy once there are moral experts? If, in all other areas of expertise, experts guide, advise, and teach nonexperts, so that laymen need not flounder as they would if left to their own devices, ought we not to expect the same in the

---

1. We may compare to this problem in moral inquiry what Socrates says in the *Republic* about geometry and other sciences that proceed from hypotheses for which their practitioners can give no account: "When the beginning is what one does not know and the end and what comes in between are woven out of what is not known, what contrivance is there for ever turning such an agreement into knowledge?" (*Rep.* 7.533c, trans. Bloom [1968]). If this is the sorry state of mathematics when it lacks grounding in Forms, how could moral reasoning in the Cave possibly be thought to yield knowledge?

moral realm? I will argue here that in the *Republic*, where philosophers do not merely love wisdom but are actually wise, the notion of the philosophical life as the examined one is abandoned; philosophy is no longer merely love of wisdom—it *is* wisdom.

Let us begin by comparing the value of true opinion with that of knowledge in the *Meno* and the *Republic*. In the *Meno*, as we saw in Chapter 4, Section v, true opinion is a highly valued thing, particularly from the perspective of action. Indeed, from the perspective of action, it is, according to the *Meno*, difficult to see in what way knowledge is better than true opinion—at least for as long as one actually has hold of the true opinions. True opinion is inferior to knowledge in that it lacks stability; since one does not *know* that one's opinions are true, one's opinions are vulnerable to competing opinions, as well as to passions, and must be repeatedly examined and tested. But insofar as one's opinions are true, they fare, as a practical guide, no worse than knowledge.

We recall the example used in the *Meno* to illustrate the equal value of knowledge and true belief with respect to action, the case of someone guiding others to Larisa:

> If someone who knows the road to Larisa or anywhere else you like went there and guided others, would he not guide them aright and well? . . . But what if someone had the right opinion as to which is the road, though he had never gone there and had no knowledge of it? Would not this man, too, guide people aright? . . . And, I suppose, as long as he has a right opinion about the matters about which the other man has knowledge, then, even though he thinks what is true but does not have understanding (*phronōn de mē*), he will be no worse a guide than this one who has understanding about this matter (*tou toutou phronountos*). . . . So, then, true opinion is no worse a guide to right action than *phronēsis*. (*M.* 97a9–b10)

A bit further on, in a context in which Socrates is explaining to Meno why true opinion, despite its equal practical worth to knowledge, is nevertheless inferior to knowledge, Socrates says:

> For true opinions, too, are a fine thing as long as they stay in their place, and they produce all sorts of good things. (*M.* 97e6–7)

If true opinions in the *Meno* are not worth as much as knowledge, it is not because they are not themselves fine; it is only because it is difficult to hold on to them.

If we turn to the *Republic,* we find a radical departure from the *Meno*'s view of true opinions. At *Rep.* 6.506c6–9, we find the following:

> What? . . . Have you not noticed that all opinions without knowledge are ugly (*aischrai*)? The best of them are blind. Or do men who opine something true without intelligence (*aneu nou*) seem to you any different from blind men who travel the right road? (trans. Bloom [1968], very slightly modified)

In this passage, the *Republic* frankly reverses the *Meno*'s take on true opinion: true opinions were "a fine thing," *kalon to chrēma,* in the *Meno;* but all opinions, including true ones, are ugly things, *aischrai,* in the *Republic.* Moreover, the guide who possesses true opinion and guides others along the road to Larisa is said in the *Meno* to be as good a guide as the guide who has knowledge; the *Republic,* however, regards one who has true opinion without intelligence, *aneu nou,* as a blind man who happens to travel the right road.

It is not difficult to explain the disdain for true opinion displayed by Socrates in the *Republic* as compared with the esteem in which he holds it in the *Meno.* In the *Meno,* as was argued, Socrates does not envision anyone's transcending the realm of opinion in moral matters: when the best that people can do is inquire, in the hope of replacing incorrect opinions with correct ones, true opinions become very valuable indeed. There is no denying that the tendency of true opinions toward flightiness is a problem: how does one hold on even to the truths one does have in the face of a host of other opinions that clamor for acceptance? When one lacks knowledge, one has to work all one's life to hold firm to one's right, though likely unpopular, opinions, by subjecting them repeatedly to the challenge of critical examination. Nevertheless, there is, in the Cave, no other life that can rival in worthiness the life of relentless self-examination. In the *Republic,* by contrast, Socrates envisions godlike human beings who transcend the Cave and "see" the Forms. In comparison with the achievement of these men, the achievements of ordinary human beings who pit opinion against opinion, groping in semidarkness for the better of the two, seem suddenly paltry. From the perspective of one whose powers of vision are enhanced by the light of the sun, those who strain to make out shadows in the dim light of the Cave are little better than blind men. Opinions are "a fine thing" when they are the best one can do; they are, however, "ugly" when one can do far, far better.

The allusion in the *Republic* passage to blind men who happen to travel the right road points rather unmistakably to the road to Larisa passage in the *Meno,* in which guides who lack knowledge can, as long as they have true opinion, nevertheless guide aright. In this respect, too, the *Republic*'s divergence from the *Meno* is easily accounted for. In the *Meno,* one is grateful to be able both to find one's own way and to lead others successfully: one's hitting upon the truth even without knowing evokes commendation rather than scorn, because there is no shame in one's not knowing what no human being can know. In the *Republic,* however, where knowledge is imagined to be possible, where escape for some from the Cave is presented as an attainable goal, it is contemptible indeed merely to stumble upon the truth in the dark of the Cave.

In the *Republic,* then, true opinion, which is in the Socratic dialogues the coveted end result of moral inquiry, is for the hopelessly benighted. But what of moral inquiry itself? Should the prisoners in the Cave debate endlessly about the shadows on the wall they face or is there a better course open to them? What ramifications does the philosopher's intellectual grasp of the Forms of the virtues have for the many farmers, artisans, and auxiliaries whose souls will never be turned?

Throughout the Socratic dialogues, nonexperts regularly benefit from the presence of experts: whether there are shoes to be made, ships to be built, musical instruments to be mastered, illnesses to be cured, or mathematical problems to be solved, the appropriate expert is available to furnish the answer. In none of these fields is it best that one be a do-it-yourselfer: far better to consult the expert whose advice, guidance, or actual taking up of the task at hand will ensure a superior result. Is the situation any different with respect to virtue? To be sure, in the absence of experts, moral do-it-yourselfers are admirable; they are the most worthy of human beings. But once there are experts, is it not foolhardy, even dangerous, to rely on one's inexpert and inconclusive arguments about shadows of justice when one can turn to someone who has seen Justice Itself?

Shorey (1980), 45, contends, quite rightly in my judgment, that insofar as the function of the political art is to "make others good," it is a twofold function: with reference to the multitude, the political art makes others good "through habit, discipline, and instinctive conformity to models set for them from above"; with respect to the elite, the political art means "the training up of a succession of philosophic statesmen to maintain and perpetuate the ideally best social organism."[2] Is not the statesman who exercises this dual art reminiscent of the *Apology*'s "overseer," *epistatēs*, of human beings, who, on analogy with the trainer of colts and calves (*Ap.* 20a), makes human beings noble and good in their appropriate virtue, namely, in human and political virtue? Would such an *epistatēs*, if there were one, permit his charges to determine on their own what is best for them? For Plato, one goal of a good ruler is to domesticate men, to make them tame and gentle, as seen in the following passage from the *Gorgias*:

> A man like that [like Pericles] who cared for donkeys or horses or cattle would at least look bad if he showed these animals kicking, butting, and biting because of their wildness, when they had been doing none of these things when he took them over. Or do you not think that any caretaker of any animal is a bad one who will show his animals to be wilder than when he took them over, when they were gentler? . . . Was Pericles not a caretaker of men? . . . Should he not . . . have turned them out more just instead of more unjust, if while he cared for them he really was good at politics . . . the just are gentle. . . . So on this reasoning Pericles was not good at politics. (*Gorg.* 516a–d, trans. Zeyl [1987], very slightly modified)

In the *Gorgias*, moreover, no less than in the *Republic*, a politician who knows what is best for the people will make them better "using persuasion or constraint" (*Gorg.* 517b6): "That alone is the task of the good citizen" (*Gorg.* 517c1–2). There is no implication that the successful ruler will strive to create a multitude of seekers after truth.

---

2. Kraut (1984), 242, who argues that there is no incompatibility between there being, on the one hand, authoritarian philosopher-kings and, on the other, a populace that lives the examined life, suggests that for Socrates moral experts "should not simply give commands to the rest of the citizens; they must also try to get the others to understand, as far as possible, the ethical theory that lies behind the commands." Socrates, Kraut thinks, thus "leaves a good deal of work for nonexperts to do": it is their job to gain understanding of what the moral expert commands. I show in what follows that Socrates reserves no such work for nonexperts; nor does he conceive of philosopher-kings as encouraging the ordinary man to understand moral matters. On the contrary, for Socrates in the *Republic*, the only thing nonexperts must understand is that they lack the moral expertise that the philosopher-kings possess and that they ought, therefore, to obey their rulers. Grote (1875), I, 239, Popper (1966), 129–30, Gulley (1968), 177, and Vlastos (1971), 20, think Socrates limits the rulers' role to guidance, leaving it to each individual to think for himself about matters of virtue and to make up his own mind. This view, too, will be shown to be unsupported by the *Republic*, as it is as well by both the *Apology* and the *Gorgias*.

As we turn to the *Republic,* we find the following statement, un-ambiguous in its intent:

> Thus, when they [the philosophers] have come plainly to light, one will be able to defend oneself, showing that it is by nature fitting for them both to be engaged in philosophy and to lead a city, *and for the rest not to engage in philosophy and to follow the leader.* (*Rep.* 5.474b–c, trans. Bloom [1968]; emphasis mine)

And at *Rep.* 9.590c–d, we find the following with respect to a man in whom the best part of his soul is too weak to rule the beasts in it and, consequently, serves and flatters them instead:

> In order that such a man also be ruled by something similar to what rules the best man, do we not say that he must be the slave of that best man who has the divine rule in himself? It is not that we suppose the slave must be ruled to his own detriment, as Thrasymachus supposed about the ruled, but that it is better for all to be ruled by what is divine and prudent, especially when one has it as his own within himself; but if not, [it must be] set over one from outside, so that insofar as possible all will be alike and friends, piloted by the same thing. (trans. Bloom [1968], very slightly modified)

It is clear from *Rep.* 6.500c–d that "it is the philosopher, keeping company with the divine and the orderly, who becomes orderly and divine, to the extent that is possible for a human being." Moreover, such a philosopher will, by "*putting* what he sees there *into* the dispositions of men," be a good craftsman of moderation, justice, and demotic virtue as a whole (*Rep.* 6.500d).

In the *Republic,* then, the philosopher alone is to practice philosophy and, in his role as ruler, to implant virtue, as it were, into the souls of those he rules. Nonphilosophers are not to engage in philosophy; they are to be the passive recipients of the virtue instilled into them from without.

This view in the *Republic* is completely consonant with that expressed consistently throughout the "Socratic" dialogues: when there is an expert, an *epaïōn,* a *beltiōn,* in a particular domain, he is to be obeyed, be he god or man. It is only for as long as there is no moral expert to be found that elenctic (or other) moral inquiry bestows value upon human life. But in the event that some do attain the godlike status of moral expert, the others are to abandon moral inquiry in favor of unquestioning submission. "The unexamined life," Socrates says, "is not worth living *for a man*," that is, when all men are but men. Yet when some men are virtual gods, there is no place for the examined life: the men who are gods have knowledge and need not inquire; the rest lack knowledge and may not inquire:

> And thus always educating other like men and leaving them be-
> hind in their place as guardians of the city, they go off to the Isles
> of the Blessed and dwell. The city makes public memorials and
> sacrifices to them as to divinities (*daimosin*), if the Pythia is in ac-
> cord; if not, as to happy and *divine* men. (*Rep.* 7.540b7–c2, trans.
> Bloom [1968])

If some men are godlike, if they are such that the city is to make memorials and sacrifices to them when they depart, can it be right to think that the proper comportment of the citizen body with respect to these men before they depart is anything but reverential accession to their moral directives?

> Far best is he who knows all things himself;
> Good, he that hearkens when men counsel right;
> But he who neither knows, nor lays to heart
> Another's wisdom, is a useless wight.
> Hesiod, Works and Days, 293–97

Bibliography

Ackrill, J. L. 1974. "Anamnesis in the *Phaedo*: Remarks on 73c–75c." In *Exegesis and Argument*, ed. E. N. Lee, A. P. D. Mourelatos, and R. Rorty. Assen: Van Gorcum, 177–95.

Adam, James, ed. 1969. *The Republic of Plato*. 2 vols. Cambridge: Cambridge University Press.

Adkins, A. W. H. 1960. *Merit and Responsibility*. Oxford: Clarendon Press.

Allen, R. E. 1959. "Anamnesis in Plato's *Meno* and *Phaedo*." *Review of Metaphysics* 13: 165–74.

———. 1984. *The Dialogues of Plato*. Vol. 1. New Haven: Yale University Press.

Anastaplo, George. 1975. "Law and Morality." In *Human Being and Citizen: Essays on Virtue, Freedom, and the Common Good*. Chicago: Swallow Press, 74–86, 268–81.

Anderson, D. E. 1993. *The Masks of Dionysos: A Commentary on Plato's "Symposium."* Albany: State University of New York Press.

Andic, Martin. 1971. "Inquiry and Virtue in the *Meno*." In *Plato's Meno*, ed. Malcolm Brown. New York: Bobbs Merrill, 262–314.

Apelt, Otto. 1914. *Platons Menon*. Leipzig.

Arieti, James. 1991. *Interpreting Plato: The Dialogues as Drama*. Savage, Md.: Rowman and Littlefield.

Bacon, Francis. 1868. *Novum Organum*. In *The Works of Francis Bacon*, vol. 4, ed. J. Spedding, R. L. Ellis, and D. D. Heath. London: Longman & Co.

Bedu-Addo, J. T. 1983. "Sense-Experience and Recollection in Plato's *Meno*." *American Journal of Philology* 104: 228–48.

———. 1984. "Recollection and the Argument 'From a Hypothesis' in Plato's *Meno*." *Journal of Hellenic Studies* 104: 1–14.

Benson, Hugh H. 1989. "A Note on Eristic and the Socratic Elenchus." *Journal of the History of Philosophy* 27: 591–99.

————. 1990a. "Meno, the Slave Boy, and the Elenchos." *Phronesis* 35: 128–58.

————. 1990b. "The Priority of Definition and the Socratic Elenchus." *Oxford Studies in Ancient Philosophy* 8: 19–65.

Blank, David L. 1985. "Socratics versus Sophists on Payment for Teaching." *Classical Antiquity* 4: 1–49.

Bloom, A., trans. 1968. *The "Republic" of Plato*. New York: Basic Books.

Bluck, R. S. 1961a. *Plato's "Meno."* Cambridge: Cambridge University Press.

————. 1961b. "Plato's *Meno."* *Phronesis* 6: 94–101.

Bostock, David. 1986. *Plato's "Phaedo."* Oxford: Clarendon Press.

Boter, Gerard J. 1988. "Plato, *Meno* 82c2–3." *Phronesis* 33: 208–15.

Brague, Rémi. 1978. *"Ménon," le restant*. Paris: Vrin/Belles Lettres.

Brown, Malcolm. 1971. "Plato Disapproves of the Slave-Boy's Answer." In *Plato's "Meno,"* ed. Malcolm Brown. New York: Bobbs-Merrill, 198–242. Originally published in *Review of Metaphysics* 20 (1967): 57–93.

Brumbaugh, Robert S. 1954. *Plato's Mathematical Imagination: The Mathematical Passages in the Dialogues and Their Interpretation*. Bloomington: Indiana University Press.

————. 1990. Review of David J. Melling, *Understanding Plato. Ancient Philosophy* 10: 299–301.

Buchmann, Klara. 1936. "Die Stellung des Menon in der Platonischen Philosophie." *Philologus* 29 (supp.): 16–19.

Burger, R. 1984. *The "Phaedo": A Platonic Labyrinth*. New Haven: Yale University Press.

Burnet, J. 1911. *Plato's "Phaedo."* Oxford: Clarendon Press.

Burnyeat, Myles F. 1977. "Socratic Midwifery, Platonic Inspiration." *Bulletin of the Institute of Classical Studies* 24: 7–16.

Bury, R. G. 1906. "Platonica." *Classical Review* 20: 12–14.

Calvert, Brian. 1974. "Meno's Paradox Reconsidered." *Journal of the History of Philosophy* 12: 143–52.

Canto-Sperber, Monique, trans. 1991. *Plato: "Ménon."* Paris: Flammarion.

Cherniss, Harold. 1936. "The Philosophical Economy of the Theory of Ideas." *American Journal of Philology* 57: 445–56.

————. 1947. "Some War-Time Publications Concerning Plato." *American Journal of Philology* 68: 113–46, 225–65.

————. 1951. "Plato as Mathematician." *Review of Metaphysics* 4: 395–425.

Cornford, F. M. 1934. *Plato's Theory of Knowledge*. New York: Humanities Press. Rpt. 1957. New York: Liberal Arts Press.

————. 1952. *Principium Sapientiae*. Cambridge: Cambridge University Press.

————. 1971. "Anamnesis." In *Plato's "Meno,"* ed. Malcolm Brown. Indianapolis: Bobbs-Merrill, 108–27.

Crombie, I. M. 1963. *An Examination of Plato's Doctrines.* 2 vols. London: Routledge and Kegan Paul.

Davis, Michael. 1988. *Ancient Tragedy and the Origins of Modern Science.* Carbondale and Edwardsville: Southern Illinois University Press.

Day, Jane M., trans. and ed. 1994. *Plato's "Meno" in Focus.* London: Routledge.

Desjardins, Rosemary. 1985. "Knowledge and Virtue: Paradox in Plato's *Meno.*" *Review of Metaphysics* 39: 261–81.

Devereux, Daniel T. 1978. "Nature and Teaching in Plato's *Meno.*" *Phronesis* 23: 118–26.

Diels, H., and W. Kranz. 1960–61. *Die Fragmente der Vorsokratiker.* 10th ed. 3 vols. Berlin: Weidmann.

Dodds, E. R. 1959. *Plato: "Gorgias."* Oxford: Clarendon Press.

Ebert, Theodor. 1973. "Plato's Theory of Recollection Reconsidered: An Interpretation of *Meno* 80a–86c." *Man and World* 6: 163–81.

Epictetus. 1933. *Discourses,* trans. Elizabeth Carter. London: J. M. Dent.

Ferejohn, Michael. 1982. "Socratic Virtue as the Parts of Itself." *Philosophy and Phenomenological Research* 43: 377–88.

Fine, Gail. 1992. "Inquiry in the *Meno.*" In *The Cambridge Companion to Plato,* ed. Richard Kraut. Cambridge: Cambridge University Press, 200–226.

Flew, Antony. 1971. *An Introduction to Western Philosophy: Ideas and Arguments from Plato to Sartre.* Indianapolis: Bobbs-Merrill.

Fowler, D. H. 1990. "Yet More on *Meno* 82a–85d." *Phronesis* 35: 175–81.

Friedländer, Paul. 1945. Review of Richard Robinson, *Plato's Earlier Dialectic. Classical Philology* 40: 253–59.

Gallop, D. 1993. *Plato: "Phaedo."* Oxford: Oxford University Press.

Gera, Deborah Levine. 1996. "Porters, *Paidagogoi,* Jailers, and Attendants: Some Slaves in Plato." *Scripta Classica Israelica* 15: 90–101.

Gosling, J. 1965. "Similarity in *Phaedo* 73b seq." *Phronesis* 10: 151–61.

Gould, John. 1955. *The Development of Plato's Ethics.* Cambridge: Cambridge University Press.

Grote, George. 1888. *Plato and the Other Companions of Sokrates.* Vols. 1 and 2. London: Murray.

Grube, G. M. A. 1935. *Plato's Thought.* London: Methuen.

———, trans. 1981. *Plato: Five Dialogues.* Indianapolis: Hackett.

Gulley, Norman. 1937. *Plato's Cosmology: The "Timaeus" of Plato.* London: Kegan Paul.

———. 1954. "Plato's Theory of Recollection." *Classical Quarterly* n.s. 4: 194–213.

———. 1968. *The Philosophy of Socrates.* London: Macmillan.

Guthrie, W. K. C. 1975. *A History of Greek Philosophy.* Vol. 4, *Plato: The Man and His Dialogues, Earlier Period.* Cambridge: Cambridge University Press.

————, trans. 1956. *Plato: "Protagoras" and "Meno"*. London: Penguin.

Hackforth, R., trans. 1955. *Plato's "Phaedo."* Cambridge: Cambridge University Press.

Hansing, Ovidia. 1928. "The Doctrine of Recollection in Plato's Dialogues." *Monist* 38: 231–62.

Heath, Thomas L., trans. 1925. *Euclid's "Elements."* 2nd ed. 2 vols. Cambridge: Cambridge University Press.

Hoerber, Robert G. 1960. "Plato's *Meno.*" *Phronesis* 5: 78–102.

Irwin, Terence. 1973. "Recollection and Plato's Moral Theory." *Review of Metaphysics* 27: 752–72.

————. 1977. *Plato's Moral Theory: The Early and Middle Dialogues*. Oxford: Clarendon.

Jowett, Benjamin. 1953. *The Dialogues of Plato*. 4th ed. 4 vols. Oxford: Oxford University Press.

————, trans. 1961. *Laches*. In *The Collected Dialogues of Plato*, ed. Edith Hamilton and Huntington Cairns. Princeton: Princeton University Press.

Kahn, Charles H. 1983. "Drama and Dialectic in Plato's *Gorgias.*" *Oxford Studies in Ancient Philosophy* 1: 75–121.

————. 1992. "Vlastos's Socrates." *Phronesis* 37: 233–58.

Klein, Jacob. 1965. *A Commentary on Plato's "Meno."* Chicago: Chicago University Press.

Koyré, Alexandre. 1945. *Discovering Plato*, trans. Leonora Cohen Rosenfield. New York: Columbia University Press.

Kraut, Richard. 1983. "Comments on Gregory Vlastos, 'The Socratic Elenchus.'" *Oxford Studies in Ancient Philosophy* 1: 59–70.

————. 1984. *Socrates and the State*. Princeton: Princeton University Press.

Levinson, Ronald B. 1953. *In Defense of Plato*. Cambridge: Harvard University Press.

Liddell, H. G., R. Scott, and H. S. Jones. 1966. *A Greek-English Lexicon*. 9th ed. Oxford: Clarendon.

Lloyd, G. E. R. 1992. "The *Meno* and the Mysteries of Mathematics." *Phronesis* 37: 166–83.

MacDonough, B. T. 1978. "A Study of the Conclusion of Plato's *Meno.*" *Dialogos* 31: 169–77.

McKirahan, Richard D., Jr. 1994. *Philosophy before Socrates*. Indianapolis: Hackett.

McTighe, Kevin. 1984. "Socrates on Desire for the Good and the Involuntariness of Wrongdoing: *Gorgias* 466a–468e." *Phronesis* 29: 193–236.

Moline, Jonathan. 1969. "Meno's Paradox?" *Phronesis* 14: 153–61.

Moravcsik, Julius. 1971. "Learning as Recollection." In *Plato*, vol. 1, *Metaphysics and Epistemology*, ed. Gregory Vlastos. Garden City, N.Y.: Doubleday, 53–69.

Morrison, J. S. 1942. "Meno of Tharsalus, Polycrates and Ismenias." *Classical Quarterly* 36: 57–78.

Mugler, Charles. 1948. *Platon et la recherche mathématique de son époque.* Strasbourg and Zurich: Heitz.

Nakhnikian, George. 1973. "The First Socratic Paradox." *Journal of the History of Philosophy* 11: 1–17.

Narveson, Jan. 1965. "Pacificism: A Philosophical Analysis." *Ethics* 75: 259–71.

Nehamas, Alexander. 1985. "Meno's Paradox and Socrates as a Teacher." *Oxford Studies in Ancient Philosophy* 3: 1–30.

———. 1987. "Socratic Intellectualism." In *Proceedings of the Boston Area Colloquium in Ancient Philosophy,* vol. 2, ed. John J. Cleary. Lanham, Md.: University Press of America, 275–316.

———. 1990. "Eristic, Antilogic, Sophistic, Dialectic: Plato's Demarcation of Philosophy from Sophistry." *History of Philosophy Quarterly* 7: 3–16.

Nietzsche, Friedrich. 1968. *The Twilight of the Idols,* trans. Walter Kaufmann. In *The Viking Portable Nietzsche.* New York: Viking Press.

Nussbaum, Martha. 1979. "Eleatic Conventionalism and Philolaus on the Conditions of Thought." *Harvard Studies in Classical Philology* 83: 63–108.

Penner, Terry. 1973. "The Unity of Virtue." *Philosophical Review* 82: 35–68.

Phillips, Bernard. 1965. "The Significance of Meno's Paradox." In *Plato's "Meno": Text and Criticism,* ed. Alexander Sesonske and Noel Fleming. Belmont, Calif.: Wadsworth, 77–83.

Popper, Karl R. 1966. *The Open Society and Its Enemies.* Vol. 1, *The Spell of Plato.* 5th ed. rev. Princeton: Princeton University Press.

Robinson, Richard. 1953. *Plato's Earlier Dialectic.* 2nd ed. Oxford: Clarendon Press.

———. 1971. "Elenchus." In *The Philosophy of Socrates,* ed. Gregory Vlastos. Garden City, N.Y.: Doubleday, 78–93.

Rohatyn, Dennis A. 1980. "Reflections on Meno's Paradox." *Apeiron* 14: 69–73.

Rorty, Amelie Oksenberg. 1987. "The Limits of Socratic Intellectualism: Did Socrates Teach *Aretē?*" In *Proceedings of the Boston Area Colloquium in Ancient Philosophy,* vol. 1, ed. John Cleary. Lanham, Md.: University Press of America, 317–30.

Rose, Lynn E. 1970. "Plato's *Meno,* 86–89." *Journal of the History of Philosophy* 8: 1–8.

Ross, David. 1951. *Plato's Theory of Ideas.* Oxford: Clarendon Press.

Ryle, Gilbert. 1971. "Teaching and Training." In *Plato's "Meno,"* ed. Malcolm Brown. Indianapolis: Bobbs-Merrill, 243–61.

———. 1976. "Many Things Are Odd about Our *Meno.*" *Paideia* 5: 1–9.

Santas, Gerasimos Xenophon. 1979. *Socrates: Philosophy in Plato's Early Dialogues.* London: Routledge and Kegan Paul.

Scolnicov, Samuel. 1976. "Three Aspects of Plato's Philosophy of Learning and Instruction." *Paideia* 5: 50–66.

Scott, Dominic. 1987. "Platonic Anamnesis Revisited." *Classical Quarterly* 37: 346–66.

———. 1991. "Socrate prend-il au serieux le paradoxe de Menon?" *Revue philosophique* 181: 627–41.

———. 1995. *Recollection and Experience.* Cambridge: Cambridge University Press.

Seeskin, Kenneth. 1987. *Dialogue and Discovery: A Study in Socratic Method.* Albany: State University of New York Press.

Sharples, R. W. 1989. "More on Plato, *Meno* 82c2–3." *Phronesis* 34: 220–26.

———, trans. 1985. *Plato: "Meno."* Chicago: Bolchazy-Carducci.

Shorey, Paul. 1933. *What Plato Said.* Chicago: University of Chicago Press.

———. 1980. "The Idea of the Good in Plato's *Republic.*" In *Selected Papers,* vol. 2, ed. Leonardo Taran. New York: Garland, 28–79.

Skemp, J. B. 1952. *Plato's "Statesman."* New Haven: Yale University Press.

Sprague, Rosamond Kent. 1962. *Plato's Use of Fallacy.* London: Routledge.

———, trans. 1965. *Plato: "Euthydemus."* New York: Bobbs-Merrill. Rpt. 1993. Indianapolis: Hackett.

Stalley, R. F. 1983. *An Introduction to Plato's "Laws."* Indianapolis: Hackett.

Sternfeld, Robert, and Harold Zyskind. 1978. *Plato's "Meno": A Philosophy of Man as Inquisitive.* Carbondale and Edwardsville: Southern Illinois University Press.

Stokes, Michael C. 1963. Review of Bluck, *Plato's "Meno." Archiv für Geschichte der Philosophie* 45: 292–99.

Taylor, A. E. 1948. *Plato: The Man and His Work.* 5th ed. London: Methuen.

Teloh, Henry. 1986. *Socratic Education in Plato's Early Dialogues.* Notre Dame: University of Notre Dame Press.

Thomas, John F. 1980. *Musings on the "Meno."* The Hague: Martinus Nijhoff.

Thompson, E. Seymer, ed. 1901. *The "Meno" of Plato.* London: Macmillan.

Tigner, Steven J. 1970. "On the 'Kinship' of 'All Nature' in Plato's *Meno." Phronesis* 15: 1–4.

Umphrey, Stewart. 1990. *Zetetic Skepticism.* Waterfield, N.H.: Longwood Academic.

Verdenius, W. J. 1957. "Notes on Plato's *Meno." Mnemosyne,* 4th series, 10: 289–99.

Vlastos, Gregory. 1965. "Anamnesis in the *Meno." Dialogue* 4: 143–67.

———. 1971. "The Paradox of Socrates." In *The Philosophy of Socrates,* ed. Gregory Vlastos. Garden City, N.Y.: Anchor Books, 1–21.

———. 1983. "The Socratic Elenchus." *Oxford Studies in Ancient Philosophy* 1: 27–58.

————. 1985. "Socrates' Disavowal of Knowledge." *Philosophical Quarterly* 35: 1–31.

————. 1991a. "Elenchus and Mathematics." In *Socrates: Ironist and Moral Philosopher.* Cambridge: Cambridge University Press, 107–31. Originally published in *American Journal of Philology* 109 (1988): 362–96.

————. 1991b. "Socrates *contra* Socrates in Plato." In *Socrates: Ironist and Moral Philosopher.* Cambridge: Cambridge University Press, 45–80.

Weiss, Roslyn. 1990. "Hedonism in the *Protagoras* and the Sophist's Guarantee." *Ancient Philosophy* 10: 17–39.

————. 1998. *Socrates Dissatisfied: An Analysis of Plato's "Crito."* New York: Oxford University Press.

————. 2000. "When Winning Is Everything: Socratic Elenchus and Euthydemian Eristic." In *Plato: "Euthydemus," "Lysis," "Charmides,"* ed. T. M. Robinson and Luc Brisson. Sankt Augustin: Academia Verlag, 68–75.

West, Thomas G., and Grace Starry West, trans. 1984. *Plato and Aristophanes: Four Texts on Socrates.* Ithaca, N.Y.: Cornell University Press.

White, Nicholas P. 1974–1975. "Inquiry." *Review of Metaphysics* 28: 289–310.

————. 1976. *Plato on Knowledge and Reality.* Indianapolis: Hackett.

Williams, B. A. O. 1972. "Knowledge and Reasons." In *Problems in the Theory of Knowledge,* ed. G. H. von Wright. The Hague: Martinus Nijhoff, 1–11.

Woodruff, Paul. 1976. "Socrates on the Parts of Virtue." *Canadian Journal of Philosophy* 2 (supp.): 101–16.

————. 1990. "Plato's Early Theory of Knowledge." In *Companions to Ancient Thought,* vol. 1, *Epistemology,* ed. Stephen Everson. Cambridge: Cambridge University Press, 60–84.

Zeyl, Donald J., trans. 1987. *Plato: "Gorgias."* Indianapolis: Hackett.

Zyskind, Harold, and R. Sternfeld. 1976. "Plato's *Meno* 89c: 'Virtue Is Knowledge': A Hypothesis?" *Phronesis* 21: 130–34.

Index